MW00912081

Study Guide

for

Berk

Child Development

Fifth Edition

Prepared by

Leslie M. Bach
Jessica Friedberg
Laura E. Berk
Illinois State University

Allyn and Bacon
Boston London Toronto Sydney Tokyo Singapore

Copyright © 2000, 1997 by Allyn & Bacon
A Pearson Education Company
160 Gould Street
Needham Heights, Massachusetts 02494-2130

Internet: www.abacon.com

All rights reserved. No part of the material protected by this copyright notice
may be reproduced or utilized in any form or by any means, electronic or
mechanical, including photocopying, recording, or by any information
storage and retrieval system, without the written permission of the copyright owner.

ISBN 0-205-30272-6

Printed in the United States of America

10 9 8 7 6 5 4 3 2   03 02 01 00

CONTENTS

PREFACE

As you embark on the fascinating journey of studying the development of children and adolescents, it is our hope that this Study Guide will help you master the material in your text, *Child Development*, by Laura E. Berk. Our intention in preparing the Study Guide is to provide you with active practice in learning the content in your textbook and thought-provoking questions that help you clarify your own thinking. Each chapter in the Study Guide is organized into the following six sections:

CHAPTER SUMMARY

We begin with a brief summary of the material, mentioning major topics covered and general principles emphasized in text discussion. Each text chapter includes three additional summaries: an informal one at the beginning of the chapter, Brief Reviews that serve as interim summaries throughout the text narrative, and a structured summary at the end of the chapter. Thus, the summary in the Study Guide will be your fourth review of the information covered in each chapter. It is intended to remind you of major points in the text before you embark on the remaining activities in the Guide.

LEARNING OBJECTIVES

We have organized the main points in each chapter into a series of objectives that indicate what you should be able to do once you have mastered the material. We suggest that you look over these objectives before you read each chapter. You may find it useful to take notes on information pertaining to objectives as you read. When you finish a chapter, try to answer the objectives in a few sentences or a short paragraph. Then check your answers against the text and revise your responses accordingly. Once you have completed this exercise, you will have generated your own review of chapter content. Because it is written in your own words, it should serve as an especially useful chapter overview that can be referred to when you prepare for examinations.

STUDY QUESTIONS

The main body of each chapter consists of study questions, organized according to major headings in the textbook, that assist you in identifying main points and grasping concepts and principles. Text pages on which answers can be found are indicated next to each entry. The study question section can be used in a number of different ways. You may find it helpful to answer each question as you read the chapter. Alternatively, try reading one or more sections and then testing yourself by answering the relevant study questions. Finally, use the study question section as a device to review for examinations. If you work through it methodically, your retention of chapter material will be greatly enhanced.

ASK YOURSELF AND CONNECTIONS QUESTIONS

In each chapter, we have included questions that ask you to summarize evidence on a controversial topic, argue a point of view, or apply your knowledge to real-life problems in child development. The questions are arranged so that you can write short-essay responses in the space provided and conveniently turn them in to your instructor as a class assignment. Answers to ask yourself and connections questions are included in the Instructor's Guide.

PUZZLES

To help you master the central vocabulary of the field, we have provided crossword puzzles that test your knowledge of important terms and concepts. Answers can be found at the back of the Study Guide. If you cannot think of the term that matches a clue in the puzzles, your knowledge of information related to the term may be insecure. Reread the material in the text chapter related to each item that you miss. Also, try a more demanding approach to term mastery: After you have completed each puzzle, cover the clues and write your own definitions of each term.

PRACTICE TESTS

Once you have thoroughly studied each chapter, find out how well you know the material by taking the 25-item multiple choice practice test. Then check your answers using the key at the back of the Study Guide. Each item is page-referenced to chapter content so you can look up answers to questions that you missed. If you answered more than a few items incorrectly, spend extra time rereading the chapter, writing responses to chapter objectives, and reviewing the study questions of this guide.

Now that you understand how the Study Guide is organized, you are ready to begin using it to master Child Development. We wish you a rewarding and enjoyable course of study.

Leslie M. Bach
Jessica Friedberg
Laura E. Berk

CHAPTER 1

HISTORY, THEORY, AND
APPLIED DIRECTIONS

SUMMARY

Child development is the study of all aspects of human growth and change. It is an interdisciplinary, scientific, and applied field of study. Researchers often divide the subject of development into three broad domains--physical, cognitive, and emotional and social--through five periods of development from conception through adolescence.

Theories provide organizing frameworks that guide and give meaning to the scientific study of children. Major theories can be organized according to the stand that they take on four basic issues: (1) Is the course of development continuous or discontinuous? (2) Is there one general course of development that characterizes all children, or are there many possible courses? (3) Are genetic or environmental factors more important in determining development? (4) Do individual children establish stable, lifelong patterns of behavior early in development, or are they open to change? Many theories, especially modern ones, take a balanced point of view and recognize the merits of both sides of these issues.

In recent years, the field of child development has become increasingly concerned with applying its knowledge to the solution of pressing social problems faced by children and adolescents. Public policy, laws, and government programs designed to improve current conditions are essential for protecting children's development.

LEARNING OBJECTIVES

After reading this chapter, you should be able to:

1.1 Explain the importance of the terms *interdisciplinary* and *applied* as they help to define the field of child development. (4)

1.2 Cite major domains and periods of development that help make the study of human change more convenient and manageable. (4-6)

1.3 Explain the role of theories in understanding child development, and describe the four basic issues on which major theories take a stand. (6-9)

1.4 Trace historical influences on modern theories of child development from medieval times through the early twentieth century. (11-16)

1.5 Describe and compare mid-twentieth century theories of child development, citing the contributions and limitations of each. (16-23)

1.6 Describe five recent theoretical perspectives on child development, noting the contributions of major theorists. (23-31)

1.7 Identify the stand taken by each major theory on the four basic issues of child development. (31-33)

1.8 Discuss factors that affect public policies serving children and families, noting their impact on the status of American children relative to children in other industrialized nations. (33-39)

STUDY QUESTIONS

1. Child development is a field of study that is devoted to understanding all aspects of human growth and change from _____ through _____. (4)

Child Development as a Scientific, Applied, and Interdisciplinary Field

1. Child development addresses issues of practical importance and is considered to be a(n) _____ field. (4)

Domains of Development as Interwoven

1. Identify and describe three broad domains of development. (4-5)

A._____

B._____

C._____

Periods of Development

1. List the ages that correspond to the following five periods of development. (5-6)

A. The prenatal period:_____

B. Infancy and toddlerhood:_____

C. Early childhood:_____

D. Middle childhood:_____

E. Adolescence:_____

1. Explain the two reasons theories are vital tools in the study of child development. (6)

A._____

_____

B._____

_____

2. True or False: In the field of child development, there are many theories with very different ideas about what children are like and how they develop. (6)

3. What are the four basic issues that almost all theories of child development address? (6)

A._____

B._____

C._____

D._____

Continuous or Discontinuous Development?

1. Discuss the continuous and discontinuous perspectives of the process of child development. (6-8)

A. Continuous:_____

_____

B. Discontinuous:_____

_____

2. The concept of _____ refers to qualitative changes in thinking, feeling, and behaving. (8)

One Course of Development or Many?

1. Children grow up in distinct _____; that is, they experience unique combinations of personal and environmental circumstances. (8)

Nature or Nurture?

1. Theorists who emphasize nature as the primary cause of development believe that (heredity/environment) is more important; those who emphasize nurture believe that (heredity/environment) is more important. (8)

The Individual: Stable or Open to Change?

1. True or False: Theorists who believe that change is possible and likely if new experiences support it are more likely to stress the role of nurture in child development. (9)

2. Why would investigators' opinion regarding the issue of stability versus change have implications for whether or not they believe children's early experiences influence development? (9)

_____
_____
_____

A Balanced Point of View

1. True or False: A modern theorist is more likely to take an extreme position with regard to the basic issues of child development. (9)

2. Describe three broad factors that may contribute to resilience in children. (10)

A._____
_____

B._____
_____

C._____
_____

Historical Foundations

Medieval Times

1. In medieval times, a view called preformationism regarded children as _____
_____. (11)

2. True or False: During medieval times, some laws protected children from adults who might mistreat them, and there were medical works that provided special instructions for their care. (11)

The Reformation

1. Describe how Puritan attitudes toward child rearing were shaped by religious ideology, and discuss changes that came about after the Puritans emigrated from England to the United States. (11)

_____
_____
_____
_____
_____

2. Recent historical evidence suggests that the harsh child-rearing practices recommended by the Puritan doctrine were probably (typical/not typical) of everyday practices in Puritan families. (11)

Philosophies of the Enlightenment

1. Locke viewed the child as a blank slate, or _____; in contrast, Rousseau thought that children were _____, with a natural sense of right and wrong. (12)

2. Describe the stands that Locke and Rousseau took on the basic issues of child development discussed earlier in this chapter. (12)

_____
_____
_____
_____
_____

3. The concept of _____ refers to a naturally unfolding, genetically determined course of growth. (12)

Darwin: Forefather of Scientific Child Study

1. Describe Darwin's theory of evolution. (12-13)

_____
_____
_____
_____
_____

2. True or False: The belief that the development of the human child from conception to maturity follows the same general plan as the evolution of the human species proved to be inaccurate. (13)

Scientific Beginnings

1. Describe the lasting influence of the baby biographies in the field of child development. (13)

_____

_____

2. Describe the weakness in using baby biographies for the study of child development. (13)

_____

_____

3. _____ was the founder of the child study movement. (13-14)

4. The computation of age-related averages of child growth and behavior, emphasized by G. Stanley Hall, is known as the _____ to child study. (14)

5. Discuss the contributions of Arnold Gesell to the child study movement. (14)

_____

_____

_____

_____

6. True or False: Although the work of Hall and Gesell provided descriptive facts and norms about children of different ages, it also yielded extensive information on the process of development. (14)

7. The first successful intelligence test was constructed by _____ and _____ to identify retarded children who needed to be placed in special classes. (14)

8. Binet's effort was unique because it began with a well-developed theory that defined intelligence as _____, _____, and _____ _____. (14)

9. Describe James Baldwin's view of the process of child development. (14, 16)

_____

_____

_____

_____

10. What themes have been represented by popular parenting literature throughout the past few decades? (15)

_____
_____
_____
_____

Mid-Twentieth-Century Theories

The Psychoanalytic Perspective

1. Describe the psychoanalytic approach to personality development. (16-17)

_____
_____
_____
_____
_____

2. True or False: The psychoanalytic approach assumes that the way conflicts are resolved by the child determines his or her ability to cope with anxiety. (16-17)

3. Freud's _____ theory of development was based on adult remembrances, and emphasized that management of children's _____ and _____ drives is crucial for healthy personality development. (17)

4. Describe the three parts of the personality in Freud's psychosexual theory. (17)

A._____
_____

B._____
_____

C._____
_____

5. True or False: Freud believed that the individual's basic personality was established during the period of adolescence. (17)

6. Match each of the following stages of psychosexual development with the appropriate description: (17)

_____ Stage in which sexual instincts die down and the superego develops further

    A. Genital

_____ Stage marked by the onset of puberty

    B. Latency

    C. Anal

_____ Stage in which the infant desires sucking activities

    D. Oral

    E. Phallic

_____ Stage in which the Oedipus/Electra conflict occurs and the superego is formed

_____ Stage in which toileting issues may cause conflicts between parent and child

7. Describe the Oedipus conflict, and explain how it is resolved. (17)

_____

_____

_____

_____

8. List two contributions made by Freud's theory, and list three criticisms of the theory. (18)

Contributions:

A._____

B._____

Criticisms:

A._____

B._____

C._____

9. Erikson's _____ theory viewed the ego as a positive force in development and emphasized the lifespan nature of development. (18)

10. Match each of Erikson's stages with the appropriate description: (19)

_____ The primary task in this stage is the development of an understanding of who one is and what one's place in society is.

_____ Successful resolution of this stage depends on warm, responsive care.

_____ In this stage, children experiment with adult roles through make-believe play.

_____ Successful resolution of this stage means giving to others through child rearing, caring for other people, and productive work.

_____ Successful resolution of this stage allows children to use mental and motor skills to make their own decisions.

_____ In this stage, successful resolution involves reflecting on the type of person one has been.

_____ The development of close relationships with others ensures successful resolution of this stage.

_____ Successful resolution of this stage requires developing the capacity to work and cooperate with others.

A. Autonomy vs. Doubt
B. Intimacy vs. Isolation
C. Identity vs. Diffusion
D. Industry vs. Inferiority
E. Trust vs. Mistrust
F. Generativity vs. Stagnation
G. Initiative vs. Guilt
H. Ego Integrity vs. Despair

11. Describe several differences between Freud's psychosexual theory of development and Erikson's psychosocial theory of development. (18)

_____
_____
_____
_____
_____

12. The _____, accepted by psychoanalytic theorists, combines information from a variety of sources to determine the personality functioning of a child. (18)

13. Why is psychoanalytic theory no longer in the mainstream of child development research? (18)

_____
_____
_____
_____
_____

Behaviorism and Social Learning Theory

1. American behaviorism began with the work of _____, who believed in studying (mental concepts/observable events). (19)

2. Watson applied Pavlov's concept of _____ to children's behavior in a historic experiment with Little Albert, an 11-month-old infant who was taught to fear a white rat by repeatedly presenting it together with a loud sound. (19)

3. According to Clark Hull's drive reduction theory, people continually act to satisfy _____ and reduce _____. (20)

4. The theory of operant conditioning was developed by _____, who believed that specific behaviors could be increased through the use of _____ _____ and could be decreased through the use of _____. (20)

5. True or False: Skinner rejected Hull's idea that primary drive reduction is the only way to get children to learn. (20)

6. True or False: Social learning theorists accept the traditional behaviorist principles of conditioning and reinforcement. (20)

7. Bandura demonstrated that _____, otherwise known as imitation or observational learning, is the basis for a wide variety of children's behaviors. (20)

8. Describe Bandura's most recent revision of his social learning theory. (20)

_____
_____
_____
_____
_____

9. The term _____ describes beliefs about one's abilities that guide behavior. (20)

10. Combining conditioning and modeling procedures to eliminate undesirable behaviors and increase socially acceptable responses is called _____. (21)

11. True or False: Many theorists believe that behaviorism and social learning theory offer too narrow a view of important environmental influences. (21)

Piaget's Cognitive-Developmental Theory

1. Piaget believed that development occurs as children actively construct knowledge, and cognitive development takes place in _____. (21)

2. Central to Piaget's theory is the biological concept of _____, which means that the structures of the mind develop to better fit with the environment. (21)

3. Match Piaget's stages with the appropriate descriptions: (22)

____ Language and make-believe play develop, but thinking is illogical.
____ The capacity for abstract, complex reasoning develops.
____ Recognizing and exploring objects through use of the senses and movement occurs in this stage.
____ Reasoning becomes more organized and logical in this stage.

A. Formal operational
B. Preoperational
C. Concrete operational
D. Sensorimotor

4. Piaget used open-ended _____ as his primary method to assess child and adolescent thinking. (22)

5. Piaget's cognitive-developmental perspective convinced many people that children are _____ learners, and encouraged the development of educational programs that emphasize _____ and direct contact with the environment. (22)

6. Research indicates that Piaget (overestimated/underestimated) the competencies of infants and preschoolers and that children's performance on Piagetian problems (can/cannot) be improved with training. (22)

Recent Theoretical Perspectives

Information Processing

1. According to information processing theorists, between presentation to the senses at _____ and behavioral responses at _____, information is actively coded, transformed, and organized. (23)

2. Like Piaget, information-processing researchers view the child as a(n) (active/passive) participant in development; however, unlike Piaget, they view development as a (continuous/discontinuous) process. (24)

3. True or False: Information processing emphasizes the study of imagination and creativity in children. (24)

11

Ethology

1. _____, which is concerned with the adaptive value of behavior and its evolutionary history, can trace its origins to the work of _____.
(24-25)

2. _____ refers to the early following behavior of certain baby birds that ensures that the young will stay close to the mother and be fed and protected. (25)

3. The term _____ refers to a time that is optimal for certain capacities to emerge in the child and in which the child is especially responsive to environmental influences. (25)

4. Describe Bowlby's application of ethological theory to the human infant-caregiver relationship. (25)

_____

_____

_____

_____

_____

5. True or False: Ethologists emphasize the genetic and biological roots of development and do not consider learning to be an important influence on behavior. (25)

Vygotsky's Sociocultural Theory

1. Cross-cultural research can help untangle the contributions of _____ and _____ factors to the timing, order of appearance, and diversity of children's behaviors. (26)

2. Describe Vygotsky's sociocultural theory of development. (26)

_____

_____

_____

_____

_____

3. Like Piaget, Vygotsky believed that children (do/do not) actively shape their own development; however, unlike Piaget, Vygotsky believed that direct teaching by adults was (important/not important) for cognitive growth. (26)

4. True or False: Current cross-cultural research supports Vygotsky's belief that social interaction surrounding certain tasks selected for children's learning leads to the development of knowledge and skills essential for success in a particular culture. (26)

12

Ecological Systems Theory

1. Bronfenbrenner's _____, which views the child as developing within a complex system of relationships affected by multiple levels of the environment, has recently been characterized as a(n) _____ model to account for the child's biological dispositions. (27)

2. True or False: Most researchers viewed a child's environment as broad and far-reaching, even before Bronfenbrenner's ecological systems theory. (27)

3. Match each of Bronfenbrenner's systems with the appropriate description or example: (27-29)

____ Relationship between the child's   A. Exosystem
      home and school environments   B. Chronosystem
____ Cultural influences on development   C. Mesosystem
____ Health services in the community   D. Macrosystem
____ The child's relationship with his/her father   E. Microsystem
____ Timing of environmental change

4. Describe Bronfenbrenner's concept of bidirectional relationships within the microsystem. (27-28)

_____
_____
_____
_____

5. True or False: Ecological systems theory assumes that the timing of environmental change does not affect its impact on the child. (29)

6. Describe how caregivers in the !Kung society respond to infants' play with objects and how such responses transmit societal values. (28)

_____
_____
_____
_____

New Theoretical Directions: Development as a Dynamic System

1. According to the _____ perspective, the child's mind, body, and physical and social worlds form an integrated system that guides mastery of new skills. (30)

2. True or False: Biological makeup, everyday tasks, the people who support children, and the quality of children's experiences lead to wide individual differences in specific skills. (30)

3. True or False: The dynamic systems perspective has largely been applied to children's emotional and social development. (30)

Comparing Child Development Theories
---

1. Behaviorist, social learning, information processing, and sociocultural theories view development as (continuous/discontinuous), whereas Piagetian and psychoanalytic perspectives advocate a (continuous/discontinuous) viewpoint. (32)

2. True or False: The behaviorist approach most heavily emphasizes nurture as a driving force behind development. (32)

3. True or False: Most theories assume that both nature and nurture influence development. (32)

New Applied Directions: Child Development and Social Policy
---

1. True or False: The poverty rate among American children is 10 percent. (33)

2. True or False: Poverty is three to four times higher, and more likely to persist for most of childhood, among Caucasian-Americans compared with other ethnic groups in the United States. (34)

3. The United States is (like/unlike) other industrialized countries in that it (guarantees/does not guarantee) basic health services to its population. (34)

4. For babies, _____ is a powerful predictor of serious health difficulties and early death. (34)

5. True or False: The rates of adolescent pregnancy and childbearing in the United States are the highest in the industrialized world. (34)

6. True or False: In the United States, 75 to 80 percent of mentally ill children have access to treatment. (34)

7. True or False: According to recent surveys, much child care in the United States is substandard in quality. (34)

The Policy-Making Process

1. Explain the terms social policy and public policy. (35)
A. Social policy:_____

_____

B. Public policy:_____

_____

2. True or False: In Bronfenbrenner's ecological systems theory, public policy is part of the exosystem. (35)

3. What is a nation's political culture? (36)

_____

_____

4. True or False: One reason why the United States has been slow to accept government-supported child care is the view that the care and rearing of children during the early years is the duty of parents. (36)

5. Why are children constantly in danger of becoming a "forgotten constituency"? (36)

_____

_____

_____

_____

6. In times of economic difficulty, governments are (more likely/less likely) to initiate new social programs. (36)

7. Provide three reasons scientific research does not invariably affect policy making. (37)
A._____

_____

B._____

_____

C._____

_____

15

Progress in Meeting the Needs of American Children

1. List two justifications for designing public policies to foster children's development. (38)

A._____

_____

B._____

_____

2. In 1989, the United Nations' General Assembly drew up the _____

_____, a treaty committing

participating countries to work toward guaranteeing certain rights for children. (38)

3. The Children's Defense Fund, an influential interest group committed to improving the lives of children, was founded by _____. (38)

4. What occurs once a nation's legislature ratifies the U.N. Convention on the Rights of the Child? (39)

_____

_____

_____

5. True or False: Presently, the United States is in compliance with all aspects of the U.N. Convention. (39)

ASK YOURSELF. . .

1.1 Suppose we could arrange a debate between John Locke, Jean Jacques Rousseau, and James Baldwin on the nature-nurture controversy. Summarize the argument each historical figure is likely to present. (p. 16)

1.2 Explain how behaviorism is consistent with Locke's image of the tabula rasa. Why is Bandura's social-cognitive approach a departure from that image? (p. 23)

1.3 A 4-year-old becomes frightened of the dark and refuses to go to sleep at night. How would a psychoanalyst and a behaviorist differ in their views of how this problem developed? (p. 23)

1.4 Return to the Variations box on page 10. Does the story of John and Gary illustrate bidirectional relationships within the microsystem, as described in Bronfenbrenner's model? Explain. (p. 31)

1.5 Explain how each of the following perspectives regards children as active, purposeful beings who contribute substantially to their own development: Bandura's social-cognitive theory, Piaget's cognitive-developmental theory, information processing, ethology, Vygotsky's sociocultural theory, ecological systems theory, and the dynamic systems perspective. (p. 31)

1.6 Check your local newspaper, television listings, and one or two national news magazines to see how often articles appear on the condition of children and families. Why is it important for researchers to communicate with the general public about children's needs? (p. 38)

CONNECTIONS

1.1 Although the baby biographies had flaws, they foreshadowed important research strategies--specifically, naturalistic observation and the longitudinal design. Describe the link between these first efforts to study the child and contemporary research techniques. (See Chapter 2, pages 45 and 58.)

1.2 Reread the example on page 8, which indicates that shy and sociable children experience very different contexts for development. Explain how those contexts can affect all domains of functioning--physical, cognitive, emotional and social? What can be done to help shy children develop more adaptively? (See Chapter 10, pages 417 and 420.)

1.3 What biological concept is emphasized in Piaget's cognitive-developmental approach? From which nineteenth-century theory did Piaget borrow this idea? (See Chapter 6, pages 222-223, for more information about the biological basis of Piagetian concepts.)

1.4 How might an information-processing flowchart be helpful to a researcher who wants to develop an intervention program to help children solve everyday social problems, such as how to enter an ongoing play activity or resolve a dispute over a toy? (See Chapter 11, pages 472-474.)

1.5 What kinds of public policies might help reduce the high infant mortality, teenage pregnancy and parenthood, and child abuse and neglect rates in the United States? Why is poverty linked to each of these threats to children's well-being? (See Chapter 3, page 116; Chapter 5, page 214, and Chapter 14, page 593.)

PUZZLE 1.1

Across

3 ___ behavior analysis, procedures that combine conditioning and modeling
5 Genetically determined course of growth
7 Social ___ theory offered expanded views of how people acquire new responses
11 ___-developmental theory, view of children as actively constructing knowledge
13 In a(n) ___ society, people define themselves as part of a group
15 In a(n) ___ society, people think of themselves as separate entities
18 Theory that focuses on how culture is transmitted to the next generation
19 ___ rasa, view of children as blank slates
20 ___ development, includes all aspects of human growth and change from conception through adolescence

Down

1 ___-nurture controversy: whether genetic or environmental factors are more important
2 Distinct ___ are unique combinations of personal and environmental circumstances
4 The child and the social environment form an integrated system in the ___ perspective
6 Ability to adapt effectively in the face of adversity
8 Approach that produced many descriptive facts about children
9 ___ savage, view of children as naturally endowed with a sense of right and wrong
10 Developmental process in which new ways emerge at particular time periods
12 Controversial issue: ___, lifelong patterns of behavior, versus change
14 ___ processing, view of the mind operating like a computer
16 ___ social indicators, periodic measures of children's well-being and living conditions
17 ___ policy, aims to solve social problems

PUZZLE 1.2

Across

1 The ___ system involves connections between children's immediate settings
3 Describes, explains, and predicts behavior
9 Time period optimal for certain capacities
10 Bronfenbrenner's approach to development is ___ systems theory
13 The ___ system does not contain children but affects their experiences
14 Medieval view of child as miniature adult
17 ___ development is developmental psychology in its interdisciplinary sense

Down

1 The ___ system includes activities in child's immediate surroundings
2 System that includes temporal changes
4 Perspective emphasizes conflicts between biology and society
5 Branch of psychology devoted to understanding changes throughout the lifespan
6 ___ theory, Erikson's view
7 ___ theory, Freud's developmental view
8 Emphasizes classical and operant conditioning
9 Characterized by qualitative change
11 Development viewed as a cumulative process
12 Values, laws, customs, and resources of a culture are the ___ system
15 Concerned with the adaptive value of behavior
16 Laws and government programs are ___ policy

PRACTICE TEST

1. Developmental psychology is defined as the study of: (4)
    A. behavior and characteristics of infants and toddlers.
    B. growth and mental development of children through elementary school.
    C. changes throughout the entire life span.
    D. development of children from birth to adolescence.

2. Which of the following is NOT true? (6)
    A. Theories provide organizing frameworks.
    B. Theories are influenced by cultural values.
    C. The continued existence of a theory depends on scientific verification.
    D. Theories guarantee agreement among researchers.

3. Which of the following is NOT a basic issue in child development? (6-9)
    A. Is there one course of development or many?
    B. Is the course of development continuous or discontinuous?
    C. Is development influenced by maturation or normative sequences?
    D. Is nature or nurture the more important determinant of development?

4. Qualitative changes in thinking, feeling, and behaving that characterize particular time periods of development are called: (8)
    A. stages.
    B. skills.
    C. sequences.
    D. categories.

5. A stage theorist assumes that children: (8)
    A. follow various courses of development.
    B. model their behavior after their parents.
    C. follow one course of development.
    D. grow up in distinct contexts.

6. A theory that regards nature as the primary influence on development would probably NOT agree with: (8-9)
    A. the importance of heredity.
    B. the strong likelihood of change at any time in life.
    C. the stability of characteristics and traits.
    D. one's early experiences are not crucial in establishing lifelong patterns of behavior.

7. Theorists who believe development is largely due to nurture suggest interventions: (9)
    A. provided at any time have the potential to enhance development.
    B. will enhance development only if they are provided during infancy.
    C. do not enhance development.
    D. need to be directly provided by the caregiver to enhance development.

8. The Puritans were known for their belief that: (11)
    A. children were miniature adults.
    B. children were blank slates.
    C. children were born evil and stubborn.
    D. children were noble savages.

9. Rousseau's philosophy included which two important concepts? (12)
    A. cultural relativism and social structuring
    B. tabula rasa and preformation
    C. stage and maturation
    D. natural selection and normative information

10. This theorist had an impact on the study of child development due to his observation of two evolutionary concepts: natural selection and survival of the fittest. (12)
    A. Locke
    B. Rousseau
    C. Gesell
    D. Darwin

11. G. Stanley Hall, the founder of the child study movement, launched: (14)
    A. baby biographies.
    B. the normative approach.
    C. mental testing.
    D. drive reduction.

12. Which of the following was NOT included in Binet's definition of intelligence? (14)
    A. association of ideas
    B. good judgment
    C. planning
    D. critical reflection

13. James Mark Baldwin, an early developmental theorist, believed that: (16)
    A. children must be reformed.
    B. children are like the workings of a machine.
    C. natural selection influences development.
    D. nature and nurture are of equal importance.

14. According to Freud's psychosexual theory of development, the way parents manage their child's sexual and aggressive drives has later implications for the development of the child's: (17)
    A. personality.
    B. intelligence.
    C. successful interpersonal relationships.
    D. id.

15. Which of the following is NOT true of Erikson's psychosocial theory? (18)
    A. Important developmental tasks are limited to early childhood.
    B. Normal development depends on the particular culture.
    C. The ego is a positive force.
    D. Three adult stages of development extend Freud's model.

16. Angela watches her mother bake a cake and then pretends to mix, stir, and pour the imaginary contents of a bowl when playing with her dolls. She is probably demonstrating the social learning principle of: (20)
    A. positive reinforcement.
    B. modeling.
    C. applied behavior analysis.
    D. conditioning.

17. According to Piaget's theory of development, children move through four broad stages, each of which is characterized by: (21)
    A. qualitative self-efficacy.
    B. techniques of applied behavior analysis.
    C. psychosocial conflict.
    D. qualitatively distinct ways of thinking.

18. Which of the following concepts are NOT associated with Piaget? (21-22)
    A. equilibrium
    B. information processing
    C. adaptation
    D. clinical interviews

19. Information-processing theorists believe: (23)
    A. children are passive recipients of environmental stimuli.
    B. development occurs in stages.
    C. flowcharts help explain how children think.
    D. creativity should be emphasized in developmental research.

20. Ethologists are most concerned with which aspect of behavior? (24)
    A. the preoperational stage
    B. sociocultural development
    C. its adaptive value
    D. drive reduction

21. Which of the following is NOT consistent with Vygotsky's sociocultural theory? (26)
    A. Social interaction is necessary to transmit culture to children.
    B. Children's thought and behavior are universal across cultures.
    C. Communication between adults and children becomes part of children's thinking.
    D. Children are active, constructive beings.

22. Bronfenbrenner's characterization of his perspective as a bioecological model reflects: (27)
    A. his belief in the influence of imprinting on behavior.
    B. his recognition that the biosphere is a factor in development.
    C. his combination of biological dispositions with environmental forces.
    D. his reliance on the science of ecology.

23. Jennifer's mother volunteers as a room mother. This connection between home and school illustrates Bronfenbrenner's: (28)
    A. mesosystem.
    B. exosystem.
    C. microsystem.
    D. macrosystem.

24. Which is NOT true of the dynamic systems perspective? (30)
    A. It draws on information-processing and contextual theories.
    B. Development is viewed as a single line of continuous change.
    C. Different skills vary in maturity within the same child.
    D. The child actively reorganizes her behavior in a more complex way.

25. Americans embrace individualism, a major reason they are reluctant to institute government-supported health insurance. This is an example of how: (36)
    A. cultural values influence public policy.
    B. the microsystem influences public policy.
    C. social learning contributes to social policy.
    D. special interests influence public policy.

CHAPTER 2

RESEARCH STRATEGIES

SUMMARY

Researchers face many challenges as they plan and implement studies of children. An understanding of research strategies enables students to separate dependable information from misleading results and to conduct their own investigations. Research usually begins with a hypothesis--a prediction about behavior drawn directly from a theory--or with a research question. The researcher then selects one or more research methods to use in the investigation, such as systematic observations, self-reports, psychophysiological methods, clinical methods, or ethnography. Once the researcher chooses the research methods, it is important to make sure that the procedures are reliable and valid and provide trustworthy information.

Next, the researcher chooses a research design, an overall plan for the study that permits the best possible test of the research idea. Two main types of designs, the correlational design and the experimental design, are used in research on human behavior. Longitudinal, cross-sectional, and longitudinal-sequential designs are uniquely suited for studying development. In the microgenetic design, researchers track change as it occurs.

Research involving children raises special ethical concerns. Ethical guidelines for research and special committees determine if the benefits of research outweigh the risks and help ensure that children's rights are protected.

LEARNING OBJECTIVES

After reading this chapter, you should be able to:

2.1 Describe the role of theories, hypotheses, and research questions in research, and explain why it is important to understand the research process. (44)

2.2 Describe common research methods used to study children, and explain the strengths and limitations of each. (44-50, 52, 54)

2.3 Explain why reliability and validity are keys to scientifically sound research, and indicate how these concepts apply to research methods and to the overall findings and conclusions of research studies. (54-55)

2.4 Describe correlational and experimental research designs, and explain the strengths and limitations of each. (55-58)

2.5 Describe longitudinal and cross-sectional research designs, and explain the strengths and limitations of each. (58-60, 62)

2.6 Describe longitudinal-sequential and microgenetic research designs, and explain why experimental and developmental designs are sometimes combined. (62-64)

2.7 Describe children's research rights, and explain why research involving children raises special ethical concerns. (64-68)

STUDY QUESTIONS

From Theory to Hypothesis

1. List two reasons it is important to learn about research strategies. (44)
A._____

_____

_____

B._____

_____

_____

Common Methods Used to Study Children

Systematic Observation

1. List a strength and a limitation of naturalistic observation. (45-46)
A. Strength:_____
B. Limitation:_____

2. List a strength and a limitation of structured observations. (45-46)
A. Strength:_____
B. Limitation:_____

3. Three different procedures can be used to collect systematic observations. Name and give a description of each. (46)
A._____

_____

B._____

_____

C._____

_____

4. List two ways that researchers can minimize observer influence when collecting systematic observations. (47)
A._____

_____

B._____

_____

5. Define observer bias, and explain how researchers guard against this problem. (47)

_____

_____

_____

Self-Reports: Interviews and Questionnaires

1. List two strengths and two limitations of the clinical interview. (45, 48)
A. Strength:_____

B. Strength: _____

C. Limitation:_____

D. Limitation:_____

_____

2. True or False: Interviews that focus on current rather than past information and specific characteristics rather than global judgments show a better match with observations and other sources of behavior. (48)

3. Describe three strengths and two limitations of structured interviews, tests, and questionnaires. (45, 48-49)
A. Strength:_____

B. Strength:_____

C. Strength:_____

D. Limitation:_____

E. Limitation:_____

_____

Psychophysiological Methods

1. _____ _____, which yield three-dimensional pictures of brain activity, provide the most precise information on which brain regions are specialized for certain functions. (50)

2. Describe two limitations of psychophysiological methods. (45, 50)
A._____

B._____

_____

The Clinical, or Case Study, Method

1. List one strength and two limitations of the clinical method. (45, 50, 52)

A. Strength:_____

_____

B. Limitation:_____

_____

C. Limitation:_____

_____

2. When parents of prodigies are _____ and focus only on their child's gifts rather than on the child herself, these children can end up disengaged, depressed, and resentful. (51)

Methods for Studying Culture

1. When comparing several cultural groups, researchers can draw on _____ and _____ procedures. (52)

2. Ethnography is a descriptive, qualitative research technique aimed at understanding a(n) _____, a(n) _____, or a(n) _____ _____. (52)

3. The ethnographic method achieves its goals through _____ _____, a technique in which the researcher lives with the cultural community and participates in its daily life. (52)

4. True or False: Delgado-Gaitan's ethnographic research shows that informal social ties and community organization has little effect in promoting the education of ethnic minority children. (53)

Reliability and Validity: Keys to Scientifically Sound Research

---

Reliability

1. _____ refers to the consistency, or repeatability, of measures of behavior and requires that observers _____ on what they see. (54)

2. List three ways researchers determine the reliability of self-report data. (54-55)

A._____

_____

B._____

_____

C._____

_____

Validity

1. Methods that have high _____ accurately measure characteristics that the researcher set out to measure. (55)

2. True or False: Although reliability of measures is important when conducting research, the reliability of a measure does not affect its validity. (55)

3. List two ways that researchers can ensure that the methods they use are valid. (55)

A._____

_____

B._____

_____

General Research Designs

Correlational Design

1. In a(n) _____ design, researchers gather information on already existing groups of individuals, and no effort is made to alter their experiences. (55)

2. True or False: The correlational design is preferred by researchers because it allows them to infer cause and effect. (56)

3. A(n) _____ is a number that describes how strongly two variables are associated with one another. (56)

4. True or False: A correlation of +.25 indicates a stronger relationship between variables than does a correlation of -.50. (56)

5. The correlation coefficient can range in value from _____ to _____. (56)

6. For a correlation coefficient, the magnitude, or size, of the number shows the _____ of the relationship, and the sign of the number shows the _____ of the relationship. (56)

7. For a correlation coefficient, a positive sign means that as one variable increases, the other _____; a negative sign means that as one variable increases, the other _____. (56)

Experimental Design

1. Unlike the correlational design, a(n) _____ design permits us to make inferences about cause and effect. (56)

2. The _____ variable is anticipated by the researcher to cause changes in the _____ variable. (56)

3. In experimental studies, investigators control for characteristics of participants that could reduce the accuracy of their findings by using the technique of _____, which is sometimes combined with _____. (57)

Modified Experimental Designs

1. In _____, researchers randomly assign people to treatment conditions in natural settings. (57)

2. True or False: Natural experiments differ from correlational research because groups of participants are carefully chosen to ensure that their characteristics are as much alike as possible. (57)

Designs for Studying Development

The Longitudinal Design

1. List two advantages of the longitudinal design. (58)
A._____
_____
B._____
_____

2. Researchers who used a longitudinal design to determine whether children who display angry and explosive or shy and withdrawn personality styles retain the same dispositions when they become adults found that these styles are (moderately/extremely) stable. (58-59)

3. In longitudinal research, _____ is a common problem because people move away or drop out, and the ones who remain are likely to differ in important ways from those who do not continue. (60)

4. A major threat to accuracy of longitudinal findings comes from _____, which refers to the fact that children born in one time period are influenced by a different set of cultural and historical conditions than those born in another time period. (60)

5. True or False: During the Depression, adolescent boys had greater involvement in family affairs while adolescent girls focused on college and careers. (61)

The Cross-Sectional Design

1. In the cross-sectional design, groups of people differing in _____ are studied at the same point in time. (60)

2. In cross-sectional designs, researchers (do/do not) need to worry about selective attrition, practice effects, and changes in the field of child development. (62)

3. Describe two problems associated with conducting cross-sectional research. (62)
A._____

_____

B._____

_____

Improving Developmental Designs

1. List three advantages of the longitudinal-sequential design. (62)
A._____

_____

B._____

_____

C._____

_____

2. A recent modification of the longitudinal approach, called the _____ design, allows researchers to track change while it is occurring. (63)

3. Microgenetic research is especially useful for studying _____ development and infants' _____ development. (63)

4. List three reasons why microgenetic studies are difficult to carry out. (63-64)
A._____

_____

B._____

_____

C._____

_____

5. True or False: One way to determine if microgenetic research has distorted developmental trends because of practice effects associated with repeated exposure to a task is to compare microgenetic with cross-sectional observations. (64)

6. Longitudinal and cross-sectional research provide only (correlational/causal) inferences about development, but when a longitudinal or cross-sectional design is combined with an experimental strategy, researchers have evidence for (correlational/causal) associations. (64)

Ethics in Research on Children

1. Describe children's research rights. (66)
A. Protection from harm:_____
_____

B. Informed consent:_____
_____

C. Privacy:_____
_____

D. Knowledge of results:_____
_____

E. Beneficial treatments:_____
_____

2. For children _____ years and older, their own _____ should be obtained in addition to parental consent to participation in research. (66)

3. True or False: Debriefing, in which the experimenter provides a full account and justification of the activities, is always sufficient to ensure that children suffer no serious emotional consequences as a result of the research. (68)

4. (Younger/Older) children tend to have difficulty understanding the research process, whereas (younger/older) children are more susceptible to procedures that threaten the way they think of themselves. (67)

ASK YOURSELF...

2.1 A researcher wants to study the thoughts and feelings of children who have experienced their parents' divorce. Which method is best suited to investigating this question? Explain. (p. 54)

2.2 A researcher is interested in how Pueblo Indian adolescents experience daily life in a New Mexico high school where the large majority of students are Caucasian Americans. Which method should he use, and why? (p. 54)

2.3 A researcher compares children who went to summer leadership camps with children who attended athletic camps. She finds that those who attended leadership camps are friendlier. Should the investigator tell parents that sending children to leadership camp promotes sociability? Why or why not? (p. 64)

2.4 A researcher wants to find out if children enrolled in child-care centers in the first few years of life do as well in school as those who are not in child care. Which developmental design, longitudinal or cross-sectional, is appropriate for answering this question? What precautions should the researcher take to help ensure that child care is responsible for any differences between the groups? Explain. (p. 64)

CONNECTIONS

2.1 Recall from Chapter 1 (page 5) that domains of development--physical, cognitive, emotional, and social--are not really distinct; they combine to form the living, growing child. Of the methods discussed in the preceding sections, which ones are best suited to uncovering the interconnections between domains?

2.2 Which research designs are best suited for detecting diversity in development? Which theories discussed in Chapter 1 are likely to be especially committed to those designs? Explain. (See Chapter 1, pages 26-32.)

PUZZLE 2.1

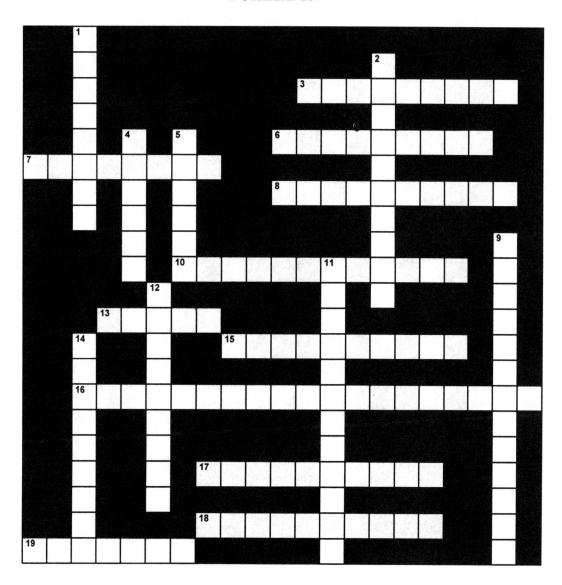

Across

3 Cross -___ design studies groups of different age people at the same time
6 Observer ___ causes a person to react in unnatural ways
7 Flexible and open-ended interview
8 Prediction about behavior drawn from a theory
10 Design modifies the longitudinal approach
13 ___ sampling records all instances of behavior
15 Children in studies should be afforded ___ from harm
16 Methods that measure the relation between physiological processes and behavior
17 Longitudinal -___ design combines two approaches
18 Experiment that achieves high control
19 Experiment that compares already existing treatments

Down

1 Risks-versus-___ ratio, which helps ensure children's rights are safeguarded
2 Interview with the same questions asked in the same way
4 Longitudinal research participants have unique characteristics in ___ sampling
5 ___ assignment protects against less accurate findings
9 Design that gathers information on already existing groups without intervention
11 Design that permits inferences about cause and effect
12 Longitudinal samples become more biased in ___ attrition
14 Variable influenced by the independent variable

PUZZLE 2.2

Across

1 ___ coefficient ranges from +1.00 to −1.00
6 ___ effects may occur after repeated testing
9 Observation method that uses natural environment
14 Method that combines interviews, observations, test scores, and psychophysiological data
15 Sampling method that records behavior during short intervals
16 Explanation of deception
17 Effects of cultural-historical change on accuracy
18 Ensures equivalency on factors likely to distort

Down

2 Design that studies participants repeatedly
3 Participants are randomly assigned in natural settings
4 Observation method that sets up situation in lab
5 Consistency or repeatability
7 Observer ___ sees and records what is expected
8 ___ consent is based on clear language
10 Variable manipulated by the experimenter
11 Record of entire stream of behavior
12 Method that measures what is intended has high ___
13 Researcher using this method lives with members of culture

PRACTICE TEST

1. An interview is an example of a research: (43)
    A. hypothesis.
    B. theory.
    C. method.
    D. design.

2. A prediction that if children eat breakfast, they will perform better at school is an example of: (44)
    A. reliability.
    B. validity.
    C. a research design.
    D. a hypothesis.

3. Which of the following is NOT a reason for learning about research strategies? (44)
    A. separating dependable information from misleading results
    B. testing hypotheses or research questions
    C. providing information to justify financial support for programs
    D. encouraging parents to test theories on their children

4. Which of the following is NOT true of naturalistic observation? (45-46)
    A. Researchers control the conditions of observation.
    B. Researchers directly observe everyday behaviors.
    C. Observations occur in the field.
    D. Observations are systematic.

5. A description of everything said and done over a certain time period is called: (46)
    A. time sampling.
    B. a specimen record.
    C. a clinical interview.
    D. a longitudinal study.

6. An observer watches children in a classroom and records each instance in which a child raises her hand. This would be: (46)
    A. time sampling.
    B. event sampling.
    C. a specimen record.
    D. a longitudinal study.

7. A researcher observes a child doing seat work at his desk for a period of 10 seconds and records his behavior on a checklist during the next 5 seconds. This is called: (46)
    A. time sampling.
    B. biased sampling.
    C. a specimen record.
    D. event sampling.

8. Which of the following is NOT true of the presence of an observer? (47)
    A. Younger children quickly get used to the observer's presence.
    B. Older children are likely to behave in a more socially desirable way.
    C. Using a familiar observer reduces observer influence.
    D. Children below the age of 3 behave more negatively.

9. Which of the following is NOT a limitation of clinical interviews? (48)
    A. Only a narrow range of information can be obtained.
    B. It is difficult to accurately assess individuals with limited verbal ability.
    C. The desire of individuals to please the interviewer distorts answers.
    D. Different responses may be due to different phrasing of questions.

10. Psychophysiological research is useful because: (49)
    A. it helps identify the emotions of infants.
    B. no inferences in interpretation need to be made.
    C. no extraneous factors can influence responses.
    D. consistent patterns of brain activity can have only one cause.

11. One limitation of ethnographic research is: (54)
    A. it is a method borrowed from biology.
    B. it tries to capture a community's values and social processes.
    C. it overturns stereotypes.
    D. a researcher's presence may alter the situation.

12. A child is given a written test of verbal ability, and then takes a different form of the same test the next day. The results of the first test are very different from the results of the second test. This test is: (54-55)
    A. standardized.
    B. predictive.
    C. unreliable.
    D. representative.

13. Two observers watch young children play and record instances of parallel play. One observer records twice as many instances as the other. This measure of play is: (54-55)
    A. standardized.
    B. predictive.
    C. unreliable.
    D. representative.

14. _____ is absolutely essential for valid research. (55)
    A. Cross-cultural study
    B. Ethnography
    C. Reliability
    D. Correlation

15. A test is intended to measure first graders' mathematical ability and includes numerous word problems. The fact that the test may measure verbal ability as well as mathematical ability means that test results may be: (55)
    A. cross-sectional.
    B. unreliable.
    C. invalid.
    D. correlational.

16. Which of the following does NOT apply to correlational designs? (55-56)
    A. They permit inference of cause and effect.
    B. The group of individuals studied already exists.
    C. Researchers do not alter participants' experiences.
    D. A third variable may account for the correlation between the variables of interest.

17. Which of the following is NOT true of experimental designs? (56-57)
    A. They do not permit inference of cause and effect.
    B. Random assignment of participants increases accuracy of findings.
    C. Groups are sometimes matched on characteristics.
    D. Researchers manipulate changes in independent variables.

18. A natural experiment differs from a field experiment because: (57)
    A. in natural experiments, researchers randomly assign participants.
    B. in natural experiments, researchers manipulate conditions.
    C. in field experiments, treatments that already exist are compared.
    D. in field experiments, researchers randomly assign participants.

19. Which of the following is NOT an advantage of using the longitudinal design? (58)
    A. Common patterns as well as individual differences can be identified.
    B. Each subject can be tracked over time.
    C. Relationships between early and later events and behavior can be examined.
    D. Cohort effects are eliminated.

20. Which of the following is NOT an advantage of using the cross-sectional design? (62)
    A. Distortions from cohort effects are eliminated.
    B. Problems with selecive attrition are eliminated.
    C. Problems with practice effects are eliminated.
    D. Problems with changes in the field of child development are eliminated.

21. Which of the following is NOT an advantage of the longitudinal-sequential approach? (62)
    A. Problems associated with biased sampling are eliminated.
    B. Researchers can determine if cohort effects are present.
    C. Researchers can make both longitudinal and cross-sectional comparisons.
    D. It is efficient.

22. An advantage of microgenetic studies is: (63)
    A. they are not subject to practice effects.
    B. they are easy to carry out.
    C. researchers can track change while it occurs.
    D. researchers can precisely determine the length of time needed.

23. Researchers sometimes combine longitudinal or cross-sectional designs with _____
    _____ designs to explore causal relationships between variables. (64)
    A. microgenetic
    B. clinical
    C. experimental
    D. self-report

24. Which of the following is NOT a research right of children? (66)
    A. knowledge of results
    B. beneficial treatments
    C. compensation
    D. privacy

25. Which of the following statements concerning research with children is NOT true?
    (66, 68)
    A. Debriefing usually works better with children than with adults.
    B. Young children rely on a basic faith in adults to feel secure.
    C. Ethical standards permit deception in research with children.
    D. Some specialists believe use of deception with children is always unethical.

CHAPTER 3

BIOLOGICAL FOUNDATIONS, PRENATAL DEVELOPMENT, AND BIRTH

SUMMARY

Human biological foundations include the genetic code and basic genetic principles that contribute to individual differences in appearance and behavior and to various abnormalities and disorders. During the most rapid phase of human growth, the prenatal period, complex transactions between heredity and environment begin to shape the course of development.

Genetic counseling and prenatal diagnosis help people make informed decisions about conceiving or carrying a pregnancy to term. The vast changes that take place during pregnancy are divided into three periods: the period of the zygote, the period of the embryo, and the period of the fetus. Environmental supports such as maternal health and nutrition are necessary for normal prenatal growth, but damaging influences such as teratogens, inadequate maternal diet, and severe maternal emotional stress can threaten the child's health and survival. Prenatal vitamin supplements can benefit women during pregnancy and also prevent certain birth complications and defects.

Childbirth takes place in three stages, beginning with contractions that open the cervix and ending with the delivery of the placenta. Natural, or prepared, childbirth tries to overcome the idea that birth is a painful ordeal that requires extensive medical intervention. Interest in home birth, which has always been popular in certain industrialized nations, has increased in the United States. In complicated deliveries, labor and delivery medication is essential; but used routinely, it can cause problems. Oxygen deprivation, prematurity, and low birth weight are serious birth complications. Infants born underweight or prematurely face developmental risks, but interventions to ensure a supportive home environment can help restore these children's growth.

The field of behavioral genetics is devoted to discovering the hereditary and environmental origins of the great diversity of complex human characteristics. These two basic determinants of development continue to influence the individual's emerging characteristics from infancy through adolescence.

LEARNING OBJECTIVES

After reading this chapter, you should be able to:

3.1 Distinguish between genotype and phenotype. (71)

3.2 Describe the structure and function of the human chromosome and the process of mitosis. (72)

3.3 Describe the process of meiosis, and explain how it leads to genetic variability. (73-75)

3.4 Describe the genetic events that result in multiple offspring and that determine the sex of the new organism. (75-76)

3.5 Describe basic patterns of genetic inheritance, give examples of each, and indicate how harmful genes are created. (76-81)

3.6 Describe the origins and consequences of Down syndrome and major abnormalities of the sex chromosomes. (81-83)

3.7 Describe reproductive choices available to prospective parents, and those that may be available in the future, and explain the controversies related to each. (83-87)

3.8 Explain the role of genetic counseling, prenatal diagnosis, and fetal medicine in the reproductive decisions of prospective parents. (83-87)

3.9 Describe the course of prenatal development, noting the major events in the period of the zygote, the period of the embryo, and the period of the fetus. (88-95)

3.10 Describe and explain the effects of teratogens on the developing organism. (95-103)

3.11 Describe how maternal nutrition, emotional well-being, and age may affect the developing organism. (103-105)

3.12 Describe the stages of childbirth, the baby's adaptation to labor and delivery, and the appearance of the newborn. (106-108)

3.13 Describe the purpose and features of the Apgar scale. (108)

3.14 Describe and evaluate various approaches to childbirth, including natural childbirth and home delivery. (109-111)

3.15 Describe effects of labor and delivery medication on the newborn baby. (111)

3.16 Describe the causes and developmental consequences of oxygen deprivation, preterm delivery, and low birth weight, along with interventions aimed at helping at-risk infants recover. (111-115)

3.17 Summarize findings on the long-term consequences of birth complications. (115-117)

3.18 Describe the goals of the field of behavioral genetics, and summarize issues of agreement and disagreement among researchers. (118)

3.19 Describe ways in which researchers determine "how much" heredity and environment contribute to complex human characteristics, and discuss the limitations of these techniques. (119-121)

3.20 Describe concepts that explain "how" heredity and environment work together to influence complex human characteristics. (121-123)

STUDY QUESTIONS

1. Directly visible characteristics of a person are called _____. They depend in part on the individual's _____, but are also affected by _____ influences. (71)

Genetic Foundations

1. _____ are rodlike structures in the nucleus of a cell that store and transmit genetic information. (72)

2. In humans, there are ____ pairs of chromosomes in each cell. (72)

The Genetic Code

1. Chromosomes are made up of a chemical substance called _____. (72)

2. Describe the process of cell duplication called mitosis. (72)

_____
_____
_____
_____
_____

The Sex Cells

1. New individuals are created when _____, or sex cells, combine. Sex cells contain ____ chromosomes. (73)

2. Place in numerical order the four steps involved in meiosis. (73-74)

____ The duplicated chromosomes separate to form gametes, each with 23 single chromosomes.
____ Crossing over takes place between the 2 innermost pair members.
____ In the original cell, 46 chromosomes each duplicate and pair with one another.
____ The pairs of chromosomes separate to form 2 cells, each with 23 duplicated chromosomes.

3. When sperm and ovum unite at fertilization, the cell that results, called a(n) _____, has ____ chromosomes. (75)

4. True or False: The genetic variability produced by meiosis increases the chances that at least some members of a species will be able to cope with changing environments and survive. (75)

Multiple Offspring

1. Sometimes a zygote that has started to duplicate separates into two clusters of cells that develop into _____, or _____, twins. In other cases, two ova are released and fertilized, producing _____, or _____ twins. (75)

2. True or False: Fraternal twins are genetically more similar than ordinary siblings. (75)

3. List and describe five maternal factors linked to fraternal twinning. (75)

A._____

_____

B._____

_____

C._____

_____

D._____

_____

E._____

_____

Boy or Girl?

1. The 22 pairs of matching chromosomes are called _____. The twenty-third pair consists of _____. In females, this pair is called _____; in males, it is called _____. (76)

2. True or False: Even though a Y-bearing sperm fertilizes the ovum, if a gene that switches on the production of male sex hormones is absent, the fetus will be female. (76)

Patterns of Genetic Inheritance

1. If the alleles from both parents are alike, the child is _____ and will display the inherited trait. If they are different, the child is _____, and relationships between the alleles determine the trait that will appear. (76)

2. In many heterozygous pairings, only one allele affects the child's characteristics. It is called _____; the second allele, which has no effect, is called _____. (76)

3. _____, a disorder that affects the way the body breaks down proteins contained in many foods, is the product of recessive alleles. (76)

4. True or False: Even though PKU can be detected shortly after birth by a blood test, there is little that can be done to prevent permanent mental retardation of a child who has the disorder. (76-77)

5. It is possible for a single gene to affect more than one trait--a genetic principle known as _____. (77)

6. _____ genes can enhance or dilute the effects of alleles controlling particular traits. (77)

7. True or False: Most serious diseases are a product of dominant alleles. (77)

8. In some heterozygous circumstances, we see _____, a pattern of inheritance in which both alleles influence characteristics. (77)

9. True or False: When a harmful allele is carried on the X chromosome, males are more likely to be affected because their sex chromosomes do not match. (78)

10. In _____, an exception to the rules of dominant- recessive and codominant inheritance, alleles are chemically marked in such a way that one pair member (either the mother's or the father's) is activated regardless of its makeup. (80)

11. An example of genetic imprinting that operates on the sex chromosomes is _____, the most common inherited cause of mild to moderate mental retardation. (80)

12. Harmful genes are created by _____, a sudden but permanent change in a segment of DNA. (81)

13. True or False: All mutations are caused by hazardous environmental agents. (81)

14. Characteristics such as height or intelligence that vary continuously are due to _____. (81)

Chromosomal Abnormalities

1. Most chromosomal defects are the result of mistakes during _____. (81)

2. The most common chromosomal abnormality is _____. In 95 percent of cases, it results from a failure of the _____ pair of chromosomes to separate during meiosis. (81)

3. What are the physical features and behavioral consequences of Down syndrome? (82)

A. Physical:_____

_____

_____

B. Behavioral:_____

_____

_____

4. True or False: Down syndrome babies are easier to care for than are normal infants. (82)

5. True or False: Early intervention programs help children with Down syndrome to make better developmental progress, especially in the areas of social, emotional, and motor skills. (82)

6. True or False: Although the incidence of Down syndrome rises dramatically with maternal age, in some cases, the extra genetic material originates with the father. (82)

7. As compared with most disorders of the autosomes, abnormalities of the sex chromosomes usually lead to (more/fewer) problems. (82)

8. Most children with sex chromosome disorders (do/do not) suffer from mental retardation. (82)

9. _____ difficulties are common among girls with triple X syndrome and boys with Klinefelter syndrome, whereas girls with Turner syndrome have trouble with _____. (82)

10. Adding to or subtracting from the usual number of X chromosomes results in (general/particular) intellectual deficits. (82)

Reproductive Choices

Genetic Counseling

1. _____ helps couples assess their chances of giving birth to a baby with a hereditary disorder. (83)

2. _____ of all couples who try to conceive discover that they are sterile. (84)

3. Define and describe three types of reproductive technologies currently in use. (84)

A. _____

_____

B. _____

_____

C. _____

_____

4. True or False: Research has shown that children conceived through the use of reproductive technologies suffer few psychological consequences. (85)

Prenatal Diagnosis and Fetal Medicine

1. Define and describe two prenatal diagnostic methods particularly useful for women of advanced maternal age. (84, 86, 87)

A. _____

_____

B. _____

2. The most widely used technique for prenatal diagnosis is _____. (86)

3. A prenatal diagnostic procedure in which a small tube with a light source at one end is inserted into the uterus to inspect the fetus is called _____. (86)

4. Advances in _____ offer new hope for correcting hereditary defects. (86)

5. True or False: Approximately 95 percent of fetuses examined through prenatal diagnosis are normal. (86-87)

6. Describe the main goals of the Human Genome Project. (88)

_____

_____

_____

7. An experimental gene-based treatment called _____ delivers DNA carrying a functional gene to the patient's cells in order to correct a genetic abnormality. (89)

Prenatal Development

Conception

1. After bursting from an ovary, an ovum is drawn into one of two _____ _____, which are long, thin structures that lead to the uterus. (88-89)

2. Most conceptions result from intercourse during a 3-day period--on the day of or the _____ days preceding _____. (89)

The Period of the Zygote

1. The period of the zygote lasts about _____ weeks. (90)

2. By the fourth day after fertilization, the ovum forms a hollow, fluid-filled ball called a(n) _____. Inner cells, or the _____, will become the new organism; the outer ring will provide protective covering. (90)

3. Sometime between the _____ and the _____ day after fertilization, implantation occurs. (90)

4. As many as _____ percent of zygotes do not make it through the first two weeks. (90)

5. The _____ is a special organ that permits food and oxygen to reach the organism, and waste products to be carried away. (91)

6. The placenta is connected to the developing organism by the _____. (92)

The Period of the Embryo

1. The period of the embryo lasts _____ weeks from implantation through the eighth week of pregnancy. (92)

2. True or False: During this period, the embryo is especially vulnerable to interference in healthy development because all parts of the body are forming. (92)

3. In the first week of this period, the _____ forms three layers of cells: (1) the _____, which will become the nervous system and skin; (2) the _____, from which will develop the muscles, skeleton, circulatory system, and other internal organs; and (3) the _____, which will become the digestive system, lungs, urinary tract, and glands. (92)

4. Describe prenatal development during the last half of the first month and the entire second month. (92-93)

A. Last half of the first month: _____

_____

_____

_____

_____

B. Second month: _____

_____

_____

_____

_____

The Period of the Fetus

1. The period of the fetus lasts from the _____ week until the end of pregnancy. (93)

2. Describe development of the fetus during the third month. (93)

_____

_____

_____

_____

_____

3. Describe development of the fetus during the second trimester. (93)

_____

_____

_____

_____

_____

_____

4. True or False: By the end of the second trimester, most neurons in the brain are in place. (93)

5. Describe development of the fetus during the third trimester. (93-95)

_____

_____

_____

_____

_____

_____

6. The _____, the point at which the baby can first survive, occurs sometime between _____ and _____ weeks. (93)

7. True or False: During the last weeks of pregnancy, the fetus learns to prefer the tone and rhythm of its mother's voice. (94)

8. In a study looking at the relationship between fetal measures and temperament after birth, findings revealed that pattern of fetal activity in the (first/last) few weeks of pregnancy was the (best/worst) predictor of infant temperament. (96)

Prenatal Environmental Influences

Teratogens

1. List four factors that influence the amount of harm done by teratogens. (95)
A._____
B._____
C._____
D._____

2. A(n) _____ is a limited time span in which a part of the body or a behavior is biologically prepared to develop rapidly and is especially vulnerable to its surroundings. (96)

3. The brain and eye have relatively (long/short) sensitive periods, and the limbs and palate have relatively (long/short) sensitive periods. (97)

4. True or False: The period of the zygote is the time when serious defects are most likely to occur in the developing organism during pregnancy. (97)

5. When taken by mothers between the fourth and sixth week after conception, the sedative _____ produced gross deformities of the embryo's developing _____ and _____. (98)

6. True or False: Heavy caffeine intake is associated with lower intelligence test scores in early childhood. (98)

7. List five problems for which babies born to users of cocaine, heroin, or methadone are at risk. (98)
A._____
B._____
C._____
D._____
E._____

8. True or False: Babies born to users of heroin, methadone, and cocaine are born drug addicted. (98)

9. True or False: Youngsters with prenatal exposure to heroin and methadone always experience long-term problems. (98)

10. _____ alters the chemical balance in the fetus's brain and may contribute to inattention, behavior problems, and a specific set of physical defects. (98-99)

11. Babies born to mothers who smoke _____ appear to be worst off in terms of low birth weight and damage to the central nervous system. (99)

12. List three behaviors of the newborn linked by researchers to prenatal exposure to marijuana. (99)
A._____
B._____
C._____

13. The most well-known effect of smoking during pregnancy is _____
_____. (99)

14. Explain how smoking can harm the fetus, and describe possible physical and behavioral consequences of prenatal exposure. (99)

_____
_____
_____
_____
_____

15. True or False: Although smoking by the mother during pregnancy has been linked to complications in the newborn, researchers have detected no adverse effects associated with passive smoking. (99-100)

16. Describe mental and physical symptoms associated with fetal alcohol syndrome. (100)

_____
_____
_____
_____
_____

17. Explain two ways alcohol produces its devastating consequences during prenatal development. (100)
A._____
_____
B._____
_____

18. True or False: Although heavy alcohol consumption by the mother during pregnancy may result in serious consequences to the baby, it is believed that moderate consumption of alcohol is safe. (100-101)

19. Prenatal exposure to the synthetic hormone _____ results in an increased rate of _____ defects and cancer. (101)

20. Among metallic elements, _____ and _____ are established teratogens. (101)

21. _____ (3-day German measles) is a teratogen that inflicts the greatest damage when it strikes during the _____ period of development. (102)

22. When a woman with AIDS becomes pregnant, about ____ to ____ percent of the time she passes the deadly virus to the developing organism. (103)

23. Describe the effects of AIDS on infants born infected with the virus. (103)

_____
_____
_____
_____

Other Maternal Factors

1. In healthy women, regular moderate exercise is related to (increased/ decreased) birth weight; however, very frequent, vigorous exercise is related to (increased/decreased) birth weight. (103)

2. Prenatal malnutrition can cause serious damage to the _____ of the fetus, especially if malnutrition occurred during the last trimester. (104)

3. Describe the effects prenatal malnutrition has on the infant. (104)

_____
_____
_____
_____

4. Match the vitamin or mineral with the impact it has on pregnancy outcomes: (104)

____ Protect(s) against cleft lip and palate   A. Iodine
____ Reduce(s) risk of many prenatal and birth   B. Calcium
      complications   C. Magnesium and zinc
____ Help(s) prevent neural tube defects   D. Folic acid
____ Help(s) prevent maternal high blood   E. Multivitamin
      pressure and premature births
____ Prevent(s) cretinism

54

5. Excessive daily intake of vitamins _____ and _____ during pregnancy can result in birth defects. (104)

6. Describe the risks for a baby whose mother experienced severe psychological stress during pregnancy, and explain how stress affects the developing organism. (105)

_____
_____
_____
_____

7. True or False: Infants of teenagers are born with a higher rate of problems because physical immaturity of the mother's body leads to pregnancy complications. (105)

Childbirth

1. Name and describe the three stages of labor. (106-107)

A._____
_____
_____

B._____
_____
_____

C._____
_____
_____

The Baby's Adaptation to Labor and Delivery

1. Explain how stress hormones help the baby adapt to labor and delivery. (107-108)

_____
_____
_____

The Newborn Baby's Appearance

1. The average newborn is _____ inches long and _____ pounds in weight; (boys/girls) tend to be slightly longer and heavier than (boys/girls). (108)

Assessing the Newborn's Physical Condition: The Apgar Scale

1. List the five characteristics of the newborn assessed by the Apgar Scale. (108)

A._____
B._____
C._____
D._____
E._____

2. When using the Apgar Scale, doctors and nurses rate the newborn from _____ to _____ on each of five characteristics at _____ and _____ minutes after birth. A score of _____ or better indicates that the infant is in good physical condition. If the score is between _____ and _____, the baby requires special help, and if the score is _____ or below, the infant is in serious danger. (108)

Approaches to Childbirth

1. True or False: In the 1950s and 1960s, a natural childbirth movement arose in Europe and spread to the United States, but the hospitals in the United States have now largely rejected its ideas concerning childbirth. (109)

Natural, or Prepared, Childbirth

1. Describe the three parts of a typical natural childbirth program: (109)

A. _____

_____

B. _____

_____

C. _____

_____

2. True or False: Research suggests that social support may be an important part of the success of natural childbirth techniques. (110)

Home Delivery

1. True or False: If mothers are at risk for any kind of complication, the appropriate place for labor and delivery is the hospital. (111)

Labor and Delivery Medication

1. Some form of medication is still used in _____ to _____ percent of births in the United States. (111)

2. True or False: When medication is given in large doses during labor and delivery, it produces a depressed state in the newborn baby that includes symptoms such as sleepiness, poor sucking during feedings, and irritability. (111)

Birth Complications

Oxygen Deprivation

1. Describe events during the birth process that may result in infants being exposed to anoxia, or inadequate oxygen supply. (111-112)

_____

_____

_____

_____

_____

_____

_____

2. Define Rh incompatibility, and explain how it may lead to anoxia. (112)

_____

_____

_____

_____

3. True or False: Children deprived of oxygen during labor and delivery remain behind their agemates in intellectual and motor progress throughout early childhood, but by the school years, most catch up in development. (112)

4. Babies born more than 6 weeks early commonly have a disorder called _____ _____. (112)

Preterm and Low-Birth-Weight Infants

1. Babies born ____ weeks or more before the end of a full 38-week pregnancy or who weigh less than ____ pounds are referred to as "premature." (112)

2. _____ is the best available predictor of infant survival and healthy development. (112)

3. What factors may increase the risk of having a premature birth? (112-113)

_____

_____

_____

4. Researchers have divided low-birth-weight infants into two groups: _____ infants are born several weeks or more before their due date; _____ infants are below their expected weight when length of pregnancy is taken into account. (113)

5. (Preterm/small-for-date) infants usually have more serious problems. (113)

6. Describe the characteristics of preterm infants and explain how those characteristics may influence the behavior of parents. (113-114)

_____

_____

_____

_____

7. _____ is an especially important form of stimulation for preterm newborns. (114)

8. True or False: Just a few training sessions may be sufficient to enable economically advantaged parents of low-birth-weight infants so that by childhood years, their children's mental test performance is equivalent to that of full-term children. (115)

9. True or False: When preterm infants live in stressed, low-income households, short-term intervention is sufficient to reduce developmental problems. (115)

10. Black infants are more than _____ as likely as white infants to die in the first year of life. (116)

11. Describe the two factors largely responsible for neonatal mortality. (116)
A._____
B._____

12. True or False: High-quality prenatal care beginning early in pregnancy is consistently related to birth weight and infant survival. (116)

Understanding Birth Complications

1. The _____ study tells us that as long as birth injuries are not overwhelming, a _____ can restore children's growth. (116)

2. True or False: In the Kauai Study, those children with fairly serious birth complications and troubled family environments who grew into competent adults relied on factors within the family and outside themselves to overcome stress. (116-117)

Heredity, Environment, and Behavior: A Look Ahead

1. _____ is a field devoted to discovering the origins of the great diversity in human characteristics. (118)

2. All behavioral geneticists agree that both _____ and _____ _____ are involved in every aspect of development. (118)

The Question, "How Much?"

1. A(n) _____ measures the extent to which individual differences in complex traits in a specific population are due to genetic factors. (119)

2. Heritability estimates are obtained from _____. (119)

3. Heritability estimates range from ____ to ____; a value of ____ indicates that half the variation for a particular trait can be explained by individual differences in genetic makeup. (119)

4. The _____ refers to the percentage of instances in which both twins show a trait when it is present in one twin. It ranges from ____ to ____ percent. (119)

5. When a concordance rate is much higher for identical twins than for fraternal twins, _____ is believed to play a major role. (119)

6. Discuss the limitations of heritability estimates and concordance rates. (120)

_____

_____

_____

_____

_____

_____

The Question, "How?"

1. The concept of _____ emphasizes that each person responds to the environment in a unique way because of his or her genetic makeup. (121)

2. True or False: According to the concept of range of reaction, different genetic-environmental combinations can make two children look the same. (121)

3. _____ is the tendency for heredity to restrict the development of some characteristics to just one or a few outcomes. (121)

4. Infant perceptual and motor development seems to be (strongly/less strongly) canalized, while intelligence and personality are (strongly/less strongly) canalized. (121)

5. Recently, scientists have expanded the notion of canalization to include _____ influences. (121)

6. According to the concept of _____, our genes influence the environments to which we are exposed. (122)

7. Describe the two types of genetic-environmental correlation common at younger ages. (122)

A._____

_____

B._____

_____

8. At older ages, _____ genetic-environmental correlation becomes common. (123)

9. The tendency to actively choose environments that complement our heredity is called _____. (123)

10. The influence of heredity and environmental factors (is/is not) constant over time. (123)

ASK YOURSELF...

3.1 Gilbert and Jan are planning to have children. Gilbert's genetic makeup is homozygous for dark hair; Jan's is homozygous for blond hair. What proportion of their children are likely to be dark haired? Explain.
(p. 87)

3.2 Ashley and Harold both carry the defective gene for fragile X syndrome. Explain why Ashley's child inherited the disorder but Harold's did not.
(p. 87)

3.3 Why is it difficult to determine the effects of some environmental agents, such as over-the-counter drugs and pollution, on the embryo and fetus? (p. 106)

3.4 Nora, pregnant for the first time, has heard about the teratogenic effects of tobacco and alcohol. Nevertheless, she believes that a few cigarettes and a glass of wine a day won't be harmful. Provide Nora with research-based reasons to abstain from smoking and drinking. (p. 106)

3.5 How do long-term outcomes reported for anoxic and preterm newborns fit with findings of the Kauai Study? (p. 118)

3.6 Bianca's parents are both accomplished musicians. Bianca began taking piano lessons when she was 4 years old and was accompanying her school choir by age 10. When she reached adolescence, she asked her parents if she could attend a special music high school. Explain how genetic and environmental factors work together to promote Bianca's talent. (p. 123)

CONNECTIONS

3.1 Families of children with a genetic disorder, such as Down syndrome, face increased stresses. What factors, within and beyond the home, can help them cope well? (Return to Chapter 1, pages 27-30, to review ecological systems theory; also see the discussion of family functioning in Chapter 14, pages 559-562.)

3.2 Research summarized in the Variations box on page 96 suggests that highly active fetuses tend to be difficult-to-care-for babies after birth. Why are difficult babies at risk for poor parenting? What caregiving strategies can help a difficult infant calm down and achieve more adaptive functioning? (See Chapter 10, page 420.)

3.3 List prenatal environmental influences discussed earlier in this chapter that increase the chances of anoxia and preterm birth. What does your list imply about effective ways to prevent these birth complications?
(See pages 95-105.)

3.4 Why might very low-birth-weight and ill newborns face special challenges in forming a secure infant-caregiver attachment?
(See Chapter 10, page 427.)

3.5 After reading a news article about the heritability of complex traits, Ross concluded that there wasn't much he could do to influence his children's intellectual and personality development. Explain the limitations of heritability estimates to Ross. Cite evidence indicating that parents play vital roles in children's development. (See Chapter 8, pages 343-344; Chapter 10, pages 420-421 and 426-427; and Chapter 14, pages 563-566.)

PUZZLE 3.1

Across

1 Union of sperm and ovum at conception
4 22 matching chromosomes in each human cell
5 Physical and behavioral characteristics
10 Twins with the same genetic makeup
11 Heterozygous person who can pass on a recessive allele
13 23rd pair of chromosomes in the human cell
16 ___ of reaction, which emphasizes that people respond to the environment uniquely due to their genetics
17 Influence of a single gene on more than one trait
19 Twins when two ova are fertilized
23 Pattern of inheritance influenced by many genes
24 Permits exchange of nutrients and waste
26 Contains instructions for production of proteins
27 Inner membrane that forms protective covering around the prenatal organism

Down

2 Human sperm and ova
3 Has two identical alleles at the same place
6 Two or more forms of a gene at the same location
7 ___ for date defines babies below expected weight
8 Rodlike structures that store and transmit genetic information
9 Both alleles are expressed
12 ___ factor, involving incompatibility between mother and baby in a blood protein
14 ___ diagnostic methods, which make early detection of abnormalities possible
15 Genetic makeup of the individual
18 Outer membrane, which forms protective covering around the prenatal organism
20 Process of cell duplication
21 Males are more likely to be affected by X-___ inheritance
22 Process by which gametes are formed
25 ___ Scale, which quickly assesses the baby's physical condition

PUZZLE 3.2

Across

8 Infants born several weeks or more before their due date
9 ___-picking means individuals choose environments that complement their heredity
10 Restriction of development of some characteristics to one or a few outcomes
16 Sudden, permanent change in a DNA segment
18 ___ genetics is devoted to discovering the origins of diversity in humans
20 Studies of family members to determine the importance of heredity
22 White, downy hair covering the fetus
23 ___-recessive inheritance, involving heterozygous pairings where only one allele affects the child's characteristics
24 Mother of ___ babies drank alcohol in small quantities while pregnant

Down

1 Having two different alleles at the same place
2 Genetic ___, when one parent's allele is activated, regardless of its makeup
3 White, cheeselike substance covering the fetus
4 Prenatal organism from the 9th week
5 ___ estimate measures the extent to which differences in complex traits are due to genetics
6 Our genes influence the environments to which we are exposed in genetic-environmental ___
7 ___ rate, percentage of instances in which both twins show trait present in one
11 ___ counseling helps couples at risk for giving birth to children with hereditary defects
12 Age when a baby can first survive
13 Major cause of infant ___ is low birth weight
14 Damaging prenatal environmental agent
15 Long cord connecting the prenatal organism to the placenta
17 The prenatal organism from 2 to 8 weeks after conception
19 ___ genes can enhance or dilute the effects of alleles controlling particular traits
21 Position in which baby's buttocks or feet are delivered first
24 ___ babies had mothers who drank heavily during pregnancy

PRACTICE TEST

1. Which of the following is NOT true of phenotypes? (71)
   A. They depend in part on the genotype.
   B. They are affected by environmental influences.
   C. They cannot be observed.
   D. They are affected even before conception by environmental factors.

2. Which of the following is NOT true of DNA? (72)
   A. Adenine always appears with thymine.
   B. Genes are always of the same length.
   C. The bases can occur in any order along the sides of the ladder.
   D. It is the sequence of base pairs that provides genetic instructions.

3. Which of the following is NOT true of meiosis? (73-75)
   A. Genes from one chromosome are replaced by genes from another.
   B. It leads to variability among offspring.
   C. Each chromosome becomes part of a sex cell.
   D. In the male, two sperm are produced each time it occurs.

4. Fraternal twinning is: (75)
   A. more likely to occur among women with poor diets.
   B. more likely to occur among whites.
   C. more likely to occur among women who have taken fertility drugs.
   D. most likely to occur if the mother is in her 40s.

5. Which of the following is NOT true of an individual with a heterozygous makeup for a trait that follows the rules of dominant-recessive inheritance? (76)
   A. The recessive allele will not affect the individual's visible characteristics.
   B. The individual can pass the recessive trait on to his or her children.
   C. The individual is called a carrier of the recessive trait.
   D. The individual may have blond hair.

6. If both parents are heterozygous carriers of a recessive allele that follows the rules of dominant-recessive inheritance, such as the one for PKU: (77)
   A. we can predict that 50 percent of their offspring will be carriers.
   B. we can predict that 50 percent of their offspring will be normal.
   C. we can predict that all of their offspring will inherit the disorder.
   D. we can predict that 50 percent of their offspring will inherit the disorder.

7. Which of the following is NOT an X-linked disease? (79)
   A. Duchenne muscular dystrophy
   B. Cystic fibrosis
   C. Hemophilia
   D. Diabetes insipidus

8. Genetic imprinting: (80)
    A. follows the rules of dominant-recessive and codominant inheritance.
    B. is always permanent.
    C. is involved in several childhood cancers.
    D. affects only traits carried on the autosomes.

9. Which of the following is NOT true of mutations? (81)
    A. They may affect only one or two genes.
    B. Some occur by chance.
    C. They may occur as a result of fathers' occupational exposure to radiation.
    D. They result from a temporary change in DNA.

10. Children with Down syndrome: (82)
    A. have an extra X chromosome.
    B. have a normal life expectancy.
    C. benefit from early intervention.
    D. are easy to care for as infants.

11. Which of the following is NOT a sex chromosome disorder? (82-83)
    A. Down syndrome
    B. Turner syndrome
    C. Klinefelter syndrome
    D. Triple X syndrome

12. Which of the following is NOT a characteristic of new reproductive technologies? (84-85)
    A. Children conceived may be genetically unrelated to one or both of their parents.
    B. Children conceived often receive inferior parenting.
    C. Post-menopausal women may become pregnant.
    D. Donors are not always screened for genetic diseases.

13. During the period of the zygote: (90)
    A. the most rapid prenatal changes take place.
    B. the embryonic disk forms three layers of cells.
    C. cells form a blastocyst.
    D. the organism's heart begins to pump blood.

14. During the period of the embryo: (92)
    A. the organism is especially vulnerable to interference in healthy development.
    B. implantation occurs.
    C. the placenta begins to develop.
    D. the organism is covered with vernix.

15. During the period of the fetus: (94)
    A. the placenta develops.
    B. tiny buds become arms, legs, fingers, and toes.
    C. the cerebral cortex enlarges.
    D. a neural tube is formed.

16. Which of the following is NOT true of teratogens? (95, 97)
    A. The amount and length of exposure make a difference.
    B. The genetic makeup of the mother and baby is important.
    C. They are most likely to produce serious effects during the fetal period.
    D. Their effect may depend on their number and on other negative factors.

17. Which illegal drug appears more likely to cause lasting difficulties to prenatally exposed children? (99)
    A. cocaine
    B. marijuana
    C. methadone
    D. heroin

18. Which of the following is NOT true of prenatal exposure to alcohol? (100-101)
    A. Distinct physical symptoms accompany FAS.
    B. Current guidelines allow pregnant women 2 drinks per day.
    C. The defects produced vary with timing and length of exposure.
    D. Children with FAE display fewer abnormalities than those with FAS.

19. The AIDS virus: (103)
    A. is transmitted during pregnancy by infected mothers 80 percent of the time.
    B. usually progresses rapidly in infants.
    C. has infected very few children worldwide.
    D. is spread through airborne contact.

20. Which of the following is NOT assessed by the Apgar Scale? (108)
    A. color
    B. temperature
    C. reflex irritability
    D. respiratory effort

21. Which of the following is NOT a documented cause of anoxia during the birth process? (112)
    A. Rh incompatibility
    B. placenta abruptio
    C. squeezing of the umbilical cord during labor
    D. use of analgesics

22. Which of the following does NOT apply to preterm infants? (113-114)
    A. They are often irritable during infancy.
    B. Touch is an especially important stimulation.
    C. They are at lower risk for child abuse.
    D. Their outcomes depend greatly on the parent-child relationship.

23. A heritability estimate: (119)
    A. is the percentage of instances in which both twins show a trait if one does.
    B. is typically used to study emotional and behavior disorders.
    C. is obtained from kinship studies.
    D. does not need to take account of environmental influences.

24. Canalization: (121)
    A. applies strongly to infant perceptual and motor development.
    B. applies strongly to the development of intelligence.
    C. applies strongly to the development of personality.
    D. does not include environmental influences on development.

25. The intellectually gifted child who insists on visiting the public library every week and becomes an excellent student is an example of: (123)
    A. passive correlation.
    B. active correlation.
    C. evocative correlation.
    D. exposure correlation.

CHAPTER 4

INFANCY: EARLY LEARNING, MOTOR SKILLS, AND PERCEPTUAL CAPACITIES

SUMMARY

Although it comprises only 2 percent of the life span, infancy is one of the most remarkable and busiest times of development. The newborn baby enters the world with surprisingly sophisticated perceptual and motor abilities, a set of skills for interacting with people, and a capacity to learn that is put to use immediately after birth.

Reflexes are the newborn's most obvious organized patterns of behavior. Some have survival value; others form the basis for motor skills that will develop later. Infants move in and out of six states of arousal that become more organized and predictable with age. Like children and adults, infants alternate between REM and NREM sleep, although they spend far more time in the REM state than they ever will again. Young infants are believed to have a special need for REM sleep; their brain-wave activity safeguards the central nervous system, and the rapid eye movements protect the health of the eye. Crying is the first way that babies communicate, letting parents know they need food, comfort, and stimulation. An infant's cry stimulates strong feelings of arousal and discomfort in almost everyone, and controversy exists on how quickly and how often parents should respond. Abnormal crying may indicate central nervous system distress.

Babies come into the world with a built-in set of learning mechanisms that permit them to profit from experience immediately. Infants are capable of two basic forms of learning: classical and operant conditioning. Habituation and dishabituation research provides a window into infant attention, perception, and cognition, and reveals that infants are naturally attracted to novel stimulation and that their recognition memory improves steadily with age. Newborn infants also have a remarkable capacity to imitate the facial expressions and gestures of adults.

According to dynamic systems theory, motor development is energized by the baby's exploration and desire to master new tasks and jointly influenced by central nervous system maturation, movement possibilities of the body, and environmental supports. Voluntary reaching plays a vital role in infant cognitive development and is integrated into increasingly elaborate motor skills. Newborns have a built-in sense of balance that is refined with experience and motor control, and their postural adjustments to self-movement take place unconsciously.

Sensitivity to touch, taste, smell, and sound are well developed in the newborn, and vision improves during the early months. Research on infants with severe visual impairments dramatically illustrates the interdependence of vision, social interaction, motor exploration, and understanding of the world. Depth perception develops as infants detect kinetic, binocular, and pictorial cues, and gradually babies move from focusing on the parts of a pattern to perceiving it as an organized whole. The Gibsons's differentiation theory provides an overall account of perceptual development.

Research findings on the question of whether infancy is a sensitive period of development indicate that early experience combines with current conditions to affect the child's development.

LEARNING OBJECTIVES

After reading this chapter, you should be able to:

4.1 Describe the major newborn reflexes, noting their functions and the importance of assessing them. (128-130)

4.2 Describe changing states of arousal in infancy, including sleep and crying, noting ways to soothe a crying infant and the importance of caregiver responsiveness. (130-136)

4.3 Describe the usefulness of neonatal behavioral assessment. (137)

4.4 Describe four basic infant learning capacities, the conditions under which they occur, the way they change with age, and the unique value of each. (137-143)

4.5 Describe the sequence of motor development during the first 2 years. (144-146)

4.6 Describe dynamic systems theory of development and the microgenetic and cross-cultural findings that support it. (146-147)

4.7 Describe the development of reaching, grasping, and manipulation of objects, and explain how early experience affects these skills. (147-149)

4.8 Describe infants' sensitivity to touch, taste, smell, and balance and self-movement, noting how each perceptual capacity influences other aspects of development. (150-153)

4.9 Summarize the development of hearing in infancy, and explain its influence on other aspects of development. (153-154)

4.10 Describe the newborn baby's visual capacities and improvements that occur in the early months. (154-156)

4.11 Describe the development of depth perception in infancy, noting factors that contribute to it. (156-159)

4.12 Describe the development of pattern perception in infancy, noting factors that influence it. (159, 161-163)

4.13 Describe the development of object perception, including size and shape constancy and how infants learn to perceive a world of independently existing objects. (163-164)

4.14 Describe evidence supporting the conclusion that from the start, babies are capable of intermodal perception. (164, 166)

4.15 Explain differentiation theory of perceptual development. (166-167)

4.16 Discuss research on early deprivation and enrichment, and explain how it sheds light on the question of whether infancy is a sensitive period of development. (168-169)

STUDY QUESTIONS

1. Infancy refers to the period of development that begins at _____ and ends at about _____ of age with an immediate capacity to _____.
(127)

The Organized Newborn

1. True or False: A newborn has a wide variety of typically human capacities that are crucial for survival. (128)

Newborn Reflexes

1. A _____ is an inborn, automatic response to a particular form of stimulation. (128)

2. The _____ reflex helps a breast-fed baby find the mother's nipple. (128)

3. The _____, or "embracing" reflex, is believed to have helped infants cling to their mothers but no longer serves any special purpose. It disappears by _____ of age. (128-129)

4. True or False: Some newborn reflexes have survival value, some protect infants from unwanted stimulation, and some help parents and babies establish gratifying interaction. (128-129)

5. Most newborn reflexes disappear during the first ____ months. (129)

6. The _____ reflex prepares the infant for voluntary grasping, and the _____ reflex may prepare the infant for voluntary reaching. (129)

7. Discuss research findings concerning how early reflexive stimulation contributes to motor control. (130)

_____

_____

_____

_____

8. Discuss how testing reflexes may help a pediatrician assess the nervous system of a newborn. (130)

_____
_____
_____
_____

Newborn States

1. Name and describe the six different states of arousal of newborn infants. (131)
A._____
_____
B._____
_____
C._____
_____
D._____
_____
E._____
_____
F._____
_____

2. By _____ months, the nightly sleep period of many babies reared in Western nations is _____ hours, resembling that of the parents. (130)

3. True or False: Parent-infant cosleeping is found only in nonindustrialized countries. (132)

4. True or False: Parents who practice cosleeping want their babies to establish an interdependent relationship with the community. (132)

5. Describe REM and NREM sleep states. (131-132)
A. REM:_____
_____
_____
B. NREM:_____
_____
_____

6. Newborns spend far (more/less) time in the REM state than they ever will again throughout their lives. REM sleep accounts for _____ percent of the newborn baby's sleep, but it declines to _____ percent between 3 and 5 years of age. (133)

7. Explain how autostimulation theory accounts for the amount of time spent by newborns in REM sleep. (133)

_____
_____
_____
_____

8. During REM sleep, _____ movements circulate vitreous humor, ensuring the eye is fully oxygenated. (133)

9. An infant usually cries because of (social/physical) needs. (134)

10. An infant's _____ often makes a difference in whether the baby will cry in response to a stimulus. (134)

11. A sharp, piercing, sustained cry usually means the baby is in _____ and causes greater _____ arousal in adults than other cries. (134)

12. List several ways to soothe a crying newborn. (134-135)

_____
_____
_____
_____

13. According to ethological theory, quick and consistent parental responsiveness to an infant's cries is (adaptive/not adaptive) for the baby's development. (135)

14. According to researchers who endorse a behaviorist position, quick and consistent parental responsiveness to an infant's cries (strengthens/weakens) crying behavior and results in a (whiny/self-sufficient) child. (135)

15. The cries of brain-damaged babies and those who have experienced prenatal and birth complications often sound _____ and _____. They sometimes contribute to _____ of the infant by parents. (136)

Neonatal Behavioral Assessment

1. The most widely used test of overall behavioral status of the newborn is the _____ _____. The test's goal is to bring out the most complex, organized _____ of which newborns are capable. (137)

2. List three reasons why neonatal assessment is useful. (137)
A._____
B._____
C._____

3. Research indicates that a single Neonatal Behavioral Assessment Scale score (is/is not) a good predictor of later development. (137)

Learning Capacities

1. _____ refers to changes in behavior as the result of experience. (137)

2. Define classical conditioning. (138)

_____
_____
_____

3. Why is classical conditioning of great value to infants? (138)

_____
_____

4. Before learning occurs in classical conditioning, a(n) _____ must consistently produce a(n) _____. A neutral stimulus that does not lead to the reflex is presented at about the same time as the _____. If learning has occurred, the neutral stimulus by itself produces the reflexive response. The neutral stimulus is then called a(n) _____, and the response it elicits is called a(n) _____. (138)

5. In the form of learning called _____, infants act on the environment, and stimuli that follow their behavior change the probability that the behavior will occur again. (138)

6. A stimulus that increases the occurrence of a response is called a(n) _____ _____. (138-139)

7. Removing a desirable stimulus or introducing an unpleasant one to decrease the occurrence of a response is called _____. (139)

8. In the young infant, operant conditioning is limited to _____ and _____ responses. (139)

9. True or False: Young infants are not yet interested in stimulus variety and change, and prefer that stimuli remain constant. (139)

10. The leading cause of infant mortality between 1 week and 12 months of age is _____ in industrialized nations. (140)

11. Infants who (are/are not) wrapped warmly in clothes and blankets and sleep on their (stomachs/backs) are more likely to die from SIDS. (140)

12. _____ refers to a gradual (increase/decrease) in the strength of a response due to repetitive stimulation. Recovery of interest due to introduction of a new stimulus is called _____. (141)

13. As infants age, habituation and dishabituation to novel visual stimuli is (faster/slower), although gains in visual perceptions lead 2-month-olds to take (more/less) time than newborns and older infants. (141)

14. During the first 6 months, infant memory is highly _____ dependent. (142)

15. Habituation-dishabituation responses of infants are the best available predictors of _____. (142)

16. True or False: Habituation-dishabituation research requires the use of recall memory by babies. (142)

17. According to Meltzoff, the capacity of the newborn to imitate is an (automatic/voluntary) response to stimuli that is (flexible/inflexible). (143)

18. In what ways is the capacity to imitate beneficial for a baby? (143)

_____
_____
_____
_____
_____

Motor Development in Infancy

1. Discuss why mastery of motor skills by babies has powerful effects on development. (144)

_____
_____
_____
_____
_____

The Sequence of Motor Development

1. (Gross/fine) motor development refers to control over actions that help infants get around in the environment; (gross/fine) has to do with smaller movements such as reaching and grasping. (144)

2. The head-to-tail sequence of motor control is called the _____ trend, and development that proceeds from the center of the body outward is called the _____ trend. (145)

Motor Skills as Dynamic Systems

1. Mastery of motor skills involves acquiring increasingly complex _____
_____, according to dynamic systems theory of motor development. (146)

2. List four factors that jointly contribute to a new motor skill. (146)
A._____
B._____
C._____
D._____

3. True or False: Motor development is a genetically predetermined process where the behaviors are hardwired into the nervous system. (146)

4. Discuss Thelen's use of the microgenetic method to demonstrate dynamic systems theory. (146-147)

_____
_____
_____
_____
_____

5. Discuss how cross-cultural research has confirmed assumptions of dynamic systems theory. (147)

_____
_____
_____
_____
_____
_____
_____

Fine Motor Development: Voluntary Reaching, Grasping, and Manipulation of Objects

1. Of all motor skills, _____, which appears at about ____ months, is believed to play the greatest role in infant cognitive development. (147-148)

2. The _____ is a clumsy motion in which the infant's fingers close against the palm, whereas the _____ is a well-coordinated movement in which the thumb and index finger are used opposably. (149)

3. True or False: The research of White and Held with institutionalized babies confirmed that massive stimulation of babies resulted in the most advanced development of voluntary reaching. (149)

Perceptual Development in Infancy

1. Explain how perception and action are linked in development. (150)

_____

_____

_____

Touch

1. List three reasons the sense of touch is important for the newborn. (151)

A. _____

B. _____

C. _____

2. True or False: It is well established by medical research that infants do not develop sensitivity to pain until several months after birth. (151)

Taste and Smell

1. Describe the facial expressions of infants in response to several basic tastes. (151)

_____

_____

_____

2. True or False: At birth, infants prefer a salty taste to all others. (151)

3. In the newborn, (some/no) odor preferences are innate. (152)

4. True or False: All babies can recognize their mother's smell within the first week of life. (152)

Balance and Self-Movement

1. List three sources of sensory information that specify a need to adapt body position. (152)

A. _____

B. _____

C. _____

2. True or False: Research reveals that infants' postural adjustments take place consciously and therefore are not present in the first 6 months. (152)

Hearing

1. Infants as young as _____ turn their eyes and head in the general direction of a sound. (153)

2. Infants prefer a (high-pitched/low-pitched) human voice with a (rising/steady) tone at the ends of phrases and sentences. (154)

3. Infants' special responsiveness to speech encourages parents to talk to them and strengthens both _____ and the _____. (154)

4. Explain how otitis media may disrupt language and academic progress of young children. (155)

_____

_____

_____

_____

5. List four ways to prevent negative developmental outcomes of early otitis media. (155)

A._____

_____

B._____

_____

C._____

_____

D._____

_____

Vision

1. Vision is the (most/least) mature of the newborn baby's senses. (154)

2. Newborns see objects at a distance of 20 feet about as well as adults do at _____ feet, but by _____ of age, visual acuity reaches a near-adult level. (154)

3. By ____ months, infants can focus on objects just as well as adults can. (154)

4. Describe the development of color perception during the first months of life. (154-156)

_____

_____

_____

_____

5. _____ is the ability to judge the distance of objects from one another and from ourselves. (156)

6. Describe the visual cliff, devised by Eleanor Gibson and Richard Walk, and explain what it indicates and what it fails to show about the development of depth perception. (157)

_____
_____
_____
_____
_____
_____

7. Describe three depth cues, and explain when and how infants use them. (157-158)

A. _____
_____
_____

B. _____
_____
_____

C. _____
_____
_____

8. Explain why perception of depth cues emerges in a particular order. (158)

_____
_____
_____
_____
_____

9. Crawling infants are better at _____ object locations and _____ hidden objects. (158-159)

10. List aspects of development that are delayed in children with severe visual impairments. (160)

_____
_____
_____
_____

11. Describe four techniques that help infants focus attention and become aware of their physical and social surroundings. (160)

A. _____
B. _____
C. _____
D. _____

12. The principle of _____ accounts for early pattern preferences of infants. If infants can detect the contrast in two or more patterns, they prefer the one with (more/less) contrast. (159)

13. Describe the development of the infant's ability to combine pattern elements. (159, 161)

_____
_____
_____
_____
_____

14. What factors are related to the infant's increasing ability to detect more fine-grained pattern elements and integrated forms? (161)

_____
_____

15. A one-month-old infant (can/cannot) discriminate a static image of the human face from a pattern of equal complexity. (162)

16. _____ is the perception of an object's size as the same, despite changes in its retinal image size, and _____ is the perception of an object's shape as stable, despite changes in the shape projected on the retina. (163)

17. Both shape and size constancy are (learned/innate) perceptual capacities. (163)

18. It is the _____ of objects relative to one another and to their background that gradually enables infants to construct a visual world of separate objects. (164)

Intermodal Perception

1. From the start, babies perceive the world in a(n) _____ fashion and expect sight, sound, and touch to go together. (164)

2. By _____ months, vision and hearing are well coordinated. (166)

Understanding Perceptual Development

1. Describe differentiation theory of perceptual development. (166)

_____
_____
_____
_____
_____
_____

1. In his research on the development of Lebanese orphans, Dennis concluded that environmental improvement by age _____ is necessary for recovery of deprived infants. (168)

2. True or False: Although too little stimulation has been found to result in developmental delays and deficits, one cannot provide a child with too much stimulation. (169)

ASK YOURSELF...

4.1 How do the capacities of newborn babies contribute to their first social relationships? Provide as many examples as you can. (p. 144)

4.2 Jackie, who had a difficult birth, observes her 2-day-old daughter, Kelly, being given the NBAS. Kelly scores poorly on many items. Jackie wonders if this means that Kelly will not develop normally. On the basis of research evidence, how would you respond to Jackie's concern? (p. 144)

4.3 Cite an example showing that motor development is not hardwired but softly assembled. (p. 150)

4.4 Roseanne read in a magazine that motor development could be accelerated through exercise and visual stimulation. She hung mobiles and pictures all over her newborn baby's crib, and she massages and manipulates his body daily. Is Roseanne doing the right thing? Why or why not? (p. 150)

4.5 Can differentiation theory of perceptual development account for infants' changing responsiveness to sound, described on page 153? Explain, citing examples of babies' discovery of invariant features. (p. 167)

4.6 Diane hung bright wallpaper with detailed pictures of animals in Jana's room before she was born. During her first 2 months, Jana hardly noticed the wallpaper. Then, around 2 months, she showed keen interest. What new visual abilities probably account for this change? (p. 167)

4.7 What evidence presented earlier in this chapter indicates that overstimulating young infants can delay their development? (p. 169)

CONNECTIONS

4.1 Recall that fear is difficult to classically condition in young babies. When do expressions of fear typically emerge in infancy, and why is later development of this emotion adaptive? (See Chapter 10, page 403.)

4.2 Recall from Chapter 1 (see page 30) that dynamic systems theorists are interested in explaining variations in development. Describe variations highlighted by dynamic systems research on motor development. Cite factors that promote such variation.

4.3 How do gains in visual perception foster early emotional development? (See Chapter 10, pages 402 and 408.)

4.4 Does research on early brain growth support the view that infancy is a sensitive period? Explain. (See Chapter 5, pages 190-191.)

4.5 Drawing on research findings, explain why the prenatal period is a sensitive period. (See Chapter 3, pages 95-97.)

PUZZLE 4.1

Across

4 Poorly coordinated swipes or swings
7 Response elicited by the CS
9 Stimulus that increases occurrence of a response
10 Most widely accepted theory of perceptual development
11 ___ flow, a sense of motion in the visual field
15 Neutral stimulus once learning has occurred
16 Head-to-tail motor trend
17 Depth cues from slightly different views of the visual field
18 Inborn, automatic response to a stimulus

Down

1 Use of thumb and index finger opposably, in a ___ grasp
2 New stimulus that causes responsiveness to return to high level
3 Motor trend proceeding from the center of the body outward
5 Action possibilities a situation offers the individual
6 ___ sensitivity, accounting for infants' early pattern preferences
8 Perception of object's size as stable, or ___ constancy
12 ___ conditioning, associating a neutral stimulus with one that yields a reflexive response
13 Fineness of discrimination, or visual ___
14 "Irregular" sleep state
15 Apparatus used to study depth perception

PUZZLE 4.2

Across

3 Death of a seemingly healthy baby
5 Way to decrease a response
11 "Regular" sleep state
12 Theory that REM provides needed stimulation
13 Perception of an object's shape as stable, or shape ___
14 Depth cues to make a painting look three-dimensional
16 A stimulus that leads to a reflexive response
17 Assesses the behavioral status of a newborn
19 Grasp in which the fingers close against the palm

Down

1 Depth cues from movements of the body or of objects
2 ___ systems theory, which views new motor skills as reorganizations of previous ones
4 In ___ conditioning, behavior is followed by stimulus that changes likelihood the behavior will occur again
6 Gradual reduction in strength of a response due to repetitive stimulation
7 Combines information from more than one sensory system
8 Features that remain stable in the environment
9 Learning by copying another's behavior
10 Decline of the CR after presenting the CS many times without the UCS
15 States of ___, representing different degrees of sleep and wakefulness
18 A reflexive response produced by a UCS

PRACTICE TEST

1. Which of the following does NOT apply to newborn reflexes? (128-129)
   A. Some have survival value.
   B. Some support interaction between parent and infant.
   C. They are voluntary, flexible behaviors.
   D. Most disappear during the first 6 months.

2. Research on reflexive stepping indicates that: (130)
   A. reflexive practice produces a child who is a better walker.
   B. the mechanism responsible for it is later used by the brain for walking.
   C. infants who practice it do not walk any sooner.
   D. the more weight gain during the first month, the stronger the reflex.

3. During the first month, the infant spends the least sustained time in: (130)
   A. crying.
   B. regular sleep.
   C. quiet alertness.
   D. waking activity.

4. The most widely accepted explanation for the relatively large percentage of time spent by young infants in REM sleep is given by: (133)
   A. autostimulation theory.
   B. reflexive stimulation theory.
   C. cosleeping theory.
   D. ethological theory.

5. The Quechua of Peru carry their infants in a nearly sealed, warm pouch on the mother's back to: (134-135)
   A. promote wakefulness in the infant.
   B. conserve energy in the infant.
   C. adapt infants to their tropical surroundings.
   D. promote self-sufficiency in the infant.

6. Which of the following does NOT apply to infant crying? (136)
   A. It peaks in the evening mainly because of lack of parental attention.
   B. It is greatest during the first 3 months.
   C. It may indicate central nervous system distress.
   D. It sometimes occurs because of difficulties in the sleep-waking cycle.

7. Which of the following does NOT describe a reason why the Neonatal Behavioral Assessment Scale is useful? (137)
   A. It shows how a baby's reactions are changed by child-rearing practices.
   B. It has been used to investigate the effects of birth complications on behavior.
   C. It is efficient because one administration is sufficient for accurate prediction.
   D. It helps parents learn about their baby's unique characteristics.

8. Ideally, in classical conditioning, the: (138)
   A. neutral stimulus should occur just before the unconditioned stimulus.
   B. unconditioned stimulus should occur just before the neutral stimulus.
   C. conditioned response should occur just before the unconditioned response.
   D. unconditioned response should occur just before the conditioned response.

9. In classical conditioning, continually presenting the conditioned stimulus alone without the unconditioned stimulus results in: (138)
   A. negative reinforcement.
   B. extinction.
   C. neutralization.
   D. dishabituation.

10. Which of the following is NOT true of classical conditioning of infants? (138)
    A. An association with survival value is more easily conditioned.
    B. Fear is easily conditioned in young infants.
    C. An infant's state often affects classical conditioning.
    D. Most conditioned responses of infants occur in the feeding situation.

11. Research using operant conditioning of infants: (139)
    A. indicates that they prefer constancy in their environment.
    B. cannot be done until at least 6 months of age.
    C. is limited to cooing and crying responses.
    D. has enabled us to study infant memory.

12. A baby is shown a picture of a wagon followed by pictures of both the wagon and a ball. When presented with both pictures, the baby looks for a longer period at the ball. The baby has _____ to the picture of the wagon. (141)
    A. differentiated
    B. responsiveness
    C. habituated
    D. dishabituated

13. Habituation-dishabituation research measures infant: (141)
    A. motor skills.
    B. imitation.
    C. memory.
    D. extinction responses.

14. Which of the following is NOT true of infant imitative responses? (143)
    A. They are more difficult to induce in the newborn than the 3-month-old.
    B. They provide the infant with a powerful means of learning.
    C. Newborns can imitate even after short delays.
    D. Older babies tend to play social games at first.

15. Which of the following is NOT true of the development of motor skills? (144-145)
    A. Motor achievements have an important effect on social relationships.
    B. Motor skills are isolated, unrelated accomplishments that follow a fixed, maturational timetable.
    C. Motor skills follow a cephalocaudal trend.
    D. Motor skills follow a proximodistal trend.

16. Each new motor skill is a product of all of the following EXCEPT: (146)
    A. central nervous system maturation.
    B. a genetically prewired process.
    C. movement possibilities of the body.
    D. environmental supports.

17. According to dynamic systems theory: (147)
    A. infants achieve motor milestones in a systematically prewired sequence.
    B. motor skill development is primarily due to heredity.
    C. motor skill development is primarily due to experience.
    D. motor skill development is due to complex interactions of nature and nurture.

18. Which motor skill is believed to play the greatest role in infant cognitive development? (147)
    A. prereaching
    B. proprioception
    C. voluntary reaching
    D. binocular grasping

19. Which of the following is NOT true of the infants' sense of taste? (150)
    A. Infants' facial expressions reveal that they distinguish several basic tastes.
    B. Infants' preference for the salty taste develops by 4 months of age.
    C. Infants' taste preferences are important for their survival.
    D. Sweet taste develops differently from salty, sour, or bitter.

20. Which of the following is NOT true of the infant's sense of smell? (152)
    A. Some odor preferences seem to be innate.
    B. Newborns can identify the location of an odor.
    C. All newborns can recognize their mother's smell within the first week.
    D. Bottle-fed babies prefer the smell of their formula over a lactating breast.

21. Vision in newborns: (154)
    A. is the most well-developed sense.
    B. shows a visual acuity slightly inferior to that of adults.
    C. shows well-developed ability to distinguish colors.
    D. continues to develop after birth.

22. For babies: (157)
    A. binocular depth cues are the first to develop.
    B. motion provides information about depth.
    C. 4-month-olds respond to a variety of pictorial depth cues.
    D. kinetic depth cues are the last to develop.

23. When babies look at patterns: (159)
    A. they prefer ones with more detectable contrast.
    B. they look away because their eyes are irritated by contrast.
    C. very young babies limit visual exploration to the stimulus interior.
    D. they ignore them in preference to plain stimuli.

24. Which of the following is NOT true of the infant's perception of the human face?
(162-163)
    A. 1-month-olds do not inspect the eyes, nose, and mouth on a face.
    B. Infants' recognition of faces does not seem to be a built-in capacity.
    C. 3-month-olds can make fine distinctions among the features of different faces.
    D. Newborns react to happy faces differently than they do sad ones.

25. According to Gibson's differentiation theory: (166)
    A. infants actively search for inconsistent features in an environment.
    B. acting on the environment plays a minor role.
    C. over time, babies' capacity to seek out order and stability increases.
    D. babies are unable to detect invariant features.

CHAPTER 5

PHYSICAL GROWTH

SUMMARY

As time passes during the first two decades of life, the human body changes continuously and dramatically, until it reaches the mature adult state. Numerous biological and environmental factors regulate and control the course of human growth. Compared to other animals, primates (including humans) experience a prolonged period of physical growth.

Physical development during infancy and childhood follows the cephalocaudal and proximodistal trends. During puberty, growth actually proceeds in the reverse direction, and sex-related differences in body proportions appear. The best way of estimating a child's physical maturity is to use skeletal age, a measure of development of the bones of the body. Body growth is controlled by a complex set of hormonal secretions released by the pituitary gland and regulated by the hypothalamus. Individual and cultural differences in body size and rate of maturation are influenced by both heredity and environment. Physical growth is an asynchronous process because different body systems have their own unique, carefully timed patterns of maturation.

The human brain achieves its adult size earlier than other organs. Both heredity and early experience contribute to brain organization, and there may be sensitive periods in which appropriate stimulation is necessary. Studies indicate that brain growth spurts coincide with peaks in children's intelligence test performance and major cognitive changes.

Both heredity and nutrition are factors affecting physical growth. Breast-feeding is especially suited to infants' growth needs, and the importance of nutrition is evident in the dietary diseases of marasmus and kwashiorkor. In industrialized countries, obesity is a nutritional problem with health and psychological consequences, and the most effective treatment is family based and focuses on changing behaviors. Infectious disease can combine with poor nutrition to undermine healthy physical development. Nonorganic failure to thrive and deprivation dwarfism illustrate the role of love and stimulation in children's healthy physical growth.

Puberty is a time of dramatic physical change leading to an adult-sized body and sexual maturity. The psychological impact of pubertal events is a product of both biological and social forces. Adolescents' physical changes and their new powers of reasoning may lead to a rise in family tensions, but the conflict that takes place is generally mild. The timing of puberty has a major impact on psychological adjustment. For some adolescent girls, cultural ideals combine with family and individual psychological problems to produce the serious eating disturbances of anorexia nervosa and bulimia. American adolescents receive mixed messages from adults and the larger culture about sexual activity, which contributes to high rates of sexually transmitted disease and teenage pregnancy, abortion, and parenthood.

LEARNING OBJECTIVES

After reading this chapter, you should be able to:

5.1 Describe the course of physical growth from birth through adolescence for boys and girls, including changes in body size, proportions, and composition. (174-177)

5.2 Describe changes in gross motor skills during childhood and adolescence. (177-179)

5.3 Describe skeletal growth, including the usefulness of skeletal age for estimating physical maturity. (179-181)

5.4 Describe hormonal influences on physical growth. (181-184)

5.5 Discuss factors that contribute to worldwide variations, secular trends, and asynchronies in physical growth. (184-185)

5.6 Describe the functions and development of neurons and glial cells. (186-187)

5.7 Describe the lateralized organization of the cerebral cortex and evidence on its development, noting research on brain-injured children and on handedness. (187-190)

5.8 Describe the functions and development of the cerebellum, the reticular formation, and the corpus callosum. (190)

5.9 Discuss evidence supporting brain growth spurts as sensitive periods of development. (190-191)

5.10 Describe evidence indicating that heredity contributes to body size and rate of physical maturation. (192)

5.11 Discuss age-related nutritional needs, including the importance of breast-feeding and the influence of the social environment on children's food preferences. (193194)

5.12 Discuss the causes, symptoms, consequences, and treatment of marasmus and kwashiorkor. (194-195)

5.13 Discuss the incidence, causes, consequences, and treatment of obesity. (195-198)

5.14 Explain how disease interacts with malnutrition to affect physical growth, and describe the importance of oral rehydration therapy (ORT) and immunization in protecting children from infectious disease. (198-199)

5.15 Discuss the causes, symptoms, consequences, and treatment of nonorganic failure to thrive and deprivation dwarfism. (199)

5.16 Describe sexual maturation in girls and boys, noting genetic and environmental influences on pubertal timing. (200-202)

5.17 Cite evidence indicating that puberty is not an inevitable period of storm and stress. (202-203)

5.18 Discuss adolescents' reactions to the physical changes of puberty, noting factors that influence feelings and behavior. (203-206)

5.19 Discuss the impact of maturational timing on adolescent adjustment, noting sex-related differences and short- and long-term consequences. (206-208)

5.20 Describe the symptoms of anorexia nervosa and bulimia, and cite factors within the individual, the family, and the larger culture that contribute to these disorders. (209-210)

5.21 Discuss individual, family, and cultural influences on adolescent sexual attitudes and behavior. (210-212)

5.22 Discuss factors related to homosexuality and the challenges faced by gay and lesbian adolescents in forming a positive sexual identity. (212-213)

5.23 Explain the high incidence of sexually transmitted disease among adolescents, and special concerns about AIDS. (212, 214)

5.24 Discuss factors related to adolescent pregnancy and parenthood, including correlates and consequences, prevention strategies, and interventions with teenage parents. (214-217)

STUDY QUESTIONS

The Course of Physical Growth

1. Why is a prolonged period of physical growth in humans adaptive? (174)

_____

_____

Changes in Body Size

1. Compared with infancy, children's rate of growth (speeds up/slows down) in early and middle childhood. (174)

2. On average, adolescents add nearly _____ inches in height and about _____ pounds in weight. (174)

3. One type of growth curve used to track changes in height and weight is the _____ _____ curve, which plots the average height and weight of a sample of children at each age. (174-175)

4. Around age ____, the average girl becomes taller and heavier than the average boy. At age ____, she is surpassed by the average boy. (175)

5. Another type of growth curve is the _____ curve, which plots the average amount of growth at each yearly interval. (175)

6. True or False: The distance curve is better than the velocity curve in revealing the exact timing of growth spurts. (175)

7. True or False: Throughout their development, children tend to grow in spurts rather than making steady gains. (175)

Changes in Body Proportions

1. Exceptions to the basic _____ and _____ growth trends occur during puberty, when growth actually proceeds in the reverse direction. (176)

2. During adolescence, the most obvious sex-related differences in body proportions involve the _____ in boys and the _____ _____ in girls. (177)

Changes in Body Composition

1. Describe changes in body composition that occur from the last weeks of prenatal life through the teenage years. (177)

_____
_____
_____
_____
_____
_____
_____

Changes in Gross Motor Skills

1. As children's bodies become (more/less) top-heavy, their center of gravity shifts (upward/downward), toward the trunk resulting in improved balance, which will pave the way for new motor skills. (177)

2. Describe the principle of dynamic systems of action as it relates to children's motor development. (178)

_____

_____

_____

3. In early childhood, boys are slightly advanced over girls in abilities that emphasize _____ and _____. Girls have an edge in certain gross motor capacities that combine _____ and _____. (180)

4. Sex-related differences in physical growth during childhood (are/are not) enough to explain boys' superiority in so many gross motor capacities. (180)

5. What non-physical factors may help explain the sex-related differences in many gross motor capacities during childhood? (180-181)

_____

_____

_____

6. Sports influence _____ and _____ development as well as motor performance. (181)

7. What steps can be taken to raise girls' confidence that they can do well at athletics? (181)

_____

_____

_____

Skeletal Growth

1. The best way of estimating a child's physical maturity is to use _____, a measure of development of the bones of the body. (179)

2. Special growth centers in bone called _____ appear just before birth and increase throughout childhood. (179)

3. When the skeletal ages of infants and children are examined, (African-American/ Caucasian-American) children tend to be slightly ahead. (Girls/boys) are considerably ahead. (179)

4. Skull growth is especially rapid during the first ____ years because of large increases in _____ size. (180)

5. At birth, the bones of the skull are separated by ____ gaps, or "soft spots," called _____. (180)

6. True or False: By middle childhood, the sutures, or seams, between the skull bones have completely disappeared. (181)

Hormonal Influences on Physical Growth

1. The vast physical changes that take place during childhood and adolescence are controlled by the _____ of the body which manufacture _____, chemical substances secreted by specialized cells in one part of the body that pass to and influence cells in another. (181-182)

2. The most important hormones for human growth are released by the _____ _____. The _____ initiates and regulates pituitary secretions. (182)

3. _____ is the only pituitary secretion produced continuously throughout life. (182)

4. Explain how growth hormone affects development. (182)

_____

_____

_____

5. _____ is necessary for normal development of the nerve cells of the brain and for growth hormone to have its full impact on body size. (183)

6. True or False: Estrogens are found only in females, and androgens are found only in males. (183)

7. The testes release the androgen _____, which leads to muscle growth, body and facial hair, and gains in body size. (183)

8. _____ influence the girl's height spurt and stimulate growth of underarm and pubic hair. (184)

Worldwide Variations in Body Size

1. What accounts for vast differences in body size and rate of growth among children? (184)

_____

_____

Secular Trends

1. Explain what is meant by secular trends in physical growth. (184)

_____

_____

2. Biologists believe that improved _____ and _____ are largely responsible for secular gains. (184)

3. True or False: It is expected that secular gains in physical growth will continue indefinitely in countries such as the United States, Canada, and Japan. (185)

Asynchronies in Physical Growth

1. Physical growth is a(n) _____ process because different body systems have their own unique, carefully timed patterns of maturation. (185)

2. The _____ describes changes in overall body size. Outer dimensions of the body, as well as a variety of internal organs, follow the same pattern: _____ growth during infancy, _____ gains in early and middle childhood, and _____ growth during adolescence. (185)

3. Describe three exceptions to the general growth curve. (185)
A._____
B._____
C._____

Development of the Brain

Development of Neurons

1. The human brain has ____ to ____ billion nerve cells called _____. These cells release chemicals that cross the _____ between them, thereby sending messages to each other. (186)

2. What are the three developmental steps of neurons? (186)
A._____
B._____
C._____

3. The peak period of development in any brain area is marked by the greatest rate of _____. (186)

4. Neurons seldom stimulated by input from the surrounding environment soon lose their synapses, a process called _____. (186-187)

5. About _____ of the brain's volume is made up of _____. Their most important function is _____, which improves the efficiency of message transfer. (187)

6. By the age of 2, the brain is about _____ percent of its adult weight; by the age of 6, it reaches _____ percent. (187)

Development of the Cerebral Cortex

1. The _____, which is responsible for the unique intelligence of humans, is the (largest/smallest) structure of the brain, the (first/last) brain structure to stop growing, and probably (more/less) sensitive to environmental influences than other parts of the brain. (187)

2. True or False: The order in which areas of the cortex develop corresponds to the sequence in which various capacities emerge during infancy and childhood. (187)

3. Describe the different functions controlled by the left and right hemispheres of the brain. (188)
A. Left:_____
B. Right:_____

4. Specialization of the two hemispheres is called _____. (188)

5. _____ refers to the ability of parts of the brain to take over functions of a part that is damaged. (188)

6. Give examples of hemispheric specialization that are already under way at birth. (188)
_____
_____
_____

7. Although the cortex is programmed from the start for hemispheric specialization, the rate and success of this genetic program are greatly influenced by _____. (189)

8. A strong hand preference reflects the greater capacity of the _____ _____ to carry out skilled motor action. (189)

9. The brains of left-handers tend to be (more/less) strongly lateralized than those of right-handers. (189)

10. Twins are (more/less) likely than ordinary siblings to display opposite handedness. (189)

11. Hand preference, which is evident by _____ months of age, undergoes dips and recoveries that coincide with bursts in _____. (189)

12. A (large/small) number of left-handers show developmental problems. (190)

13. Left- and mixed-handed youngsters are (more/less) likely than right-handed agemates to develop outstanding verbal and mathematical talents. (190)

Other Advances in Brain Development

1. The _____ is a structure that aids in balance and control of body movement. Fibers linking it to the cerebral cortex complete myelinization by age _____. (190)

2. The _____, a structure that maintains alertness and consciousness, continues myelinization into _____. (190)

3. The _____ is a large bundle of nerve fibers that connects the two hemispheres so that they can communicate with one another. (190)

Brain Growth Spurts and Sensitive Periods of Development

1. The existence of sensitive periods in postnatal development of the cortex (has/has not) been demonstrated in studies of animals. (190)

2. Intermittent brain growth spurts are identified by gains in _____ and _____ as well as changes in _____ of the cortex. (191)

3. Brain growth spurts coincide with peaks in children's _____ _____ and major _____ changes. (191)

Factors Affecting Physical Growth

1. Physical growth results from the continuous and complex interplay between _____ and _____. (192)

Heredity

1. At birth, the differences in lengths and weights of identical twins are (greater/less) than those of fraternal twins. (192)

2. Genes influence growth by controlling the body's production of and sensitivity to _____. (192)

3. When environmental conditions are adequate, height and rate of physical growth are strongly influenced by _____. (192)

Nutrition

1. List six nutritional and health advantages of breast-feeding. (193)
A. _____
B. _____
C. _____
D. _____
E. _____
F. _____

2. Breast-fed and bottle-fed youngsters show (differences/no differences) in psychological development. (194)

3. Why is wariness of new foods by toddlers adaptive? (194)
_____
_____

4. As the result of a tendency to consume empty calories, _____ percent of North American teenagers suffer from _____ deficiency. (194)

5. _____ is a wasted condition of the body that usually appears in the first year of life and is caused by a diet that is low in all essential nutrients. (195)

6. _____ is due to an unbalanced diet that is very low in protein. (195)

7. Severe malnutrition may interfere with _____, causing a permanent loss in brain weight. (195)

8. How do the passivity and irritability of malnourished children make the impact of poor diet even worse? (195)
_____
_____

9. Obesity is a greater than _____ percent increase over average body weight, based on the child's age, sex, and physical build. (195)

10. Low-income youngsters in industrialized countries are (more/less) likely to be obese. (196)

11. Describe how parental food choices and feeding practices may contribute to obesity in young children. (197)
_____
_____
_____
_____

12. Next to already existing obesity, _____ is the best predictor of future obesity among school-age children. (197)

13. What are the psychological consequences of obesity? (197)

_____

_____

_____

14. True or False: By young adulthood, overweight individuals have lower incomes, complete fewer years of schooling, and marry less often than do individuals with other chronic health problems. (197-198)

15. The most effective intervention for obesity is _____ which focuses on _____. (198)

16. _____ is a measure of poor diet and stunting; whereas _____ is a measure of obesity. (196)

17. True or False: In each country except China, rate of overweight was greater among stunted than nonstunted children. (196)

18. What are two physiological changes researchers believe contribute to excessive weight gain among growth-stunted children? (196)

A._____

B._____

Infectious Diseases

1. Describe how disease interacts with malnutrition in developing countries in a vicious spiral. (198)

_____

_____

_____

_____

2. _____ _____ can prevent most growth retardation and deaths due to diarrhea. As a result of its use the lives of more than _____ million children are being saved annually. (198)

3. True or False: All medically uninsured American children are now guaranteed free immunizations. (198)

Emotional Well-Being

1. Describe the behavior of infants with nonorganic failure to thrive. (199)

_____

_____

2. Describe the family circumstances surrounding failure to thrive. (199)

_____

_____

_____

3. Deprivation dwarfism appears usually between _____ and _____ years. Its most striking features are _____, _____ _____, and _____. Severe emotional deprivation affects communication between the _____ and the _____, resulting in stunted growth. (199)

Puberty: The Physical Transition to Adulthood

---

1. _____ characteristics involve the reproductive organs; _____ characteristics are visible on the outside of the body. (200)

Sexual Maturation in Girls

1. _____ is the scientific name for the first menstruation, which typically happens around _____ for North American girls. (200)

2. Puberty in girls usually begins with _____ and _____ _____. (200)

3. Why is it adaptive for menarche to follow the peak of the height spurt? (200)

_____

Sexual Maturation in Boys

1. The first sign of puberty in boys is _____, accompanied by changes in the texture and color of the _____. (201)

2. The growth spurt occurs much (earlier/later) in the sequence of pubertal events for boys than girls. (201)

3. Voice change usually takes place (before/at the peak of/after) the male growth spurt. (201-202)

4. Around age ____, _____, or first ejaculation, occurs. (202)

Individual and Group Differences in Pubertal Growth

1. _____ is partly responsible for the timing of puberty. _____ and _____ also contribute. (202)

2. True or False: Variations in pubertal growth do not exist between regions of the world and income groups. (202)

The Psychological Impact of Pubertal Events

Is Puberty an Inevitable Period of Storm and Stress?

1. Emotional turbulence (is/is not) a routine feature in puberty. (202)

2. According to Mead, (biological/social) factors are entirely responsible for how teenagers adjust to puberty. (202)

3. Why is adolescence in industrialized societies usually a more difficult period than in nonindustrialized societies? (203)

_____

_____

_____

Reactions to Pubertal Changes

1. True or False: Girls' reactions to menarche depend on prior knowledge and support from family members. (203)

2. Boys report (negative/mixed/positive) feelings about spermarche, and most obtain information about it from (parents/reading material/friends). (203)

3. Girls are (more/less) likely than boys to tell friends about the physical changes of puberty. (203)

4. Unlike many tribal and village societies that celebrate puberty with a(n) _____ _____, Western societies lack a widely accepted marker of physical and social maturity. (203-204)

5. What is an adolescent initiation ceremony? (204)

_____

_____

6. Describe three features typically included in adolescent initiation ceremonies. (204-205)

A._____

B._____

C._____

Pubertal Change, Emotion, and Social Behavior

1. Research suggests that _____ factors may act in concert with _____ influences to affect teenagers' moodiness. (206)

2. Why would a youngster's more adultlike appearance and sexual maturity trigger parent-child conflict? (206)

_____

_____

_____

3. The conflict that does take place between parents and adolescents is generally (mild/severe). (206)

Early versus Late Maturation

1. Maturational timing acts in (similar/opposite) directions for boys and girls. (206)

2. Describe the findings of studies concerning the characteristics of early- and late maturing boys. (206)

A. Early maturing boys:_____

_____

B. Late maturing boys:_____

_____

3. Describe the findings of studies concerning the characteristics of early- and late maturing girls. (206-207)

A. Early maturing girls:_____

_____

B. Late maturing girls:_____

_____

4. What two factors seem to account for these trends in maturational timing? (207)

A._____

B._____

5. Early maturing girls have a(n) (less/more) positive body image than late maturing girls, whereas early maturing boys have a(n) (less/more) positive body image than late maturing boys. (207)

106

6. True or False: Adolescents feel most comfortable with peers who match their own level of biological maturity. (207)

7. True or False: The academic performance of early maturers tends to exceed that of later maturers. (207)

8. Early maturing sixth-grade girls would probably feel better about themselves if they attended a school that was (K-6/K-8). (207)

9. Describe the long-term consequences of maturational timing. (208)
A. Early maturing boys:_____
_____
B. Late maturing boys:_____
_____
C. Early maturing girls:_____
_____
D. Late maturing girls:_____
_____

10. True or False: The confidence-inducing adolescence of early maturing boys and late maturing girls tends to promote the coping skills needed to solve life's later problems. (208)

Puberty and Adolescent Health

Eating Disorders

1. Anorexia nervosa, an eating disturbance, occurs more often among (Caucasian-American/African-American) females, and occurs among teenagers from economically advantaged (and/but not) economically disadvantaged families. (209)

2. Anorexics have a(n) _____ body image. About _____ percent of those with the disorder die of it. (209)

3. Describe how the forces within the person, family, and culture give rise to anorexia nervosa. (209)

_____
_____
_____
_____
_____

4. _____ is the most successful treatment for anorexia, but still only _____ percent of anorexics fully recover. (209)

5. About 1 to 3 percent of teenage girls, including one-fifth of anorexics, develop _____, a disorder in which young people engage in binge eating followed by deliberate vomiting, purging with laxatives, and strict dieting. (209-210)

6. List two characteristics bulimics share with anorexics. (210)
A._____
B._____

7. How do bulimics differ from anorexics? (210)
_____
_____
_____

Sexuality

1. The production of _____ in both sexes leads to an increase in sex drive. (210)

2. In what ways are American teenagers given contradictory and confusing messages about sex? (210)
_____
_____
_____

3. A (substantial minority/majority) of boys and girls are sexually active by ninth grade. (211)

4. (Males/females) tend to have the earliest first intercourse, and sexual activity is especially high among (black/white) adolescents--especially (girls/boys). (211)

5. Most teenagers engage in relatively (high/low) levels of sexual activity. (211)

6. Give two examples of adolescent cognition that may explain why some sexually active teenagers do not use contraception or use it only occasionally. (211-212)
A._____
B._____

7. Teenagers who talk openly with their parents about sex (are/are not) less sexually active, and are (more/less) likely to use birth control. (212)

8. True or False: New evidence indicates that heredity makes an important contribution to homosexuality. (212)

9. True or False: Identical twins are no more likely than fraternal twins to share a homosexual orientation. (212)

10. How might heredity lead to homosexuality? (212)

_____

_____

11. Explain how family factors are linked to homosexuality. (212)

_____

_____

12. Describe a three-phase sequence adolescents and adults who are homosexual may move through when coming out. (213)

A._____

B._____

C._____

Sexually Transmitted Disease

1. _____ sexually active teenagers contract sexually transmitted diseases. (214)

2. True or False: It is twice as easy for a male to infect a female with any STD, including AIDS, as it is for a female to infect a male. (214)

Adolescent Pregnancy and Parenthood

1. The adolescent pregnancy rate in (Great Britain/Canada/the United States) is the highest in the industrialized world. (214)

2. List three ways that the United States differs from countries such as Canada, France, and the Netherlands that may affect the adolescent pregnancy rate. (214)

A._____

B._____

C._____

3. Although the total number of teenage births in the United States is actually (lower/higher) than it was 30 years ago, in 1960 ____ percent of teenage births were to unmarried females, whereas today, ____ percent are. (214)

4. Describe how early childbirth imposes lasting hardships on two generations. (215)

_____

_____

_____

_____

_____

_____

5. List three factors that often lead to more favorable outcomes for the teenage mother and her child. (216)

A._____

B._____

C._____

6. List three key elements used in more effective sex education programs. (216)

A._____

B._____

C._____

7. In Western Europe, where school-based health clinics offering contraceptive services are common, teenage pregnancy, childbirth, and abortion rates are (much lower than/the same as/much higher than) in the United States. (216)

8. School programs that provide services such as health care, child care, and instruction in life-management skills to adolescent mothers and their children (do/do not) reduce the incidence of low-birth-weight babies and the likelihood of additional rapid childbearing. (216)

ASK YOURSELF. . .

5.1 Explain why boys' childhood advantage over girls in throwing, batting, kicking, dribbling, and catching cannot be accounted for, except in small measure, by sex-related differences in physical growth. (p. 186)

5.2 When Joey was born, the doctor found that his anterior fontanel had started to close prematurely. Joey had surgery to open the fontanel when he was 3 months old. From what you know about the function of the fontanels, why was early surgery necessary? (p. 186)

5.3 Explain why overproduction of synapses and synaptic pruning are adaptive processes that foster optimal development? (p. 192)

5.4 We are used to thinking of brain growth as following a strict genetic program, but research shows that this is not so. List examples that reveal the effects of experience on brain growth and organization. (p. 192)

5.5 Explain why the United Nations engages in vigorous public education campaigns to promote breast-feeding in developing nations. (p. 200)

5.6 Sasha remembers menarche as a traumatic experience. When she discovered she was bleeding, she thought she had a deadly illness. What is the likely cause of Sasha's negative reaction? (p. 208)

5.7 How might adolescent moodiness contribute to the psychological distancing between parents and children that accompanies puberty? (Hint: Think about bidirectional influences in parent-child relationships.) (p. 208)

5.8 Fourteen-year-old Lindsay says she's pretty certain she couldn't get pregnant from having sex with her boyfriend, since he told her he'd never do anything to "mess her up." What factors might account for Lindsay's unrealistic reasoning? (p. 217)

5.9 Explain how cultural forces are involved in each of the following health concerns: adolescent eating disorders, homosexual adolescents' self-acceptance, and teenage pregnancy and childbearing. What implications does your analysis have for the accuracy of the "storm and stress" view of adolescence? (p. 217)

CONNECTIONS

5.1 What do secular trends in physical growth and cohort effects, discussed on page 60 of Chapter 2, have in common? Why would a researcher engaged in a longitudinal or cross-sectional study of physical growth need to be concerned about cohort effects?

5.2 Are findings on early brain plasticity consistent with the modular view of the mind, introduced in Chapter 6 (see page 234)? Explain.

5.3 Select one of the following growth problems of childhood: malnutrition, obesity, or nonorganic failure to thrive. Use ecological systems theory to show how bidirectional influences between caregiver and child combine with factors in the surrounding environment to compromise children's development. (See Chapter 1, pages 27-30.)

5.4 Are infants with nonorganic failure to thrive likely to develop a secure attachment with the familiar caregiver? Explain. (See Chapter 10, pages 426-427.)

5.5 At puberty, many boys and girls display a rise in gender-stereotyped beliefs and behaviors. Why is this so? (See Chapter 13, page 541.)

5.6 Cite commonalities in the life circumstances of adolescents who engage in early and unprotected sex, who commit delinquent acts, and who abuse alcohol and drugs. Explain why these risk behaviors often co-occur. (See Chapter 12, pages 511-514, and Chapter 15, pages 613-615.)

PUZZLE 5.1

Across

5 ___ cerebral hemisphere has greater capacity to carry out skilled motor action
7 ___ callosum connects the two cerebral hemispheres
9 Specialization of the cerebral hemispheres
11 Condition due to an unbalanced diet low in protein
15 Solution children with diarrhea are given that quickly replaces fluids the body loses
16 Aids in balance and control of body movement
17 Affects the development of almost all body tissues
18 ___ age, or measure of physical maturity
19 Wasted condition of the body caused by a diet low in all essential nutrients
20 Nonorganic failure to ___, due to lack of affection and stimulation

Down

1 Process by which neural fibers are coated with an insulating fatty sheath
2 ___ cortex, the brain's largest structure
3 Tribal and village societies celebrate puberty with adolescent ___ ceremonies
4 ___ trends in physical growth, changes from one generation to the next
6 Children with ___ dwarfism are below-average in stature
8 Peak period of brain development is marked by the greatest rate of ___ cell death
10 People with ___ nervosa starve themselves out of fear of getting fat
12 Children who lag behind in body size show ___-up growth under improved conditions
13 ___ formation, the brain stem structure that maintains alertness and consciousness
14 Body ___, conception of and attitude toward one's own physical appearance
17 General ___ curve, describes changes in overall body size

PUZZLE 5.2

Across

1 Biological changes during adolescence leading to sexual maturity
6 ___ sexual characteristics, involving reproductive organs
8 Hormones produced chiefly by the testes, influencing male sex characteristics
13 Initiates and regulates pituitary secretions
17 ___ sexual characteristics, not involving reproductive organs
18 Cells serving the function of myelinization
19 Growth curve that plots average yearly growth
20 Nerve cells that transmit information

Down

2 Leads to binges, purges, and dieting
3 Six soft spots separating the bones of the skull
4 Thyroid hormone necessary for central nervous development
5 Synaptic ___, occurring when neurons seldom stimulated lose their synapses
6 Gland near the base of the brain that releases hormones affecting physical growth
7 First ejaculation of seminal fluid
9 Bone growth centers
10 Gap between neurons
11 Ability of intact brain regions to take over the functions of damaged regions
12 Hormones produced by the ovaries
14 More than 20 percent over average weight
15 Growth curve that plots average height and weight
16 First menstruation

PRACTICE TEST

1. Which of the following is NOT true of the body's muscle-fat makeup? (177)
   A. Around age 5, girls start to add relatively more fat than boys.
   B. At birth, girls have slightly more body fat than boys.
   C. Both sexes gain in muscle at puberty.
   D. The arm and leg fat of adolescent boys decreases.

2. Which of the following is NOT true of sex-related differences in motor skills? (180)
   A. Preschool boys can run a little faster than girls.
   B. Preschool girls are relatively advanced in hopping and skipping.
   C. During middle childhood, differences in skill levels decrease.
   D. 12-year-old boys can throw a ball much farther than 12-year-old girls can.

3. During childhood, boys' superiority in so many gross motor capacities: (180)
   A. can be explained by sex-related differences in physical growth.
   B. can be explained by their overall superior physical maturity.
   C. can be explained by adult encouragement and example.
   D. cannot be explained.

4. When the skeletal ages of infants and children are examined: (179)
   A. Caucasian-American children are ahead of African-American children.
   B. boys are considerably ahead of girls.
   C. the gap between the sexes widens over infancy and childhood.
   D. at birth, there is no difference between the sexes.

5. Growth hormone: (182)
   A. is produced until the end of puberty.
   B. affects prenatal growth.
   C. stimulates the release of somatomedin.
   D. is produced by the thyroid gland.

6. The secular trends in physical growth occurring in industrialized nations are best explained by: (184)
   A. genetic mutations.
   B. increasing numbers of large families.
   C. improved nutrition and health.
   D. the increase in single-parent families.

7. Neurons in the brain: (186-187)
   A. send messages to each other by electrical means.
   B. are generated until the end of puberty.
   C. engage in a process called synaptic pruning.
   D. number in the millions.

8. Lateralization of the brain: (187-188)
   A. begins after age 2.
   B. increases brain plasticity.
   C. is not influenced by experience.
   D. means that areas are committed to specific functions.

9. A highly plastic cortex: (188)
   A. will never lateralize.
   B. is adaptable because many areas are not yet committed to specific functions.
   C. is only present during adulthood.
   D. is necessary for optimal mental and motor development.

10. Hand preference: (189)
   A. is more likely to be the same in twins than in ordinary siblings.
   B. is not stable until age 5.
   C. for those who are left-handed indicates a more strongly lateralized brain.
   D. undergoes dips and recoveries that coincide with language development.

11. Which of the following is NOT true of nutrition? (193-194)
   A. It is especially critical during infancy.
   B. Breast-fed babies in developing countries are less likely to survive the first year.
   C. Breast- and bottle-fed babies show no differences in psychological development.
   D. Preschoolers' wariness of new foods may be adaptive.

12. Obese children: (198)
   A. are not likely to remain overweight as adults.
   B. are more responsive to internal hunger cues than normal-weight children.
   C. are as physically active as normal-weight children.
   D. are best treated with family-focused intervention.

13. Female puberty usually begins with: (200)
   A. menarche and budding of the breasts.
   B. the growth spurt and budding of the breasts.
   C. underarm hair development and pubic hair development.
   D. menarche and underarm hair development.

14. Male puberty usually begins with: (201)
   A. the growth spurt.
   B. voice changes.
   C. emergence of facial hair.
   D. enlargement of the testes.

15. Research indicates that: (203)
    A. girls' feelings about menarche depend on prior knowledge and support.
    B. when fathers are told about pubertal changes in girls, more problems occur.
    C. boys get their information about spermarche from parents.
    D. boys usually tell peers about spermarche within a few weeks.

16. Which of the following is NOT true during adolescence? (205-206)
    A. Adolescents' moods tend to be stable compared to adults'.
    B. Negative life events probably influence moods.
    C. Psychological distancing from parents is adaptive.
    D. Conflict between parents and adolescents is generally mild.

17. Early maturing girls: (208)
    A. are regarded as physically attractive and sociable in school.
    B. are leaders at school.
    C. often develop into adults who are independent, cognitively competent, and satisfied.
    D. have a more positive body image when young.

18. Which of the following does NOT apply to early maturing boys? (208)
    A. As adults, many are independent, flexible, and satisfied.
    B. They seek out older companions.
    C. They hold leadership positions in school.
    D. They are popular in school.

19. Anorexia nervosa is: (209)
    A. more common among African-Americans.
    B. fatal in about 30 percent of cases.
    C. the result of individual, family, and cultural forces.
    D. fully cured in about 90 percent of cases.

20. Bulimics differ from anorexics in that they: (210)
    A. have a pathological fear of getting fat.
    B. persist in weight loss to an extreme.
    C. tend to have a family background with high expectations.
    D. typically lack self-control in other areas of their lives.

21. Early sexual activity is more common: (211)
    A. among more affluent adolescents.
    B. among adolescents who talk openly with parents about sex.
    C. among adolescents who come from small families.
    D. among adolescents whose parents are divorced.

22. Which of the following is NOT true of adolescent contraceptive use? (211)
  A. Adolescent cognition may have something to do with a reluctance to use contraception.
  B. Adolescent contraceptive use has decreased in recent years.
  C. Adolescents who talk openly with their parents about sex are more likely to use birth control.
  D. The social environment appears to contribute to adolescents' reluctance to use contraception.

23. Homosexuality: (212)
  A. is the sexual orientation of about 10 percent of young people.
  B. is more likely to be shared by fraternal twins than identical twins.
  C. in males is more common on the paternal side of families.
  D. may in some cases be an X-linked characteristic.

24. Which of the following is NOT true of AIDS? (214)
  A. AIDS symptoms typically take 8 to 10 years to emerge in a person infected with HIV.
  B. Heterosexual spread of AIDS is increasing, especially among females.
  C. It is possible to tell whether people have AIDS by looking at them.
  D. It is easier for a male to infect a female with AIDS than for a female to infect a male.

25. In comparison to Great Britain, Sweden, and the Netherlands, the United States: (214)
  A. has a lower rate of adolescent pregnancy.
  B. has more convenient, low-cost contraceptive services.
  C. has more families who live in poverty.
  D. reaches more teenagers with effective sex education.

CHAPTER 6

COGNITIVE DEVELOPMENT:
PIAGETIAN AND VYGOTSKIAN PERSPECTIVES

SUMMARY

Piaget's cognitive-developmental stage theory stands as one of three dominant twentieth-century positions on cognitive development. Piaget conceived of human cognition as a network of mental structures created by an active organism constantly striving to make sense of experience. Piaget believed that children move through four stages of development--sensorimotor, preoperational, concrete operational, and formal operational--during which the exploratory behaviors of infants are transformed into the abstract, logical intelligence of adolescence and adulthood. Piaget's stage sequence, which emphasizes that stages are invariant and universal, groups together similar qualitative changes in many schemes that occur during the same period of development.

According to Piaget, specific psychological structures, or schemes, change with age through the exercise of two important intellectual functions: adaptation and organization. Piaget described infants' special means of adapting their first schemes as the circular reaction--stumbling onto a new experience caused by the baby's own motor activity, and then trying to repeat the event. He considered revisions in the circular reaction so important that he named the six sensorimotor substages after them.

Some researchers believe that important schemes develop through perceptual means--by looking and listening--rather than just through acting on the world. Other researchers take a nativist view, believing that infants' built-in, core understanding become more elaborate as they come in contact with new information. A growing number of researchers have a modular view of the mind, viewing the mind as a collection of separate modules, or genetically prewired, special-purpose neural systems in the brain, which trigger new understandings with exposure to stimulation.

Recent research challenges many of Piaget's conclusions, often finding that infants and children develop cognitive capacities earlier than Piaget had believed. Today, virtually all experts agree that children's cognition is not as broadly stagelike as Piaget believed. Information-processing theorists believe that thought processes are similar at all ages--just present to a greater or lesser extent--and that uneven performance across tasks can largely be accounted for by variations in children's knowledge and experience. The neo-Piagetian perspective combines Piaget's stage approach with information-processing ideas.

Piaget's theory has had a major impact on education with its emphasis on discovery learning, sensitivity to children's readiness to learn, and acceptance of individual differences. Vygotsky's sociocultural theory, a second major theory of cognitive development, also views children as active seekers of knowledge, but rich social and cultural contexts profoundly affect the way their cognitive world is structured. Whereas Piaget concluded that young children's language is egocentric and nonsocial, Vygotsky reasoned that children speak to themselves for self-guidance and self-direction. Because language helps children think about their own behavior and select courses of action, Vygotsky regarded it as the foundation for all higher cognitive processes.

Vygotsky believed that through joint activities with more mature members of society, children come to master activities and think in ways that have meaning in their culture. He believed that children learn best when tasks are in their zone of proximal development, a range of tasks that the child cannot yet handle alone but can accomplish with the help of adults and more skilled peers.

Vygotsky's theory has also influenced education through concepts and techniques such as assisted discovery, peer collaboration, reciprocal teaching, and cooperative learning. A new Vygotsky-inspired educational approach transforms classrooms into communities of learners, where no distinction is made between adult and child contributions; all collaborate and develop. An evaluation of Vygotsky's theory indicates that its emphasis on the role of language may not accurately describe cognitive development in all cultures. Also, by focusing on the cultural line of development, his theory does not describe exactly how elementary cognitive processes contribute to higher cognitive processes derived from social experience.

LEARNING OBJECTIVES

After reading this chapter, you should be able to:

6.1 Explain Piaget's cognitive-developmental view of what changes with development and how cognitive change takes place. (221-223)

6.2 Describe the sensorimotor infant's means of building schemes and state the major achievements of Piaget's six sensorimotor substages. (224-227)

6.3 Evaluate the accuracy of Piaget's sensorimotor stage on the basis of recent evidence, and describe alternative ideas about how early cognitive development takes place. (227-235)

6.4 Describe advances in representation during the preoperational stage. (235-240)

6.5 Describe the limitations of preoperational thought from Piaget's point of view. (240-242)

6.6 Discuss recent research on preoperational thought and its implications for the accuracy of Piaget's preoperational stage. (242-248)

6.7 Describe major achievements and limitations of the concrete operational stage. (249-252)

6.8 Discuss recent research on concrete operational thought and its implications for the accuracy of Piaget's concrete operational stage. (252-253)

6.9 Describe major features of abstract thought during the formal operational stage and the consequences of new reasoning powers for thinking about the relation between self and other. (254-256)

6.10 Discuss recent research on formal operational thought and its implications for the accuracy of Piaget's formal operational stage. (256-257)

6.11 Summarize questions raised about Piaget's theory along with current alternatives to his view of development. (257-258)

6.12 Describe educational implications of Piaget's theory. (258-259)

6.13 Explain Vygotsky's view of cognitive development, noting the importance of social experience and language. (259-260)

6.14 Describe features of social interaction that promote transfer of culturally adaptive ways of thinking to children. (261-262)

6.15 Discuss Vygotsky's view of the role of make-believe play in development. (262-263)

6.16 Describe educational implications of Vygotsky's theory. (263-266)

6.17 Cite strengths and limitations of Vygotsky's theory. (266-267)

STUDY QUESTIONS

1. _____ refers to the inner processes and products of the mind that lead to "knowing." It includes remembering, symbolizing, categorizing, problem solving, creating, fantasizing, and dreaming. (221)

2. The three dominant twentieth-century positions on cognitive development include Piaget's _____, Vygotsky's _____ _____, and _____. (221)

3. Vygotsky viewed the acquisition of _____ as crucial for cognitive change. (221)

4. Piaget claimed that cognitive development was a matter of (domain-general/domain-specific) changes. (222)

Piaget's Cognitive-Developmental Theory

1. Piaget conceived of human cognition as a network of _____ structures created by a(n) (active/passive) organism, and viewed the child as an (intrinsically/extrinsically) motivated learner. (222)

2. Piaget's stage sequence has two important characteristics: it is _____, which means the stages always emerge in a fixed order, and the stages are _____, which means that they describe the cognitive development of children everywhere. (222)

What Changes with Development

1. According to Piaget, specific psychological structures, or _____, change with age. (222)

How Cognitive Change Takes Place

1. One important intellectual function identified by Piaget is _____, which involves building schemes through direct interaction with the environment. (223)

2. During the process of _____, we interpret the external world in terms of our current schemes; during the process of _____, we adjust old schemes or create new ones. (223)

3. In a state of cognitive _____, children assimilate more than they accommodate; in a state of _____, children shift toward accommodation as they engage in rapid cognitive change. (223)

4. _____ describes the back-and-forth movement between equilibrium and disequilibrium. (223)

5. A second important intellectual function identified by Piaget is _____, a process in which the child rearranges new structures and links them to other schemes so that they are part of a strongly interconnected cognitive system. (223)

The Sensorimotor Stage (Birth to 2 Years)

1. The term _____ describes a sensorimotor response that first occurs by chance, and through repetition becomes strengthened into a new scheme. (224)

2. The capacity of _____ first appears during this period and was regarded by Piaget as the purest form of assimilation. The capacity of _____ also appears during this time and emphasizes accommodation. (224)

The Sensorimotor Substages

1. The first substage of Piaget's six sensorimotor substages is _____ (birth to _____ month). In this period, infants behave in the _____, no matter what experiences they encounter. (224)

2. Describe the important achievements of the primary circular reactions substage (_____ to _____ months). (224-225)

_____
_____
_____

3. During the _____ substage (_____ to _____ months), infants sit up, reach, grasp, and manipulate objects. In addition, they try to repeat interesting sights and sounds caused by their own actions and imitate the behaviors of others. (225)

4. In substage 4: _____ of Secondary Circular Reactions (_____ to _____ months), infants begin to attain the cognitive milestones of _____ behavior and _____ but make the _____ error. In addition, infants anticipate events more effectively and may try to change them and also _____ behaviors slightly different from those they usually perform. (225-226)

5. During substage 5: _____ Circular Reactions (_____ to _____ months), toddlers repeat behaviors with _____, provoking new outcomes. They also have an advanced understanding of _____ and _____ many more behaviors. (226)

6. Substage 6: _____ (_____ months to _____ years) brings with it the ability to make _____ of absent objects and past events. Children can solve problems (symbolically/by trial-and-error) and better understand object permanence so that they solve the _____ task easily. They also begin to engage in _____ in which they reenact familiar activities. (226-227)

Recent Research on Sensorimotor Development

1. Habituation-dishabituation research indicates that infants grasp the idea of _____ _____ as early as 3 1/2 months of age. An explanation for why older infants do not try to search for hidden objects is that they cannot coordinate the _____. (227-228)

2. One explanation for the AB search error is that infants have difficulty _____ _____ a previously rewarded response. (228)

3. Describe aspects of physical reasoning displayed by infants during the first year. (228-229)

_____

_____

_____

_____

_____

4. Research indicates that _____, a form of representation, is present by the second month of life. (230)

5. As shown by the less vigorous response of infants to changed stimuli, the beginning of the ability to _____ objects and events is present in the early months. (230)

6. Based on similar overall appearance or prominent object part, infants' earliest categories are _____ while later categories become _____, the focus on common function and behavior. (231)

7. Present in 10-to-12-month infants, _____ is extracting a solution strategy from one problem-solving context and applying it in other appropriate contexts. (231)

Evaluation of the Sensorimotor Stage

1. The cognitive attainments of infancy (do/do not) develop in the neat stepwise fashion predicted by Piaget's substages. (232)

2. Some researchers believe that important schemes develop through _____ means rather than solely through acting on the world. (232)

3. Some researchers, who take a nativist approach, believe that infants' remarkable cognitive skills are based on _____. This perspective regards the mind as a collection of separate _____, or genetically prewired, independent, special-purpose systems. (234)

The Preoperational Stage (2 to 7 Years)

1. The preoperational stage involves an extraordinary increase in _____ activity. (235)

Language and Thought

1. Although he acknowledged that _____ is our most flexible means of mental representation, Piaget did not regard it as responsible for more advanced forms of cognition because he believed that _____ leads to internal images of experience which children then label with words. (235-236)

Make-Believe Play

1. Describe three important changes in make-believe play that occur during early childhood. (236-237)

A. _____

_____

B. _____

_____

C. _____

_____

2. List three functions of make-believe play emphasized by Piaget. (237)

A. _____

B. _____

C. _____

3. True or False: Make-believe play appears to strengthen memory, language ability, logical reasoning, imagination, and creativity. (237)

Drawings

1. The three stages that preschoolers' drawings progress through are _____, _____, and _____. (238)

2. A major milestone in children's artwork occurs when they begin to use _____ to represent the _____ of objects. (238)

3. The culture in which children are raised (does/does not) influence their drawings. (239)

Spatial Symbols

1. Explain how 3-year-olds grasp the meaning of spatial symbols. (240)

_____

_____

Limitations of Preoperational Thought

1. In the preoperational stage, according to Piaget, children (are/are not) capable of operations, mental representations of actions that obey logical rules. (240)

2. According to Piaget, the most serious deficiency of this stage is _____, which means that children are unaware of any symbolic viewpoints other than their own. This limitation is responsible for _____ thinking. (240)

3. _____ refers to the idea that certain physical characteristics of objects remain the same, even when their outward appearance changes. (240)

4. Preoperational children's understanding is _____, characterized by _____, and focuses on _____ rather than _____. (241)

5. _____ is the ability to go mentally through a series of steps and then reverse direction, returning to the starting point. (241)

6. _____ refers to the tendency to link together two events that occur close in time and space in a cause-and-effect fashion. (241)

7. _____ refers to the ability to organize objects into classes and subclasses on the basis of similarities and differences between the groups. (241)

Recent Research on Preoperational Thought

1. True or False: Even when researchers use familiar objects in visual displays, young children consistently give egocentric responses. (242-243)

2. True or False: Research indicates that many of children's apparent animistic responses result from incomplete knowledge about some objects, not from a rigid belief that the objects are alive. (243)

3. A realistic understanding of death is based on _____, _____, and _____. (244)

4. Describe how parents should discuss death with their children. (245)

_____

_____

_____

5. When given simplified and relevant tasks, preschoolers (do/do not) perform better on conservation tasks. (244-246)

6. The capacity to classify hierarchically (is/is not) present in early childhood. (247)

7. At age ____, children can separate the way an object appears to feel from the way it truly feels, but it is not until age ____ or ____ that children do well on problems involving sights and sounds. (247)

8. The idea that logical operations develop gradually poses a challenge to Piaget's _____ concept. (248)

The Concrete Operational Stage (7 to 11 Years)

Operational Thought

1. Piaget regarded children's ability to pass _____ as an important achievement of the concrete operational stage, since it provides clear evidence of _____. (249)

2. During middle childhood, children are capable of _____ as they recognize that a change in one aspect of a substance is compensated for by a change in another aspect, an explanation that also illustrates _____. (249)

3. True or False: By the end of middle childhood, children still do not possess the cognitive development sufficient to pass Piaget's class inclusion problem. (249)

4. The ability to order items along a quantitative dimension is called _____. The ability to perform this task mentally is called _____. (249)

5. Between 7 and 8, children start to perform _____, in which they align the self's frame to match that of a person in a different orientation. (251)

6. Mental representations of large-scale spaces are called _____. By the end of middle childhood, children form a(n) _____ _____ in which landmarks and routes are interrelated. (251)

Limitations of Concrete Operational Thought

1. An important limitation of concrete operational thought is difficulty in applying mental operations to _____ idcas. (252)

2. The term _____ describes the gradual mastery of logical concepts. For example, children usually grasp conservation problems in the following order: first _____, then _____, and finally _____. (252)

Recent Research on Concrete Operational Thought

1. True or False: Recent research supports Piaget's assumption that operational thinking does not depend on particular kinds of experiences. (252)

2. True or False: Although schooling is helpful in many areas of cognitive development, it does not appear to promote mastery of Piagetian tasks. (252)

3. The phrasing of questions and the objects to which they refer (do/do not) have an important effect on Piagetian task performance. (253)

4. Research findings indicate that adults (do/do not) always use concrete operations. This indicates that concrete operational reasoning may be a product of _____, _____, and _____. (253)

The Formal Operational Stage (11 Years and Older)

Hypothetico-Deductive Reasoning

1. In hypothetico-deductive reasoning, a person starts with a(n) _____ of all possible factors that might affect an outcome and _____ from it specific _____ (or predictions) about what might happen. (254)

Propositional Thought

1. True or False: Because adolescents are capable of propositional thought, they can evaluate the logic of verbal statements without referring to real-world circumstances. (254)

Consequences of Abstract Thought

1. Egocentrism in teenagers results in two distorted images of the relation between the self and other: the _____ in which young teenagers believe that they are the focus of everyone else's attention and concern, and the _____ in which they develop an inflated opinion of their own importance. (255)

Recent Research on Formal Operational Thought

1. Although school-age children show the glimmerings of abstract reasoning, they cannot sort out evidence that bears on ____ or more variables at once. (256)

2. About ____ to ____ percent of college students fail Piaget's formal operations problems. (256)

3. True or False: Although in some cultures formal operational reasoning appears later than in others, it appears sometime during adolescence in all known cultures. (256)

Larger Questions About Piaget's Theory

Issues of Clarity and Accuracy

1. True or False: Aspects of Piaget's concept of equilibration seem vague and imprecise. (257)

Are There Stages of Cognitive Development?

1. Information-processing theories regard development as _____, but reject the existence of _____ change. (257)

2. Neo-Piagetians who combine Piaget's stage approach with information-processing ideas believe that as long as the _____ of tasks is controlled, children and adolescents approach physical and social reasoning problems in similar, _____ ways. (258)

3. The nativist perspective rejects Piaget's _____ and his belief that the human mind is made up of _____. (258)

Piaget and Education

1. List three educational principles that have served as the foundation for a variety of Piagetian-based curricula. (258-259)
   A._____
   B._____
   C._____

Vygotsky's Sociocultural Theory

1. Vygotsky believed that social and cultural contexts (do/do not) affect the way children's cognitive world is structured. (259)

2. According to Vygotsky, once children become capable of mental representation, especially through _____, their ability to participate in social dialogues is enhanced. (260)

Private Speech

1. Utterances made by young children as they go about their daily activities were called _____ by Piaget. In contrast, Vygotsky called it private speech and reasoned that children speak to themselves for _____ and _____. (260)

2. Vygotsky regarded _____ as the foundation for all higher cognitive processes. (260)

3. True or False: Research shows that children use more private speech when tasks are difficult, after they make errors, or when they are confused. (260)

4. Children with learning problems engage in especially (high/low) rates of private speech. (260)

Social Origins of Cognitive Development

1. The concept of _____ refers to a range of tasks that the child cannot yet handle alone but can accomplish with the help of adults and more skilled peers. (261)

2. _____ refers to the process whereby two participants who begin a task with different understandings arrive at a shared understanding. (261)

3. _____ refers to a changing quality of social support over the course of a teaching session. (261)

4. Deaf children of (hearing/deaf) parents are often delayed in language process and in complex make-believe play. (263)

5. Describe the parent-child communication between hearing parents and their deaf child. (263)

_____
_____
_____
_____

Vygotsky's View of Make-Believe Play

1. Describe two ways that make-believe play promotes development. (262)
A._____
_____
B._____
_____

2. An observational study of middle-class American toddlers at play in their homes revealed that 75 to 80 percent of make-believe during the second year involved _____. (264)

3. In many cultures, make-believe is more frequent, as well as more complex, with _____ than with mothers. (264)

Vygotsky and Education

1. A Vygotskian classroom promotes _____. (264)

2. Describe Vygotsky's major educational message. (265)

_____
_____
_____
_____
_____

Reciprocal Teaching

1. In reciprocal teaching, collaborative learning group members apply four cognitive strategies: _____, _____, _____, and _____. This method creates a _____ in which children gradually assume more responsibility. (265)

Cooperative Learning

1. A crucial factor in peer collaboration is _____, structuring the peer group so that students work together toward a common _____. (265)

2. Working in groups come easier for children reared in (collectivist/ individualistic) cultures. (266)

The Classroom as a Community of Learners

1. The _____ is based on the assumption that different people have different expertises that can be helpful to other members of the community. (266)

Evaluation of Vygotsky's Theory

1. Vygotsky's theory leads us to expect (universal/variable) development. (266)

2. In contrast to adults in middle-class communities, who emphasize verbal interaction with children, adults in Mayan and Indian communities interact emphasizing _____ and _____. (267)

3. Vygotsky stated that the _____ and _____ lines of development join, forming a single developmental path. (267)

ASK YOURSELF. . .

6.1 While sitting in her high-chair, 7-month-old Mimi dropped her rattle, which fell out of sight on her lap. Mimi looked around but did not try to retrieve it. Does Mimi know that the rattle still exists? Why doesn't she search for it? (p. 235)

6.2 At 14 months, Tony pushed his toy bunny through the slats of his crib onto a nearby table. To retrieve it, he tried jerking, turning, and throwing the bunny. What kind of circular reaction is Tony demonstrating? If Tony's parents showed him how to get the bunny, could he use that procedure to retrieve a different toy in another context? Explain, using research findings. (p. 235)

6.3 At home, 4-year-old Will understands very well that his tricycle isn't alive and can't move by itself. Yet when Will went fishing with his family and his father asked, "Why do you think the river is flowing along?" Will responded, "Because it's alive and wants to." What explains this contradiction in Will's reasoning?
(p. 248)

6.4 Mastery of conservation problems provide one illustration of Piaget's horizontal decalage. Review the preceding sections. Then list additional examples showing that operational reasoning develops gradually in middle childhood. (p. 253)

6.5 Thirteen-year-old Cassie insisted that she had to have high-heeled shoes to wear to the school dance. "No way I can wear those low heels, Mom. They'll make me look way too short, and the whole evening will be ruined!" Why is Cassie so concerned about a detail of her appearance that most people would be unlikely to notice? (p. 259)

6.6 Review the interaction between Sammy and his mother on page 261. Is Sammy's mother engaging in scaffolding? How might her assistance change as Sammy improves at the task? How would it differ were she and Sammy engaged in make-believe play rather than working a puzzle? (p. 267)

CONNECTIONS

6.1 Cite evidence that supports a nativist, modular account of language development. What questions have been raised about this explanation? (See Chapter 9, pages 359-364.) Do those questions resemble reservations about the modular view raised earlier in this chapter?

6.2 Do children separate appearance from reality in the emotional domain--that is, realize that an emotion a person expresses may not be the one he or she truly feels--at about the same time they solve the appearance-reality tasks discussed in this chapter? (See Chapter 10, page 410.)

6.3 Gains in perspective-taking skill are vital for self- and social understanding. Explain how the development of perspective taking in middle childhood contributes to self-concept and moral reasoning. (See Chapter 11, page 448, and Chapter 12, pages 495-496.)

6.4 How do school-age children's flexible classification skills affect their gender-stereotyped thinking? (See Chapter 13, page 543.)

6.5 The transition to abstract thinking at adolescence is widely regarded as stagelike. After reviewing the concept of stage in Chapter 1 (see page 8), cite evidence that supports this conclusion.

PUZZLE 6.1

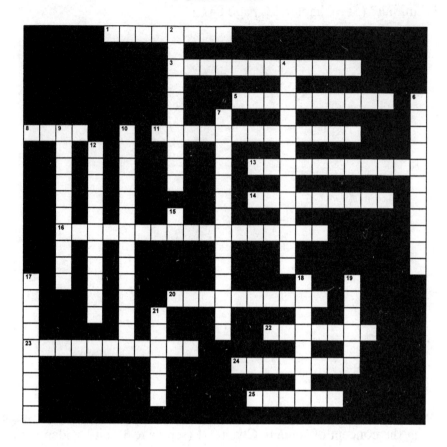

Across

1 Copying the behavior of models not present is ___ imitation
3 Idea that an object's physical characteristics always remain the same
5 Easily distracted by the concrete appearance of objects, or ___-bound
8 In make-believe ___, children represent familiar activities
11 ___ play combines pretend schemes with those of peers
13 Working together toward a common goal in ___ learning
14 Adolescents regard themselves as always on stage in the ___ audience
16 Starting a task with different understandings and arriving at shared ones
20 ___ décalage, or gradual mastery of logical concepts
22 Children's "speech to self"
23 Changing quality of adult support
24 ___ causality, the action one object exerts on another through contact
25 Preoperational children focus on ___ rather than transformations

Down

2 ___ teaching, a collaborative learning group
4 Adjustment of old schemes or creation of new ones
6 Lack of awareness of other's viewpoints
7 Belief that children learn through their own activity
9 Problem-solving method of using a solution strategy from a previous context
10 Stage with rapid advances in mental representation
12 Goal-directed behavior
15 ___ search error occurs when object permanence is not complete
17 Objects change location when out of sight in an ___ displacement task
18 Belief in innate knowledge
19 Internal images of objects and past events, or ___ representation
21 ___ participation provides learning opportunities through involvement with others

PUZZLE 6.2

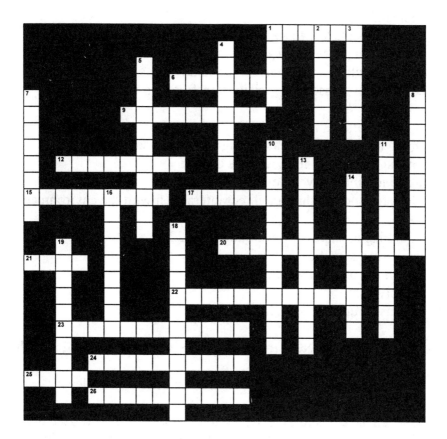

Across

1 Stage in which abstract thinking develops
6 Common changes across all knowledge are domain-___
9 ___-of-learners model assumes different expertises can be helpful to others
12 Piagetian stage from age 7 to 11, called ___ operational
15 Belief in lifelike qualities of inanimate objects
17 Specific structure that changes with age
20 Movement from equilibrium to disequilibrium
21 Mental representations of large-scale environments, or cognitive ___
22 External world seen in terms of current schemes
23 Reasoning from particular to particular
24 ___ inference is seriating mentally
25 Tasks the child does with assistance are in the ___ of proximal development
26 Focusing on only one aspect of a situation

Down

1 Personal ___, an early adolescent belief
2 Regards the mind as genetically prewired
3 Conclusions drawn from the rules of logic in ___ necessity
4 Domain-___ changes lead to separate abilities
5 Adolescents first become capable of ___-deductive reasoning
7 ___ reaction involves repeating a chance event
8 Build schemes by direct interaction with the environment
10 Ability to mentally go through aspects of steps and return
11 Piaget's stage spanning the first 2 years
13 Linking schemes so they form an interconnected cognitive system
14 Object ___, or understanding the continued existence of invisible objects
16 Ability to arrange items quantitatively
18 Organization based on likeness and difference
19 Mental representations of actions obeying logical rules

139

PRACTICE TEST

1. Piaget claimed that: (221)
   A. language is the key to spurring cognitive development.
   B. information processing explains much of human cognition.
   C. acting directly on the physical world advances cognition.
   D. cognitive processes are socially transferred to children.

2. According to Vygotsky's theory: (221)
   A. children first master ideas through the exercise of schemes.
   B. language is crucial for cognitive change.
   C. the mind builds psychological structures.
   D. adaptation occurs through direct interaction with the environment.

3. According to Piaget, stages of development: (222)
   A. are culture-specific.
   B. vary in the order in which they emerge.
   C. are universal.
   D. emphasize quantitative change.

4. Which of the following is NOT true of schemes, according to Piagetian theory? (222-223)
   A. Schemes move from a mental level to an action-based level.
   B. Schemes change with age.
   C. Children have a natural tendency to exercise schemes repeatedly.
   D. When equilibration occurs, more effective schemes are produced.

5. According to Piaget: (223)
   A. when children are not changing very much, they accommodate more than they assimilate.
   B. assimilation produces more effective schemes.
   C. schemes change through adaptation and organization.
   D. the cognitive structures of young children and adults are essentially equal.

6. If Tyrone sees a sheep and calls it a horse, he is: (223)
   A. assimilating.
   B. accommodating.
   C. transforming.
   D. modifying.

7. Which of the following is NOT a capacity that appears during the sensorimotor stage? (224)
   A. operations
   B. circular reactions
   C. play
   D. imitation

140

8. According to Piaget, the AB search error occurs during sensorimotor _____ because infants' awareness of _____ is not yet complete. (225-226)
- A. substage three/physical causality
- B. substage four/object permanence
- C. substage three/sensorimotor egocentrism
- D. substage six/mental representations

9. Recent research indicates that: (227)
- A. there is little evidence that infants understand object permanence before 8 months.
- B. early in the first year, infants are sensitive to principles of object permanence.
- C. primary circular reactions do not occur until 6 months.
- D. Piaget overestimated infant capacities.

10. Researchers have used the _____ to find out what young babies know. (227)
- A. clinical interview
- B. habituation-dishabituation sequence
- C. horizontal décalage
- D. imaginary audience

11. Categorization begins during the: (230)
- A. preoperational stage.
- B. concrete operational stage.
- C. sensorimotor stage.
- D. formal operational stage.

12. Which of the following is NOT true of the nativist view of cognitive development? (234)
- A. It views perceptual and reasoning abilities as based on innate knowledge.
- B. It has a modular view of the mind.
- C. It views the child as a far less active participant in the construction of knowledge than did Piaget.
- D. It views interaction between the child and the environment as the primary force behind cognitive development.

13. Piaget regarded _____ as responsible for more advanced forms of cognition. (236)
- A. language
- B. sensorimotor activity
- C. scaffolding
- D. animistic thinking

14. Which of the following is NOT true of sociodramatic play, according to Piaget? (236-237)
   A. It increases children's cognitive and social skills.
   B. It becomes increasingly attached to the real-life conditions associated with it children.
   C. It is emotionally integrative.
   D. It allows children to become familiar with social role possibilities.

15. Research findings on the preoperational stage: (244)
   A. confirm Piaget's notion of stage.
   B. indicate that Piaget underestimated preschoolers' animistic beliefs.
   C. confirm an absence of ability in young children to classify hierarchically.
   D. often differ from Piaget's conclusions when tasks are simplified and made relevant.

16. Which of the following is NOT a feature of cognitive development attained during the concrete operational stage, according to Piaget? (249, 251)
   A. decentration
   B. transitive inference
   C. transductive reasoning
   D. mental rotations

17. The imaginary audience and the personal fable are examples of _____ during the formal operational stage. (255)
   A. intersubjectivity
   B. egocentrism
   C. cooperative learning
   D. animistic thinking

18. Research indicates that: (256)
   A. in many tribal cultures, formal operational reasoning does not appear at all.
   B. about 5 percent of college students fail Piaget's formal operational problems.
   C. formal operational thought emerges in all contexts at once.
   D. people are most likely to think abstractly in situations in which they have had little experience.

19. Which of the following is NOT an educational principle of a Piagetian-based curriculum? (258-259)
   A. reciprocal teaching
   B. discovery learning
   C. acceptance of individual differences
   D. sensitivity to readiness to learn

20. Private speech: (260)
   A. was viewed as egocentric and nonsocial by Vygotsky.
   B. decreases when tasks are difficult.
   C. was viewed by Vygotsky as a central force in cognitive development.
   D. is used less and for a shorter time by children with learning problems.

21. The term _____ refers to a changing quality of social support over the course of a teaching session. (261)
   A. intersubjectivity
   B. zone of proximal development
   C. horizontal décalage
   D. scaffolding

22. Vygotsky regarded make-believe play as a(n) _____ that encouraged children to learn _____ . (262)
   A. transformation/propositional thought
   B. zone of proximal development/self-restraint
   C. egocentric construction/self-interest
   D. preoperational stage/accommodation

23. A classroom following Vygotskian educational principles differs from one using a Piagetian curriculum in emphasizing: (263-264)
   A. assisted discovery.
   B. active participation.
   C. acceptance of individual differences.
   D. transformational learning.

24. Questioning, summarizing, clarifying, and predicting are cognitive strategies used in _____. (265)
   A. animistic thinking
   B. conservation
   C. reciprocal teaching
   D. seriation

25. Which of the following does NOT describe Vygotsky's community-of-learners model? (266)
   A. broadens the concept of the zone of proximal development
   B. lessons are the focus of classroom activities
   C. enables participants to gain a multifaceted understanding of the topic
   D. children and adults draw on one another's expertise

CHAPTER 7

COGNITIVE DEVELOPMENT:
AN INFORMATION-PROCESSING PERSPECTIVE

SUMMARY

The information-processing view of cognition seeks to find out how children and adults operate on different kinds of information. Most information-processing theorists view the mind as a complex, symbol-manipulating system through which information flows, much like a computer. Two general models of adult information processing have influenced research on children's cognition. Atkinson and Shiffrin's store model assumes that information is held, or stored, in three parts of the system for processing: the sensory register, short-term memory, and long-term memory. The levels-of-processing model assumes that transfer of information from working to long-term memory depends on the depth to which information is processed.

Several developmental models of information processing exist. Case's theory reinterprets Piaget's theory within an information-processing framework. He views cognitive development as a matter of increases in information-processing capacity that result from brain development and more efficient strategy use. Connectionism tries to explain development by means of computer-simulated learning tasks, using large numbers of interconnected, simple processing units, which are organized in layers, much like the brain's neurological structure. Siegler's model of strategy choice suggests that children generate a variety of strategies for solving challenging problems; with experience, some strategies are selected and survive, whereas others die off.

Attention is fundamental to human thinking because it determines the information that will be considered in any task. Attention improves greatly during early and middle childhood, becoming more selective, adaptable, and planful. Improved cognitive inhibition and effectiveness of attentional strategies are important for the refinement of selective attention. Refinement of attentional strategies occurs in four phases: production deficiency, control deficiency, utilization deficiency, and effective strategy use.

Memory strategies also improve with age as children gradually develop a variety of techniques—such as rehearsal, organization, and elaboration--to increase the likelihood of holding information in working memory and transferring it to the long-term knowledge base. During infancy, retrieval changes from recognition of previously experienced stimuli to include recall in the presence of few retrieval cues or none at all beyond the context in which the information was previously experienced. Over childhood and adolescence, recall improves steadily as the knowledge base becomes better organized and memory strategies are applied more effectively.

When people are given complex, meaningful material to remember, condensations, additions, and distortions appear that are not just the result of memory failure but due to a radical transformation of the information--a process called reconstruction. Fuzzy-trace theory suggests that when we first encode information, we reconstruct it automatically, creating both a vague, fuzzy version that preserves essential content without details, and a verbatim version adapted to answering questions about specifics.

Children's metacognitive knowledge changes from a passive to an active, constructive view of mental functioning as awareness of cognitive capacities, strategies for processing information, and task variables expands. Cognitive self-regulation develops slowly during childhood and adolescence. Recently, information-processing researchers have turned their attention to children's academic learning.

A major strength of the information-processing approach is its explicitness and precision in breaking down complex cognitive performance into its separate elements so each can be studied. However, by analyzing cognition into its components, information processing has had difficulty putting them back together into a broad, comprehensive theory of development. Also, computer models of cognitive processing do not reflect the richness of real-life learning experiences. A final shortcoming is the slowness of information-processing research to respond to the growing interest in the biological bases of cognitive development.

LEARNING OBJECTIVES

After reading this chapter, you should be able to:

7.1 Describe the unique features of the information-processing approach to cognitive development. (272)

7.2 Describe the store and levels-of-processing models, noting their implications for cognitive development. (272-276)

7.3 Describe and evaluate three developmental theories of information processing: Case's neo-Piagetian theory, connectionism, and Siegler's model of strategy choice. (276-282)

7.4 Describe the development of attention in terms of selective, adaptable, and planful strategies, noting the role of gains in processing capacity. (283-287)

7.5 Describe the development of the memory strategies of rehearsal, organization, and elaboration, noting the influence of task demands and culture. (287-291)

7.6 Describe the development of three approaches to memory retrieval: recognition, recall, and reconstruction. (291-294)

7.7 Discuss the role of knowledge in memory performance. (294-295)

7.8 Describe the role of scripts in everyday life, and explain how they may serve as the developmental link between episodic and semantic memory. (295-296)

7.9 Describe alternative theories of infantile amnesia, and explain how autobiographical memory emerges and develops. (296-297)

7.10 Describe the development of metacognitive knowledge and cognitive self-regulation, and explain why self-regulation is vital for success on complex tasks. (299-302)

7.11 Discuss development in reading, mathematics, and scientific reasoning, noting the implications of research for teaching in each academic domain. (302-309)

7.12 Summarize strengths and limitations of the information-processing approach. (310-311)

STUDY QUESTIONS

The Information-Processing Approach

1. Information-processing theorists view the mind like a(n) _____ _____. (272)

2. Some information-processing investigators use _____ simulations to test their ideas. All hold a strong commitment to explicit _____ of cognitive functioning which must be tested with _____. (272)

General Models of Information Processing

The Store Model

1. Atkinson and Shiffrin's store model of assumes information is stored in three parts of the system for processing: _____, _____, and _____. As information enters each store, it can be operated on and transformed using _____ processes. (272)

2. According to Atkinson and Shiffrin, stores are (inborn/learned); mental strategies are (inborn/learned). (272)

3. We apply _____ to retain information in _____. The capacity limit is not a matter of physical pieces of information, but of _____ _____. The longer information is retained in working memory, the greater the chances it will be transferred to _____. (273)

4. We also apply _____ to retrieve information in _____. The capacity of this component is (limited/unlimited). (273)

5. The _____, which occurs when you try to memorize a list of items, supports the distinction between working- and long-term memory. Items located at the (beginning/middle/end) are less likely to be remembered initially, but over time, items located at the (beginning/middle/end) decay, whereas those at the (beginning/middle/end) continue to be retained. (274)

146

6. True or False: The capacity limits of the sensory register and short-term memory have been found to vary only slightly from study to study. (274)

The Levels-of-Processing Model

1. The levels-of-processing model assumes that transfer of information depends on the _____ to which information is processed by the system. We can encode a written word (deeply/superficially) according to how it looks or sounds, or we can encode the word (deeply/superficially) according to its meaning or _____ features by relating it to other information. (274)

2. True or False: Automatic cognitive processes require little attentional resources. (274)

Implications for Development

1. Research indicates that strategy use (deteriorates/improves) with age, and the hardware, or absolute capacity of the cognitive system, (increases/decreases). (275)

2. True or False: Myelinization and synaptic pruning in the brain may contribute to age-related gains in information-processing resources. (275-276)

Developmental Theories of Information Processing

1. True or False: Developmental models of information processing differ from the store and levels-of-processing models because the former focus on how children's thinking changes with age. (276)

Case's Neo-Piagetian Theory

1. According to Case's _____ theory, each major stage involves a distinct type of _____ structure. As children become more efficient cognitive processors, the amount of information they can hold onto and combine in _____ expands. (276)

2. Describe three factors Case believes are responsible for the increasing capacity of working memory. (276-277)
A._____
_____
B._____
_____
C._____
_____

3. Case's theory accounts for horizontal décalage by assuming that each successive task requires more _____ for mastery. (277)

4. True or False: Case's theory accounts for the uneven nature of cognitive development because it is a domain-general approach; it does not acknowledge domain-specificity in development. (278)

Connectionism

1. _____ tries to explain development by means of computer-simulated learning tasks; computers are set up to learn and presented with tasks that children encounter. (278)

2. A typical neural network includes a(n) (hidden/input/output) layer to encode the task; a (hidden/input/output) layer to combine information into internal representations; and a(n) (hidden/input/output) layer to generate a response to the situation. (278)

3. Computer-simulated learners are sometimes called _____
_____. (278)

4. Explain how researchers program an artificial neural network to learn and how the system's responses are used to describe children's learning. (278)

_____
_____
_____
_____

5. Connectionists have depicted children's development on the following tasks:
_____, _____,
_____, and _____.
(279)

6. Connectionist models highlight (internal/external) learning as essential for changes in many skills that appear (gradual/abrupt) when viewed from (inside/outside) the system. (280)

7. True or False: Connectionism presents powerful support for the nativist, modular view of the mind. (280)

8. Describe three shortcomings of connectionism that make its account of mechanisms of development incomplete. (280)
A._____

_____
B._____

_____
C._____

_____

Siegler's Model of Strategy Choice

1. Siegler's _____ applies an _____
perspective to children's cognition. _____ and _____
characterize children's mental strategies yielding adaptive problem-solving techniques.
(281)

2. Describe several examples of strategy use children engage in when solving basic math
facts. (281)

_____
_____

3. True or False: Siegler found that strategy use for many types of problems progresses
in a stagelike way. (281)

4. Children tend to make adaptive strategy choices based on two criteria: _____
and _____. (281)

5. True or False: Siegler's model reveals that no child thinks in just one way. (282)

6. Explain what speech-gesture mismatches are and what they reveal about children's
learning. (283)

_____
_____
_____
_____

Attentional Processing

1. Attention improves greatly during early and middle childhood and becomes more
_____, _____, and _____. (284)

Selectivity and Adaptability

1. Preschoolers tend to become (increasingly/decreasingly) attentive as a play session
progresses. (284)

2. True or False: Research indicates that selectivity of attention improves sharply during
infancy. (284)

3. Individuals who are skilled at _____ can prevent the mind from
straying to alternate thoughts. This capacity fosters performance on a wide variety of
tasks. (284)

4. Researchers believe that maturation of the _____ are largely
responsible for gains in cognitive inhibition. (285)

5. A failure to use a selective attentional strategy in situations where it could be helpful is called a(n) _____. (285)

6. An inability to execute a strategy effectively is called a(n)_____. (285)

7. A(n) _____ occurs when children apply a strategy consistently, but their performance does not improve. (285)

8. True or False: A reason why strategies do not work effectively when first applied by young children is that the strategies take too much of the children's attentional resources. (285)

Planning

1. _____ involves thinking out a sequence of acts ahead of time and allocating attention accordingly to reach a goal. (285)

2. ____ to ____ percent of school-age children have attention-deficit hyperactivity disorder. (288)

3. Describe symptoms of ADHD. (288)

_____
_____
_____
_____

4. The diverse symptoms of ADHD appear to be unified by a common theme: _____. (288)

5. True or False: The intelligence of ADHD children is below normal. (288)

6. _____ plays a major role in ADHD, since the disorder runs in families. (288)

7. The most common treatment for ADHD is _____. (289)

8. Combining _____ with _____ seems to be the most effective approach to treatment of ADHD. (289)

Working Memory

1. _____ are deliberate mental activities we use to increase the likelihood of holding information in working memory and transferring it to our long-term knowledge base. (287)

Strategies for Storing Information

1. Three strategies that enhance memory for new information are
_____, _____, and _____. (287)

2. Young children (are/are not) very adept at rehearsal. Both _____ and
_____ deficiencies are evident. (287)

3. True or False: Nonrehearsing children who are taught to rehearse use the strategy in
new situations. (287)

4. Preschoolers (do/do not) use _____--grouping objects or words
into meaningful categories--to aid recall. (289)

5. Before age 9 or 10, children tend to link items together by _____. (289)

6. For children age 8 and younger to use the memory strategy of organization, items
must be _____ and _____. (289)

7. _____ involves creating a relationship, or shared meaning, between
two or more pieces of information that are not members of the same category. This skill
rarely appears before age ____. (290)

8. True or False: When children under age 11 elaborate, they usually produce active
images that are memorable. (290)

Cultural and Situational Influences on Memory Strategies

1. When they play, children engage in many spontaneous organizations that aid in recall.
These include _____ use of objects and _____. (290)

2. The development of memory strategies is a product of _____ and
_____, as well as a competent information- processing system.
(291)

Long-Term Memory

Retrieval of Information

1. Information can be retrieved from memory in three ways: through _____,
_____, and _____. (291)

2. Noticing that a stimulus is identical or similar to one previously experienced is called
_____. This is the (simplest/most complex) form of retrieval. By age
____, it is highly accurate. (291)

3. _____ involves generating a mental image of an absent stimulus. It is a (more/less) challenging task than recognition. (291)

4. Compared to recognition, recall shows much (less/greater) improvement with age. (292)

5. A(n) _____ approach to information processing maintains that much information is selected and interpreted in terms of our existing knowledge. (292)

6. Like adults, when children retell a story, they _____, _____, and _____. (293)

7. According to _____ theory, when we first encode information, we reconstruct it automatically, creating a version called a(n) _____ and retaining a(n) _____ version. (293)

8. _____ memory often allows us to reason effectively without recalling specifics. (293)

9. True or False: Research indicates that both preschoolers and second graders are better at answering verbatim- than gist-dependent questions. (293)

10. Fuzzy traces are (less/more) likely than verbatim memories to be forgotten. (294)

Knowledge and Memory Performance

1. Many researchers believe that cognitive development is largely a matter of acquiring _____, knowledge in a specific area that makes new, related information more meaningful so it is easier to _____ and _____. (294)

2. True or False: In areas in which children are more knowledgeable than adults, they show better recall. (294)

3. Experts are more likely to apply organizational strategies during _____. (294)

4. Another factor involved in strategic memory processing is _____, which prompts children to actively use what they know to add more knowledge. (294-295)

Scripts: Basic Building Blocks of Structured Knowledge

1. The vast, intricately organized general knowledge system is referred to as _____ memory. It grows out of _____ memory, or memory for personally experienced events. (295)

2. _____ are general representations of what occurs and when it occurs in a particular situation. (295)

3. Scripts are a special form of _____ memory. They serve as a basic means through which we organize and interpret everyday experiences. (295)

4. Scripts may be the developmental link between early _____ memory and a(n) _____ organized long-term memory store. (295)

Autobiographical Memory

1. A special form of _____ memory is autobiographical memory, representations of one-time events that are long-lasting and particularly meaningful. (296)

2. Almost no one can retrieve experiences that happened to us before age ____--a phenomenon called _____. (296)

3. One explanation for infantile amnesia is that two levels of memory exist, one that is _____ and another that is _____. (296)

4. Another explanation for infantile amnesia is that, for episodic memories to become autobiographical, the child must have a well-developed image of the _____ and must learn to structure memories as _____. (296)

5. As early as 11/2 to 2 years, children begin to form a(n) _____ by talking about the past with adults who expand on their fragmented recollections. (296)

6. Until recently, it was rare for children under age ____ to be asked to testify in court, whereas those age ____ and older did. (298)

7. True or False: Children will not be easily misled into giving false information, even when a long delay is combined with suggestions about what happened. (299)

8. True or False: When anatomical dolls are combined with repeated interviewing, false reports by young children in cases of sexual abuse decreases. (299)

Metacognition

1. _____ refers to awareness and understanding of various aspects of thought. (299)

2. Children construct a naive _____, a coherent understanding of people as mental beings. (299)

Metacognitive Knowledge

1. True or False: Children cannot distinguish thinking from other activities until age 5. (300)

2. Preschoolers (do/do not) understand that mental inferences can be a source of knowledge. (300)

3. True or False: Preschoolers seem to view the mind as a passive container of information. (301)

4. True or False: School-age children are slightly more conscious of strategies for processing information than are preschoolers. (301)

Cognitive Self-Regulation

1. _____ is the process of continuously monitoring progress toward a goal, checking outcomes, and redirecting unsuccessful efforts. (301)

2. Difficulties children experience in engaging in self-regulation on complex tasks are evident in their _____, or sensitivity to how well they understand a spoken or written message. (302)

3. True or False: Current evidence indicates that cognitive self-regulation develops quickly. (302)

4. List three ways that parents and teachers can foster children's self-regulatory skills. (302)
A._____
B._____
C._____

5. _____ theory has been a source of inspiration for metacognitive training. (302)

Applications of Information Processing to Academic Learning

1. Describe common features of research on the application of information processing to academic learning. (304)

_____
_____
_____
_____

Reading

1. Children's active efforts to construct literary knowledge through informal experiences are called _____. (304)

2. How does Siegler's strategy-choice model help to explain the literacy developments of early childhood? (305)

_____

_____

_____

3. The _____ approach to reading instruction parallels natural language learning, whereas the _____ approach gives children simplified text materials and teaches them _____. (305)

Mathematics

1. ____ to ____ month-old infants display a beginning grasp of ordinality. (306)

2. Between the ages of ____ and ____, children grasp the principle of cardinality, which quickly increases the efficiency of counting. (306)

3. Cross-cultural evidence suggests that basic arithmetic knowledge (does/does not) emerge universally around the world. (306)

4. True or False: In learning basic math facts, poorly performing pupils move too quickly toward trying to retrieve answers automatically. (307)

5. List six factors that contribute to the sharp skill advantage of Asian over American pupils in mathematics. (308)

A._____

_____

B._____

_____

C._____

_____

D._____

_____

E._____

_____

F._____

_____

Scientific Reasoning

1. Describe what it means to reason scientifically. (309)

_____

_____

2. The ability to distinguish _____ from _____ and use _____ rules to examine their relationship in multi-variable situations improves from childhood into adulthood. (309)

3. Thinking about thought, or _____, is especially important in supporting skill at coordinating theory with evidence. (309)

4. Scientific reasoning (is/is not) the result of an abrupt, stagewise change. (309)

Evaluation of the Information-Processing Approach

1. List three strengths and four limitations of the information-processing approach. (310-311)

Strengths:

A._____

B._____

C._____

Limitations:

A._____

B._____

C._____

D._____

ASK YOURSELF . . .

7.1 A researcher gave 5-year-old Kayla several conservation-of-number problems and told her whether her answer was right or wrong. On the first one, she gave a nonconserving response. On the second one, she said, "The rows have the same number because you didn't add any pennies." On the third one, she said, "I counted the pennies. The rows have the same number." Why is it beneficial for Kayla to use several strategies? Which strategy is she likely to emphasize over time, and why? (p. 282)

7.2 At age 7, Jonah played each of his piano pieces from beginning to end instead of picking out the hard parts for extra practice. Around age 8, he began to devote more time to sections he knew least well, but his performance did not improve for several months. What explains Jonah's gradual strategy development and gains in performance? (p. 287)

7.3 Cite research findings that show utilization deficiencies as children master each of the memory strategies discussed in the preceding sections? (p. 291)

7.4 Given a list of baseball players' names to learn, Tyrone, a baseball expert, recalled many more than did Hal, who knows little about baseball, even though both boys used an organizational strategy in learning the items. Explain Tyrone's superior memory. (p. 298)

7.5 What characteristics of the parent-child conversation about the past on pages 296-297) are likely to promote the development of autobiographical memory? Explain. (p. 298)

7.6 "Mom, let's go!" pleaded 4-year-old Tom, waiting for his mother to take him to the park. "Tom, just a minute. I'm thinking about where I put my keys." Tom responded, "You can't think about keys that way. You're just standing there." What does Tom's statement reveal about his metacognitive knowledge? (p. 302)

7.7 Using information-processing mechanisms of development and research discussed in this chapter, explain why attention to both basic skills and understanding is important in reading and math instruction. (p. 310)

7.8 Review Heidi's thinking about the impact of diverse variables on the bounce of her tennis balls on page 307. What features of her reasoning suggest that she is beginning to reason scientifically? (p. 310)

CONNECTIONS

7.1 Return to Chapter 6, page 239, to review the drawings of nonschooled Jimi 10- to 15-year-olds of Papua New Guinea. Use Case's theory to explain why these drawings resemble the one-dimensional artwork of much younger children. Are these Jimi children likely to be one-dimensional thinkers on many other tasks? Explain.

7.2 How can bidirectional influences between child and environment explain the development of defiant, aggressive behavior in about one-third of children with ADHD? In what ways do the child-rearing experiences of such children resemble those known to foster aggression? (see Chapter 1, page 27, and Chapter 12, pages 512-514.)

7.3 How can gains in cognitive inhibition during middle childhood support the development of memory strategies? (See page 284.)

7.4 Review the development of deferred imitation on page 230 of Chapter 6.   What does it tell us about gains in recall memory during the first 2 years?

7.5 Self-regulation develops in other domains besides cognition. For example, children must learn how to regulate their emotions. Why is emotional self-regulation important? (See Chapter 10, pages 404-406.)

7.6 Describe cultural values, child-rearing attitudes and practices, and educational methods that lead Asian children to outperform American children in math achievement. (See Chapter 15, page 637-639.)

PUZZLE 7.1

Across

2 Theory of ___, a coherent understanding of people as mental beings

8 ___ conceptual structures allow children to think in more advanced ways

13 ___ self-regulation, continuously monitoring progress toward a goal

14 Long-lasting representation of one-time events

15 ___-skills approach teaches reading through simplified text first

17 ___-trace theory proposes information is encoded in vague and verbatim versions

18 Cognitive ___ controls internal and external distracting stimuli

19 ___-Piagetian theory reinterprets Piaget's stages within an information-processing framework

Down

1 Disorder involving inattention and impulsivity

2 Operating on and transforming information using ___ strategies

3 Determines amount of attention a person allocates to an activity

4 Type of memory that reinterprets complex material in terms of existing knowledge

5 Using a strategy consistently

6 Using informal experiences to construct literacy knowledge in ___ literacy

7 Explains development through computer-simulated learning tasks

9 General representations of what occurs and when it occurs in a particular situation

10 Order relationships between quantities

11 Increases the efficiency of counting

12 ___-of-processing model assumes memory depends on how deeply information is processed

16 ___ deficiency, producing a helpful strategy inconsistently

PUZZLE 7.2

Across

1 Preserves essential content without details
6 Part of the system in which information is consciously operated on
7 Model having three information-processing parts
13 ___ deficiency, failure to use a helpful strategy
14 Awareness of thought
17 Sights and sounds held briefly in the ___ register
18 Thinking out and allocating attention to a goal
19 Model of ___ choice shows how strategies change
20 ___-term memory, part of the system containing permanent knowledge base
21 Memory involving remembering an absent stimulus

Down

2 ___ position effect, remembering items at the end of a list better than the middle ones
3 ___-language approach, teaching reading in a manner similar to natural language learning
4 Memory strategy of repeating information
5 Memory for personally experienced events
8 Grouping information into meaningful chunks
9 Memory involving noticing whether a stimulus is identical or similar to a previous one
10 ___ comprehension, sensitivity to how well one understands a spoken or written message
11 Strategy of creating a relationship between items in different categories
12 ___ memory, failure to benefit from the use of a mental strategy
16 Infantile ___, inability to remember personal experiences that happen before age 3

PRACTICE TEST

1. The sensory register, short-term memory, and long-term memory in Atkinson and Shiffrin's store model can be thought of as the _____ of the mental system. (272)
   - A. hardware
   - B. software
   - C. merchandise
   - D. control processes

2. Working, or short-term, memory is: (273)
   - A. where information first enters the information-processing system.
   - B. unlimited in capacity.
   - C. enhanced through the use of strategies.
   - D. increased by combining information into meaningful chunks.

3. The serial position effect: (274)
   - A. is inconsistent with the store model of mental functioning.
   - B. supports the distinction between working and long-term memory.
   - C. explains why middle items on a list are more likely to be remembered.
   - D. explains why items at the beginning of a list decay from memory over time.

4. The levels-of-processing model views: (274)
   - A. information as flowing through three components where it is processed or stored.
   - B. encoding by perceptual features as deeper processing than encoding by semantic features.
   - C. information as being retained much longer if it is interpreted meaningfully.
   - D. encoding by phonemic features as deeper processing than encoding by rehearsal.

5. Recent research by Kail on processing speed indicates that: (275-276)
   - A. processing time does not decrease with age for perceptual-motor tasks.
   - B. there is a rapid decline in processing time until age 20.
   - C. the use of more effective strategies accounts for age-related differences in processing time.
   - D. similarity in development across cultures implies an age-related gain in basic information-processing resources.

6. Which of the following is NOT a factor responsible for gains in the capacity of working memory, according to Case's neo-Piagetian theory? (276-277)
   - A. brain development
   - B. range of environmental exposures
   - C. formation of central conceptual structures
   - D. practice with schemes and automatization

7. Which of the following is NOT true of connectionism? (278, 280)
   A. It explains development by means of computer-simulated learning tasks.
   B. It presents an argument against the nativist, modular view of the mind.
   C. It suggests that the human cognitive system is a domain-general processor.
   D. Its learning procedures fully capture how humans make use of feedback.

8. Siegler's model of strategy choice applies a(n) _____ perspective to children's cognition. (281)
   A. evolutionary
   B. connectionist
   C. learning
   D. sociocultural

9. Which of the following is NOT true of Siegler's model of strategy choice? (281-282)
   A. When children are aware of a more adaptive strategy, they do not always use it.
   B. It reveals that no child thinks in just one way.
   C. Strategy use progresses in a stagelike way.
   D. Strategy variability is vital for devising more adaptive ways of thinking.

10. The failure to use an attentional strategy in situations in which it could be helpful is indicative of a(n): (285)
   A. utilization deficiency.
   B. production deficiency.
   C. control deficiency.
   D. location deficiency.

11. Which of the following is NOT true of children with ADHD? (288-289)
   A. Their intelligence is normal.
   B. They appear to have an impairment in inhibition.
   C. They are best treated with a combination of medication and behavioral interventions.
   D. Approximately 20 percent of school-age children have the disorder.

12. Three strategies that enhance memory for new information include: (287)
   A. skill manipulation, reevaluation, and automaticity.
   B. rehearsal, organization, and elaboration.
   C. serial-position, revision, and recognition.
   D. self-regulation, ordinality, and skills training.

13. To remember the words "lamp" and "elephant," Shauna imagines an elephant with a big, bright lamp balanced on her trunk. This is an example of: (290)
   A. gist.
   B. ordinality.
   C. organization.
   D. elaboration.

14. Recognition as a form of memory retrieval: (291)
    A. is first present around age 2.
    B. is highly accurate by age 4.
    C. is the most complex form of retrieval.
    D. depends on a deliberate search of long-term memory.

15. When retrieving information: (292)
    A. older children recall more accurately and completely after a time lapse than younger children.
    B. condensations, additions, and distortions are solely the result of memory failure.
    C. radical transformations of material are rare.
    D. reconstruction first occurs after age 12.

16. According to fuzzy-trace theory: (293)
    A. the version of encoded information called the gist uses more working memory than the verbatim version.
    B. over time, gist memory decays more quickly than verbatim memory.
    C. both verbatim and gist memories are present from the onset.
    D. with age, children rely more on verbatim memory and less on gist.

17. Which of the following is NOT true of scripts? (295)
    A. They are used primarily by preschool-age and school-age children and are seldom referred to after adolescence.
    B. They are a special form of reconstructive memory.
    C. They are used to predict what will happen in the future.
    D. They may be the developmental link between early episodic memory and semantically organized long-term memory.

18. Which of the following is NOT a hypothesis which seeks to explain infantile amnesia? (296)
    A. Two separate levels of memory exist, one unconscious and largely used by infants, and the other conscious.
    B. Early childhood illnesses often erase memory traces.
    C. Until about age 3, the psychological self is not mature enough to serve as an anchor for memories.
    D. In order to remember, a person must be able to organize personally relevant events in narrative form.

19. When children give eyewitness testimony: (298-299)
    A. the use of anatomically correct dolls improves accuracy.
    B. they are seldom affected by the courtroom setting.
    C. a long delay combined with suggestions about what happened can easily mislead children into giving false information.
    D. they are presumed competent by law to testify at ages 3 and older.

20. Research on metacognitive knowledge indicates that: (301)
    A. young children have difficulty distinguishing between mental events and external reality.
    B. young children realize that people are constantly engaged in thought.
    C. below age 4 or 5, children believe that physical experience determines mental experience.
    D. 4-year-olds do not know that noise can interfere with attention to a task.

21. Which of the following is NOT true of cognitive self-regulation? (301-302)
    A. Cognitive self-regulation develops rapidly in early childhood.
    B. It can be assessed by looking at comprehension monitoring.
    C. It combines with metacognition to influence progress toward a goal.
    D. It can be strengthened by pointing out the special demands of tasks and encouraging the use of strategies.

22. The whole-language approach to reading instruction advocates exposing children to text in _____ form, whereas the basic-skills approach argues that children should be given _____ text. (305)
    A. deciphered/natural
    B. complete/simplified
    C. translated/original
    D. simplified/original

23. Research indicates that in mathematics: (308)
    A. multidigit problems are introduced later in Asian schools than in American schools.
    B. American math instruction emphasizes numerical understanding over computational drill.
    C. children in Asian nations are ahead of American students only at the high-school level.
    D. the use of the metric system helps children think in ways consistent with place value.

24. Scientific reasoning ability: (309)
    A. is commonly found in children as early as third grade.
    B. requires metacognitive skills.
    C. usually derives from direct instruction in scientific reasoning in school.
    D. results from an abrupt, stagewise change.

25. Which is NOT a limitation of the information-processing approach? (311)
    A. Its lack of explicitness and precision in breaking down complex cognitive performance into components.
    B. Its difficulty in constructing a broad comprehensive theory.
    C. Its inability to explain aspects of cognition such as imagination and creativity.
    D. Its lack of consideration of the biological bases of cognitive development.

CHAPTER 8

INTELLIGENCE

SUMMARY

Researchers interested in intelligence testing seek to determine what factors, or dimensions, make up intelligence, and how they change with age. They are interested in how cognitive development can be measured so that scores are useful for predicting future academic achievement, career attainment, and other aspects of intellectual success.

The psychometric approach to cognitive development is the basis for the wide variety of intelligence tests used to assess individual differences in children's mental abilities. Factor analysis emerged as a statistical method to identify the mental abilities that contribute to successful performance on intelligence tests. However, factor analysts have been criticized for devoting too much attention to identifying factors and too little to clarifying the cognitive processes that underlie them. To overcome the limitations of factor analysis, some researchers have combined psychometric and information-processing approaches and conduct componential analyses of children's test scores. Sternberg's triarchic theory of intelligence extends these efforts. Gardner's theory of multiple intelligences identifies eight distinct domains of ability, each defined by unique processing operations.

A wide variety of tests are currently available to assess children's intelligence. Accurately measuring the intelligence of infants is an especially challenging task. IQs obtained after age 6 show substantial correlational stability. IQ is an effective predictor of scholastic performance, occupational attainment, and certain aspects of psychological adjustment.

The relationship of socioeconomic status to intellectual development has sparked the IQ nature-nurture debate. Heritability estimates support a moderate role for heredity in accounting for individual differences in IQ. However, they cannot be used to explain ethnic and social-class differences in test scores. Shared and nonshared environmental influences also contribute to individual differences in intelligence.

Family attitudes toward intellectual success and academic performance are powerful predictors of academic success. Research on early intervention programs indicates that lasting benefits occur in school adjustment and in the ability to meet basic educational requirements. Conceptions of giftedness have recently expanded to include creativity.

LEARNING OBJECTIVES

After reading this chapter, you should be able to:

8.1 Describe changing definitions of intelligence, from Binet's first successful test to the modern factor analysts. (316-320)

8.2 Explain why researchers have conducted componential analyses of intelligence test scores, and cite contributions of Sternberg's triarchic theory and Gardner's theory of multiple intelligences to contemporary definitions of intelligence. (320-324)

8.3 Cite commonly used intelligence tests for children, and discuss prediction of later IQ from infant tests. (324-326)

8.4 Describe the computation and distribution of IQ scores. (326)

8.5 Discuss the stability of IQ and its prediction of scholastic performance, occupational attainment and performance, and psychological adjustment. (326-331)

8.6 Describe ethnic and socioeconomic variations in IQ, including evidence on Jensen's Level I-Level II theory. (331-333)

8.7 Describe and evaluate the contributions of heredity and environment to individual and group differences in IQ. (333-338)

8.8 Evaluate evidence on whether IQ is a biased measure of the intelligence of ethnic minority children, and discuss efforts to reduce test bias. (338-342)

8.9 Summarize the impact of shared and nonshared environmental influences on IQ. (342-345)

8.10 Discuss the impact of early intervention on intellectual development. (346-349)

8.11 Describe and evaluate evidence on the development of creativity, including the psychometric view and the multifaceted approach of investment theory. (349-353)

STUDY QUESTIONS

1. The _____ approach to cognitive development is the basis for the wide variety of intelligence tests available for assessing children's mental abilities. It is more (process-oriented/product-oriented) and focuses on (procedures/results). (315)

Definitions of Intelligence

1. Both experts and laypeople view intelligence as made up of _____, _____, and _____. (316)

Alfred Binet: A Holistic View

1. The most important influence leading to the rise of the intelligence testing movement was the beginning of _____ in Europe and the United States. (316)

2. The first successful intelligence test was devised by _____ and _____ _____ in the year _____. Its purpose was to identify pupils with _____ who required assignment to special classes. It took a(n) _____ approach to test construction and predicted _____. (316-317)

3. In the year_____, _____ adapted the Binet test for use with American schoolchildren. The American version is known as the _____ _____. (317)

The Factor Analysts: A Multifaceted View

1. _____ is a complicated statistical procedure in which scores on many separate items are combined into a few factors, which substitute for the separate scores. (317)

2. The first influential factor analyst was _____ who proposed the existence of a common underlying _____, or _____. He also identified _____, called _____. His view of mental abilities was called the _____. (317)

3. _____ argued that separate, unrelated intellectual abilities exist. He concluded that intelligence consists of seven distinct _____. (317)

4. _____ accepts "g" and divides it into two factors. _____ intelligence depends on culturally loaded, fact-oriented information. _____ intelligence involves the ability to see complex relationships and solve problems. (318-319)

5. _____ proposed a(n) _____ that represents the structure of intelligence as a pyramid, with "g" at the top and eight broad abilities in the second stratum. At the lowest stratum are narrow abilities. (319-320)

Combining Psychometric and Information-Processing Approaches

1. The _____ approach combines psychometric and information-processing approaches to provide process-oriented explanations of mental test performance. (320)

2. True or False: Individuals whose nervous systems function more efficiently have an edge when it comes to intellectual skills. (320)

3. The metabolic rate of the cortex when solving complex tasks is (higher/lower) for more intelligent people. (320)

4. True or False: Although adaptive strategy use in solving mathematical problems helps children retrieve answers more accurately, it is not related to mental test scores. (321)

5. Awareness of problem-solving strategies and organizational and planning skills (are/are not) good predictors of general intelligence. (321)

6. A major shortcoming of the componential approach is its attribution of intelligence entirely to causes _____. (321)

Sternberg's Triarchic Theory

1. The _____ subtheory of Sternberg's triarchic theory spells out the information-processing skills that underlie intelligent behavior. These include _____, _____, _____, and _____. (321)

2. The _____ subtheory states that highly intelligent individuals, compared to less intelligent ones, process information more skillfully in novel situations. (322)

3. The _____ subtheory proposes that intelligent people skillfully _____ their information-processing skills to fit with personal desires and demands of the world. Alternatively, they may try to _____ a situation to meet their needs or _____ new contexts consistent with their goals. (322)

4. The contextual subtheory emphasizes that intelligent behavior (is/is not) culture-free. (322)

Gardner's Theory of Multiple Intelligences

1. Gardner believes intelligence should be defined in terms of distinct sets of
_____. He dismisses the idea of a single overarching mental
ability, or "g," and proposes _____ independent intelligences. (322-323)

2. List three reasons why neurological support for the independence of intelligences, as
proposed by Gardner, is weak. (323-324)
A._____
B._____
C._____

Representative Intelligence Tests for Children

1. _____ tests permit many children to be tested at once and
require very little training of teachers who give them. _____ tests
demand considerable training and experience to give well. In addition to considering the
child's answers, the examiner also carefully observes _____. (324)

The Stanford-Binet Intelligence Scale

1. The Stanford-Binet Intelligence Scale is appropriate for individuals between _____
years of age and _____. It measures both _____
and four _____. The verbal and quantitative factors
emphasize _____ intelligence, whereas the abstract/visual reasoning factor taps
_____ intelligence. (324)

The Wechsler Intelligence Scale for Children

1. The Wechsler Intelligence Scale for Children-III (WISC-III) is used for children ages
_____ through _____. The Wechsler Preschool and Primary Scale of Intelligence-Revised
(WPPSI-R) is appropriate for children ages _____ through _____. (325)

2. True or False: Psychologists and educators prefer the Stanford-Binet for individual
assessment of children. (325)

3. Both the WISC-III and the WPPSI-R measure two broad intellectual factors:
_____ and _____. (325)

Infant Intelligence Tests

1. Most infant measures consist largely of _____ and _____
responses. (325)

2. The _____, a commonly used infant test, was inspired by the early normative work of _____. It consists of two parts: the _____ Scale and the _____ Scale. (325)

3. Infant perceptual and motor behaviors (do/do not) represent the same aspects of intelligence assessed in childhood. (325)

4. The most recent version of the Bayley test includes items that emphasize

_____, _____, _____, and _____. (325)

5. Traditional infant tests show some predictability for very (high-scoring/low-scoring) babies. (325)

6. Speed of _____ and _____ to visual stimuli is an effective infant correlate of childhood intelligence. The _____ is a test made up entirely of this kind of item. (325)

7. The _____ is based on Piaget's theory and assesses an important _____. (326)

The Computation and Distribution of IQ Scores

1. The _____ indicates the extent to which a raw score on an intelligence test deviates from the typical performance of same-age individuals. (326)

2. If we know the mean and standard deviation of an IQ test, we can determine the _____ of individuals at each age who fall above or below a certain score. (326)

What and How Well Do Intelligence Tests Predict?

Stability of IQ Scores

1. One way to examine the stability of IQ is to _____ scores obtained from repeated testings. The (older/younger) the child at time of first testing, the better the prediction of later IQ. The closer in time two testings are, the (stronger/weaker) the relationship between the scores. (327)

2. Explain why preschool IQ scores predict less well than later scores. (327)

_____
_____
_____

3. Longitudinal research reveals that the majority of children experience (minor/substantial) IQ fluctuations over childhood and adolescence. (328)

4. Describe the characteristics of children whose IQ scores change the most. (328)
Gainers: _____
_____

Decliners:_____
_____

5. (Heredity/environment) seems to be the overriding factor in the decreasing IQ scores
of poverty-stricken children. According to the _____,
the effects of underprivileged rearing conditions worsen the longer the children remain in
them. (328)

6. What evidence supports the cumulative deficit? (328)
_____
_____

IQ as a Predictor of Scholastic Performance

1. Correlations between IQ and academic achievement are typically around _____.
(328)

2. Discuss two theories that may explain why IQ is an effective predictor of scholastic
performance. (328)
_____
_____
_____
_____

3. In addition to IQ, factors such as _____ and _____ also account
for individual differences in scholastic performance. (329-330)

4. Using Ceci's research, list 5 results from the studies that show that schooling has a
major impact on IQ. (329)
A._____
B._____
C._____
D._____
E._____

5. Schooling influences IQ by teaching children _____ relevant to test
questions, promoting _____ skills, and encouraging _____
that foster successful test taking. (329)

IQ as a Predictor of Occupational Attainment and Performance

1. True or False: IQ scores have a much lower correlation with adult occupational
attainment than with academic achievement. (330)

2. Years of schooling is a (weaker/stronger) predictor of occupational success than is IQ. (330)

3. List three factors that characterized the individuals in Terman's study who fared best in their occupations. (330)

A._____

B._____

C._____

4. In addition to IQ, _____ predicts on-the-job performance. Ethnic-group differences in this type of intelligence (do/do not) exist. (330)

5. True or False: IQ and practical intelligence are highly correlated. (330)

IQ as a Predictor of Psychological Adjustment

1. True or False: During middle childhood, children with higher IQs tend to be better liked by their agemates. (330-331)

2. Adjustment disorders such as high anxiety, fearfulness, social withdrawal, and depression (are/are not) related to mental test scores. (331)

Ethnic and Socioeconomic Variations in IQ
---

1. Researchers assess a family's social position and economic well-being through an index called _____. (331)

2. Jensen published a controversial article in which he argued that (environment/heredity) was largely responsible for individual, ethnic, and SES differences in IQ. Recently, Herrnstein and Murray published _____, in which they concluded that the contribution of (heredity/environment) to individual and SES differences in IQ is substantial. (332)

Differences in General Intelligence

1. American black children score, on the average, ____ points below American white children on measures of general intelligence. SES accounts for (some/all) of the difference. (332)

2. True or False: There is little variability within each ethnic and SES group. (332)

3. Ethnicity and SES account for about _____ of the total variation in IQ. (332)

Differences in Specific Mental Abilities

1. Jensen distinguishes two types of intelligence. _____ refers to items emphasizing short-term and rote memory; _____ involves abstract reasoning and problem solving. (332-333)

2. According to Jensen, black-white and SES differences in IQ are due to (Level I/Level II) abilities. (333)

Explaining Individual and Group Differences in IQ

1. List the three broad classes of research aimed at uncovering the origins of individual, ethnic, and SES differences in mental abilities. (333)

A._____
B._____
C._____

Genetic Influences

1. _____ studies compare individuals of differing degrees of genetic relationship to one another. (333-334)

2. What is a heritability estimate? (334)

_____
_____

3. True or False: The greater the genetic similarity between family members, the more they resemble one another in IQ. (334)

4. The correlation in mental test performance for identical twins reared apart is (much higher/the same/much lower) than for fraternal twins reared together. (334)

5. Correlations in IQ for identical twins (increase/decrease) modestly into adulthood; those for fraternal twins (increase/decrease) sharply at adolescence. (334)

6. Correlations in IQ for identical twins reared together are considerably (higher/lower) than for those reared apart, indicating that _____ factors contribute to IQ. (334-335)

7. List four other comparisons found in kinship studies that stress the role of environment in IQ. (334)

A._____
B._____
C._____
D._____

8. Explain why using within-group heritabilities to explain between-group differences is like comparing different seeds in different soil. (335-336)

_____
_____
_____

9. Describe the findings of Skodak and Skeels's adoption research. (336)

_____
_____
_____

10. Research conducted by the Texas Adoption Project on the IQs of adopted children indicates that (heredity/environment/both heredity and environment) contribute(s) significantly to IQ. (336)

11. True or False: Adoption studies repeatedly reveal stronger correlations between the IQ scores of biological than adoptive relatives. (336)

12. Discuss the research of Scarr and Weinberg which examined IQs of transracially adopted black children. (337)

_____
_____
_____
_____

13. Moore's research on the test-taking behavior and parent-child interaction of two groups of black adoptees (does/does not) support the position that rearing environment accounts for the black-white IQ gap. (337)

Are Ethnic Groups Biologically Based?

1. DNA analyses reveal wide genetic variation _____ ethnic groups and insignificant variation _____ them. (338)

2. True or False: Using genetic, racial differences to determine ethnic differences in psychological traits are often arbitrary. (338)

Ethnicity and Test Bias

1. Briefly indicate the arguments regarding the influence of ethnicity and test bias on IQ scores. (338)

_____
_____
_____
_____

2. Efforts to make tests fairer to ethnic minorities (have/have not) raised their scores significantly. (338)

3. True or False: Cambodian, Filipino, Vietnamese, and Mexican immigrant parents value cognitive attributes in children over noncognitive ones. (339)

4. Black parents tend to ask _____ questions. Often these are _____ or _____ questions. Their language differs from that of white middle-SES children in emphasizing _____ and _____ topics rather than _____ about the world. (339)

5. True or False: When tested by an unfamiliar adult, children from poverty backgrounds are often wary. (340)

6. Research indicates that IQs of minority children (do/do not) improve when testing conditions are modified. (340)

Reducing Test Bias

1. When evaluating minority children for educational placement, assessments of _____--their ability to cope with the demands of their everyday environments--should be obtained. (340)

2. _____, an innovative approach to testing, narrows the gap between actual and potential performance. List 3 factors that distinguish this type of testing from traditional approaches. (340-341)
   A. _____
   B. _____
   C. _____

3. True or False: Evidence on dynamic testing reveals that the IQs of ethnic minority children underestimate their ability to perform intellectual tasks after adult assistance. (341)

4. List two limitations of dynamic testing. (341)
   A. _____
   B. _____

5. An approach that measures intellectual progress by examining students' real performance in school over time is _____. (342)

6. SES, ethnicity, and gender (do/do not) affect the relationship of classroom experiences to authentic academic achievement. (342)

Home Environment and IQ

1. Home influences can be divided into two broad types. The first, _____ environmental influences, are factors that pervade the general atmosphere of the home. The second, _____ environmental influences, refers to factors that make siblings different from one another. (342-343)

2. The _____ is a checklist for gathering information about the quality of children's home lives through observation and parental interview. (343)

3. In infancy, the HOME indicates that _____ and _____ show the strongest relationships with mental test scores. During the preschool years, _____, _____ _____, and _____ are the best predictors. (343)

4. Regardless of ethnic and SES background, the HOME indicates that amount of _____ during the first 3 years is a powerful predictor of early language progress. (344)

5. Based on white middle-SES families, researchers estimate that as much as half of the correlation between HOME and IQ is due to _____. (344)

6. Among students from immigrant families in America, valuing educational endeavors was a (more/less) powerful predictor of academic performance than were parental education and occupational status. (344)

7. Give three examples of nonshared environmental influences. (345)
   A._____
   B._____
   C._____

8. Some investigators conclude that the most potent nonshared influences on IQ are _____ events. (345)

Early Intervention and Intellectual Development

1. On what two assumptions are early intervention programs based? (346)
   A._____
   B._____

2. The most extensive early intervention program is _____. (346)

3. Describe a typical Head Start program. (346)

_____
_____
_____
_____

Benefits of Early Intervention

1. What did the Consortium for Longitudinal Studies find with respect to the long-term benefits of Head Start? (346)

_____
_____
_____
_____
_____

Evaluations of Head Start

1. Explain why studies of Head Start centers located in American communities may be biased. (347)

_____
_____

2. An investigation found that, compared to other preschool and no preschool groups, Head Start children showed (greater/the same/smaller) gains. (347)

3. Explain why almost all children in Head Start experience an eventual washout effect. (347)

_____
_____
_____

4. Children in the treatment group of the Carolina Abecedarian Project, an early intervention experiment, (did/did not) maintain their advantage in IQ over controls during middle childhood. (348)

A Two-Generation Program Strategy

1. A typical parent component of early intervention emphasizes teaching _____ _____ and encourages parents to act as _____ for their child. (347)

2. By expanding intervention to include _____ goals for both parents and children, program benefits might be extended. (347)

3. What is New Chance, and what gains have participants made? (349)

_____

_____

_____

_____

The Future of Early Intervention

1. Head Start serves only about _____ of the children eligible. (349)

2. Why is Head Start highly cost-effective? (349)

_____

_____

Development of Creativity

1. The standard definition of giftedness based on intelligence test performance includes youngsters with IQ scores above _____. An expanded definition also includes children who are _____. (349)

2. What are the characteristics of creative work? (349)

_____

_____

_____

The Psychometric View

1. _____ thinking involves generating multiple and unusual possibilities; _____ thinking involves arriving at a single correct answer. (350)

2. Researchers have devised _____, _____, and _____ tests of divergent thinking. (350)

3. List two limitations and three strengths of tests of divergent thinking as measures of creativity. (350)
Limitation: _____
Limitation: _____
Strength: _____
Strength: _____
Strength: _____

A Multifaceted View

1. Cite the main features of Sternberg and Lubart's investment theory of creativity. (351)

_____
_____
_____

2. Contrary to popular belief, creativity (is/is not) determined at birth and (is/is not) limited to an elite few individuals. (351)

3. Creativity requires both problem solving and _____. It also requires the ability to _____, and the more effort devoted to this step, the more original the final product. (351)

4. Creativity involves alternating between _____ and _____ thinking. (351)

5. _____ processes combine and restructure elements in sudden but useful ways. Examples include the use of _____ and _____. (351)

6. _____ is necessary to make creative contributions. As a result, individuals usually demonstrate creativity in (many/few) domains. (352)

7. The correlation between IQ and creativity is around _____ to _____. (352)

8. List four crucial personality characteristics of creative individuals. (352)
A._____
B._____
C._____
D._____

9. Motivation for creativity must be _____ focused rather than _____ focused. An example of the former is _____; an example of the latter is _____. (352)

10. What are characteristics of the home environments of talented children and adults? (353)

_____
_____
_____

11. What types of classrooms facilitate the development of creativity? (353)

_____
_____

12. Recently, _____ theory of multiple intelligences has served as the basis for several model programs that provide domain-specific enrichment to all pupils. (353)

ASK YOURSELF...

8.1 Use the experiential and contextual subtheories of Sternberg's triarchic theory to explain why a child might do poorly on an intelligence test but display superior mental abilities in everyday life. (p. 324)

8.2 Fifteen-month-old Joey's score on the Bayley Scales of Infant Development is 115. His parents want to know exactly what this means and whether the score is likely to forecast Joey's childhood IQ. How would you respond to these questions? (p. 331)

8.3 Seven-year-old Scott's father is concerned about how high his son's IQ is, since he wants Scott to go to college and enter a high-status occupation. What other factors in addition to IQ are likely to contribute to Scott's life success?
(p. 331)

8.4 IQ correlations for fraternal twins and siblings decline from childhood to adolescence. What does this suggest about the impact of shared and nonshared environmental influences on IQ? (p. 345)

8.5 Desiree, and African-American child, was quiet and withdrawn while taking an intelligence test. Later, she remarked to her mother, "I can't understand why that lady asked me all those questions. She's a grown-up. She must know what a ball and stove are for!" Explain Desiree's reaction to the testing situation. Why is her score likely to underestimate her intelligence? (p. 345)

8.6 Explain why educational programs inspired by Gardner's theory of multiple intelligences require authentic assessment of children's intellectual accomplishments. (Refer to the From Research to Practice box on page 346.) (p. 353)

CONNECTIONS

8.1 In his second-grade classroom, Tony can often be seen experimenting with strategies in reading, spelling, and math. How might Tony's adaptive strategy use contribute to both his speed of processing and his intelligence test performance? (See Chapter 7, page 281.)

8.2 Cite similarities between Gardner's theory of multiple intelligences and the modular view of the mind. (See Chapter 6, page 234.) What questions raised about the modular view also apply to Gardner's theory?

8.3 What family experiences linked to poverty probably contribute to the environmental cumulative deficit in IQ? (See Chapter 14, page 569.)

8.4 Explain how dynamic testing is consistent with Vygotsky-based concepts, including the zone of proximal development and scaffolding. (See Chapter 6, page 261.)

8.5 Using what you learned about brain development in Chapter 5 (see pages 186-191), explain why intensive intervention for poverty-stricken children beginning in the first 2 years has a greater impact on IQ than intervention at a later age.

8.6 How do findings on factors that contribute to creativity fit with research on the development of prodigies? (See Chapter 2, page 51.)

PUZZLE 8

Across

2 ___ assessment uses a pretest-intervene-retest procedure
4 ___-Binet Intelligence Scale
5 ___ analysis, a statistical procedure used to identify mental abilities
7 ___ I-___ II theory attributes ethnic and SES differences to heredity
8 Common factor that represents abstract reasoning
12 Score on an intelligence test
13 Generation of a single correct answer to a problem
14 A theory stating that information processing, experience, and culture determine intelligence
15 Abilities apparent in the read world, not in testing situations, that involve "knowing how"
17 ___ analysis clarifies the cognitive processes responsible for IQ scores
18 Index referring to social position and economic well-being
21 Creativity theory emphasizing diverse resources
24 Ability to produce original, appropriate work
25 ___ thinking, generation of multiple and unusual possibilities for a task
26 Home environment that similarly affects all children

Down

1 ___ effect, loss of IQ gains resulting from early intervention
3 Three-___ theory, comprehensive classification of mental abilities
4 Mental ability factor unique to a particular task
6 ___ intelligence involves the ability to see complex relationships
9 Environmental influences that make siblings different from one another
10 The ___ approach to cognitive development focuses on construction of tests to assess mental abilities
11 ___ intelligence depends on culturally loaded facts
16 ___, a checklist for gathering information on quality of home life
19 ___, an individual intelligence test that measures general intelligence and a variety of verbal and performance scores
20 Theory of ___ intelligences includes eight intelligences
22 Intelligence consists of seven distinct ___ mental abilities
23 The cumulative ___ hypothesis attributes declines in IQ to underprivileged conditions

PRACTICE TEST

1. The problem of defining children's intelligence is especially challenging because: (316)
   A. no IQ tests are standardized for children.
   B. IQ tests for children lack representative norm groups.
   C. behaviors that reflect intelligence change with age.
   D. children do not understand the questions on IQ tests.

2. To what need did the intelligence test completed by Binet and Simon respond? (316)
   A. the need to identify gifted children
   B. the need to identify mentally retarded pupils
   C. the need to compare the IQs of French and American pupils
   D. the need to measure reaction time

3. The first influential factor analyst was _____, who proposed the two-factor theory of intelligence. (317)
   A. Spearman
   B. Guilford
   C. Cattell
   D. Thurstone

4. _____ intelligence depends on culturally loaded, fact-oriented information; _____ intelligence involves the ability to see complex relationships and solve problems. (318-319)
   A. general/specific
   B. crystallized/fluid
   C. primary/secondary
   D. solid/flowing

5. Componential analyses indicates that: (320)
   A. speed of processing has zero correlation with general intelligence.
   B. the metabolic rate of the cortex when solving complex problems is higher for more intelligent people.
   C. response speed and strategy use both influence mental test performance.
   D. organizational skills are good predictors of general intelligence.

6. What three interacting subtheories comprise Sternberg's triarchic theory? (321-322)
   A. componential, experiential, and contextual
   B. metacognitive, strategic, and skill level
   C. adaptive, behavioral, and hereditary
   D. crystallized, conditional, and environmental

7. Both the WISC-III and the WPPSI-R measure: (325)
   - A. sensorimotor skills.
   - B. habituation/dishabituation.
   - C. verbal and performance abilities.
   - D. simultaneous and sequential processing.

8. The best available infant correlate of childhood intelligence is: (325)
   - A. speed of habituation and dishabituation to visual stimuli.
   - B. auditory central processing.
   - C. fine motor skills.
   - D. gross motor skills.

9. Most intelligence tests set the mean at _____ and the standard deviation at _____. The IQs of the great majority of the population (95.5 percent) fall between _____ and _____. (326)
   - A. 50/10/40/60
   - B. 100/15/85/115
   - C. 95/10/85/105
   - D. 100/15/70/130

10. Which of the following is NOT true of the stability of IQ scores? (327-328)
    - A. The majority of children experience minor or no IQ fluctuations over childhood and adolescence.
    - B. The older the child when tested, the better the prediction of later IQ.
    - C. Ethnic minority children who live in poverty often show IQ declines.
    - D. The closer in time two testings are, the stronger the relationship between the scores.

11. Which of the following is NOT true of IQ? (328-330)
    - A. It is an effective predictor of scholastic achievement.
    - B. It is increased by years of schooling.
    - C. Childhood IQ is an effective predictor of adult occupational attainment.
    - D. It is highly correlated with practical intelligence.

12. The two types of intelligence distinguished by Jensen were: (332-333)
    - A. academic and practical.
    - B. general and specific.
    - C. Level I and Level II.
    - D. contextual and experiential.

13. The contribution of heredity to intelligence _____ with development. (334)
    - A. strengthens
    - B. weakens
    - C. remains the same
    - D. has no relationship

14. Adoption research shows that: (336)
    A. heredity is the primary determinant of IQ.
    B. environment is the primary determinant of IQ.
    C. both heredity and environment contribute significantly to IQ.
    D. adopted children show an increasing tendency to resemble their adoptive parents in IQ as they grow older.

15. Which of the following is NOT a factor that may contribute to test bias on IQ tests? (338-340)
    A. lack of experience with games and objects that promote intellectual skills
    B. unique language customs
    C. lack of opportunity to study for the test
    D. wariness toward the examiner and test situation

16. The dynamic testing approach uses _____ in the testing situation. (340-341)
    A. motion
    B. teaching
    C. videotapes
    D. factor analysis

17. An example of a nonshared environmental influence is: (343)
    A. availability of books in the home.
    B. modeling by parents of intellectual activities.
    C. birth order.
    D. type of neighborhood.

18. Which of the following is NOT consistent with evidence provided by HOME? (343-344)
    A. Stimulation provided by parents is linked to mental development.
    B. The strength of the association between HOME and IQ increases in middle childhood.
    C. Low HOME scores during infancy predict declines in IQ.
    D. The amount of verbal interaction in the home during the first 3 years predicts language progress.

19. The most potent nonshared influence on IQ is: (345)
    A. birth order.
    B. the size of the family.
    C. an unpredictable, one-time event.
    D. being raised by a single parent.

20. Research by the Consortium for Longitudinal Studies shows that, compared with controls, children who attended early intervention programs: (346)
  A. showed lasting benefits in attitudes and motivation.
  B. maintained significantly higher scores in IQ and achievement throughout their school years.
  C. were more likely to be placed in special-education classes.
  D. were less likely to graduate from high school.

21. One way to prevent washout effects is to: (347)
  A. begin intervention programs at a later age.
  B. begin intervention programs at an earlier age.
  C. shorten the time spent in intervention programs.
  D. exclude parents from participating in intervention programs.

22. Tests of divergent thinking: (350)
  A. are referred to as the psychometric approach to creativity.
  B. are useful because they measure motivational factors influencing creativity.
  C. do not tap skills relevant to creativity.
  D. are excellent predictors of creative accomplishment in everyday life.

23. Creativity: (352)
  A. requires little knowledge.
  B. is usually limited to one or a few related domains.
  C. demands that the individual refrain from evaluating ideas.
  D. has a high positive correlation with IQ.

24. Which of the following is NOT a personality characteristic that fosters creativity? (352)
  A. independence of judgment
  B. willingness to take risks
  C. high self-esteem
  D. preference for structured activities

25. Classrooms providing conditions that help develop creativity would: (353)
  A. stress knowledge acquisition.
  B. give assignments that are short and well-defined.
  C. give time to reflect on ideas without rushing to the next assignment.
  D. focus on grades.

CHAPTER 9

LANGUAGE DEVELOPMENT

SUMMARY

Language--the most awesome of universal human achievements-- develops with extraordinary speed over the early childhood years. In mastering language, children acquire four components--phonology, semantics, grammar, and pragmatics--that they combine into a flexible communication system.

Three theories provide different accounts of how children develop language. According to Skinner and other behaviorists, language is learned through operant conditioning and imitation. In contrast, Chomsky's nativist view regards children as biologically equipped with a language acquisition device that supports rapid early mastery of the structure of language. Interactionist theories offer a compromise between these two views, stressing that innate abilities and social contexts combine to promote language development.

During infancy, biological predispositions, cognitive development, and a responsive social environment join together to prepare the child for language. Newborn babies have a built-in capacity to detect a wide variety of sound categories in human speech. By the second half of the first year, infants become increasingly sensitive to the phonemes, words, and phrase structure of their native tongue.

Semantic development takes place with extraordinary speed as preschoolers fast-map thousands of words into their vocabularies. Children's language comprehension develops ahead of production. Lexical contrast theory is a recent controversial account of how semantic development takes place. Preschoolers draw on many sources of information to deduce word meanings.

Children are active, rule-oriented learners whose earliest word combinations begin to reflect the grammar of their native tongue. In first combining words, children are preoccupied with figuring out the meanings of words and in getting their thoughts across to others. By age 6, children have mastered most of the grammar of their native tongue. Certain complex forms, however, continue to be refined in middle childhood.

During early and middle childhood, children acquire a variety of pragmatic devices that permit them to engage in more sustained and effective conversation with others. Parents the world over realize the importance of socially appropriate communication and tutor children in social routines from an early age. Although preschoolers show the beginnings of metalinguistic awareness, major advances do not take place until middle childhood.

Historically, Americans have held negative attitudes toward childhood bilingualism. A large body of research shows that children who are fluent in two languages are advanced in a variety of cognitive and metalinguistic skills.

LEARNING OBJECTIVES

After reading this chapter, you should be able to:

9.1 Describe the four components of language. (358)

9.2 Describe and evaluate three major theories of language development on the basis of research evidence. (358-366)

9.3 Describe receptivity to language, development of speech sounds, and conversational skills during infancy, noting ways that adults can support prelinguistic development. (366-369)

9.4 Describe the course of phonological development. (370-372)

9.5 Describe the course of semantic development, noting individual differences. (372-377)

9.6 Discuss ideas about how semantic development takes place, including the influence of memory and strategies for word learning. (377-378)

9.7 Describe the course of grammatical development. (379-384)

9.8 Discuss ideas about how grammatical development takes place, including strategies and environmental supports for new structures. (384-385)

9.9 Describe the course of pragmatic development, including social influences. (386-389)

9.10 Describe the course of metalinguistic awareness, noting its influence on language and literacy skills. (389-392)

9.11 Describe the impact of bilingualism on language and cognitive development, and summarize evidence justifying bilingual education. (392-393)

STUDY QUESTIONS

Components of Language

1. There are _____ components of language. The first component, _____, refers to the rules governing the structure and sequencing of speech sounds. The second component, _____, involves vocabulary. (358)

2. The third component is _____, which consists of two parts: _____, the rules by which words are arranged into sentences; and _____, the use of grammatical markers that indicate number, tense, case, person, gender, active or passive voice, and other meanings. (358)

3. The fourth component, _____, refers to the communicative side of language. It also involves _____, since society dictates how language should be spoken. (358)

Theories of Language Development

1. The regularity of achievements in language development suggests it is a process largely governed by (maturation/learning). However, the fact that children who are born deaf or who are severely neglected do not acquire verbal communication suggests that language is a product of (maturation/learning). (359)

The Behaviorist Perspective

1. Skinner proposed that language is acquired through _____. Behaviorists also believe that _____ can combine with reinforcement to promote language. (359)

2. True or False: The behaviorist perspective on language development is still the leading theory. (359)

3. Children's novel utterances (do/do not) conform to behaviorist assumptions about language development. (359)

The Nativist Perspective

1. _____ argued that mental structures are at the heart of our capacity to interpret and generate language. His theory is a(n) _____ account that regards language as biologically based. (359)

2. Chomsky suggests that humans are born with a(n) _____, a biologically based, innate module for picking up language that is triggered by verbal input from the environment. (359)

3. Within the LAD is a(n) _____, a built-in storehouse of rules that apply to all human languages. (359)

4. The nativist perspective regards deliberate training by parents as (necessary/unnecessary) for language development. (360)

5. Researchers found that children whose parents discouraged manual signing spontaneously produced a gestural communication system called _____. (361)

6. _____ are languages that arise rapidly from _____, minimally developed "emergency" tongues that result when several language communities migrate to the same area, and no dominant language exists to support interaction among them. (361)

7. The structure of creole languages (is/is not) similar around the world. (361)

8. True or False: Creole grammar resembles the linguistic structures children first use when acquiring any language. (361)

9. The ability of apes to acquire a humanlike language system is (limited/unlimited). In addition, evidence indicates that chimpanzees (can/cannot) master complex grammatical forms. (360)

10. What factors other than specialized language capacity could account for the linguistic gap between chimpanzees and humans? (360, 362)

_____

_____

11. Pygmy chimps (can/cannot) attain the basic linguistic understandings of human 2- to 3-year-olds. (362)

12. Humans have evolved specialized regions in the _____ that support language skills. For most individuals, language is housed in the _____ hemisphere of the _____. (362)

13. There are two language-specific structures in the cerebral cortex. _____, located in the _____ lobe, controls language production. _____, located in the _____ lobe, is responsible for interpreting language. (362-363)

14. Damage to _____ results in a specific _____, or communication disorder, in which the person has good comprehension but speaks in a slow, labored, ungrammatical, and emotionally flat fashion. (362)

15. Damage to _____ results in speech that is fluent and grammatical, but it contains many nonsense words. Comprehension of others' speech is also impaired. (362-363)

16. As children acquire language, the brain becomes increasingly _____ for language processing. This is (consistent/inconsistent) with the idea that a language _____ develops in a specific part of the brain. (363)

17. _____ proposed that children must acquire language during the age span of _____. Studies of severely abused children (do/do not) fit with this hypothesis. (363)

18. True or False: Studies of people who acquire a second language indicate that those who acquire the language as adults score as well on tests of grammatical knowledge as those who learn it as young children. (363)

19. It (is/is not) now widely accepted that a uniquely human biological predisposition plays a powerful role in language learning. (363)

20. List four challenges to Chomsky's theory of language development. (363-364)
A._____
B._____
C._____
D._____

21. True or False: Individuals with Williams syndrome are more advanced in their language skills than are individuals with Down syndrome. (365)

22. List the strengths and weaknesses in language development displayed by individuals with Williams syndrome. (365)
A. Strengths:_____
B. Weaknesses:_____

The Interactionist Perspective

1. True or False: The interactionist perspective on language development emphasizes the interactions between inner predispositions and environmental inputs. (364)

2. Interactionist models stress the _____ of language learning. (364)

3. According to the interactionist perspective, what three factors combine to assist children in discovering the functions of language? (364, 366)
A._____
B._____
C._____

4. Describe two views held by interactionist theorists concerning the precise nature of children's innate abilities. (366)
A._____
_____
B._____
_____

5. True or False: Today many theorists believe that biology, cognition, and social experience may operate in different balances with respect to each component of language. (366)

Prelinguistic Development: Getting Ready to Talk

Receptivity to Language

1. Adults analyze the speech stream into _____, the smallest sound units with distinctive features that can signal a difference in meaning. (367)

2. Phonemes (are/are not) the same across all languages. (367)

3. The tendency to perceive as identical a range of sounds that belong to the same phonemic class is called _____. (367)

4. True or False: Infants are sensitive to a much wider range of speech categories than exists in their own language environment. (367)

5. True or False: Within a few days after birth, babies distinguish the overall sound pattern of their native tongue from that of other languages. (367)

6. Adults in many countries speak to infants and toddlers in _____ --a form of language made up of short sentences with high-pitched, exaggerated expression, clear pronunciation, and distinct pauses between speech segments. _____ mothers show a similar style of communication with their babies. (367)

7. Why do adults use child-directed speech? (367-368)

_____

_____

8. How do parents fine-tune child-directed speech to fit with children's cognitive needs? (368)

_____

_____

First Speech Sounds

1. Around __ months, babies begin to make vowel-like noises, called _____. Around ___ months, _____ appears, in which infants repeat consonant-vowel combinations in long strings. (368)

2. The timing of early babbling seems to be due to _____. (368)

3. Deaf babies (do/do not) start babbling at the same age as those who can hear. (368)

4. Around ____ months, babbling starts to include the sounds of mature spoken languages. If a baby is hearing impaired, these speechlike sounds emerge (at the same time/later), and if a baby is deaf, they are _____ . (368)

5. True or False: Even when deaf infants are exposed to sign language from birth, they do not use it during the babbling period of speech development. (368)

6. Language input (is/is not) necessary for babbling to be sustained. (368)

7. By 1 year of age, _____ reflects the consonant-vowel and _____ patterns of the child's language community. (368)

Becoming a Communicator

1. By ____ months, the beginnings of conversation can be seen. Around ____ months, turn-taking games, such as _____ and _____ appear. By ____ months, infants participate actively. (369)

2. A preverbal gesture used by infants to influence the behavior of others is the _____, in which the baby touches an object, holds, it up, or points to it while looking at others to make sure they notice. A second gesture, the _____, occurs when the infant gets another person to do something by reaching, pointing, and often making sounds at the same time. (369)

3. Early in the second year, _____ and _____ come together. (369)

4. True or False: Cross-cultural research confirms that adult molding of infant communication is essential if children are to acquire language within the normal time frame of development. (369)

Phonological Development

The Early Phase

1. Early _____ and _____ development are related because the words children choose to say are influenced partly by what they can pronounce. (370)

Appearance of Phonological Strategies

1. By the middle of the second year, children apply systematic strategies to words so they fit with their _____ . (370-371)

2. Describe the general pattern of strategies children apply to words so they fit with their phonological capacities. (371)

_____

_____

_____

3. _____ and _____ are largely responsible for improved pronunciation during the preschool years. Phonological errors (do/do not) improve with adult correction. (371)

Later Phonological Development

1. True or False: Phonological development is far from complete when children begin school. (371)

2. List two aspects of phonological development that are not mastered until later childhood or adolescence. (371)
A._____
B._____

Semantic Development

1. On the average, children say their first word at ____ months of age. By age 6, they have a vocabulary of about _____ words. (372)

2. From infancy on, children's _____, the language they understand, develops ahead of _____, the language they use. (372)

3. Comprehension requires that children (recall/recognize) the meaning of a word; production demands that they (recall/recognize) the word, as well as the concept for which it stands. (372)

The Early Phase

1. Early language builds on the _____ foundations Piaget described and on categories children construct during the first 2 years. First words refer to

_____, _____, _____, or
_____. In their first 50 words, toddlers rarely name things that _____. (372)

2. A spurt in vocabulary usually takes place between ____ and ____ months. (373)

3. Children can connect a new word with an underlying concept after only a brief encounter, a process called _____. (373)

4. True or False: TV watching is sufficient for language development, as shown by the fact that hearing children of deaf parents exposed to spoken language only on television acquire normal speech. (373-374)

5. (Girls/Boys) are slightly ahead in vocabulary growth until 2 years of age. (374)

6. True or False: The more words caregivers use when talking to young children is not related to the number of words integrated into the child's vocabulary. (374)

7. How do the early vocabularies of children who use a referential style of language learning differ from those of children who use an expressive style? Which style results in faster growth of vocabulary? (374)

_____

_____

_____

_____

8. (Biological/Environmental/Both biological and environmental) factors account or a toddler's choice of a particular language style. In addition, language styles are linked to _____. (374)

9. Three types of words are most common in young children's vocabularies--
_____, _____, and _____. (374)

10. Why do early language learners have far more object than action words in their beginning vocabularies? (375)

_____

_____

_____

11. Describe the development of state words. (375)

_____

_____

_____

_____

12. When young children apply a new word too narrowly, they make an error called _____. A more common error between 1 and 2 1/2 years of age is _____--applying the word to a wider collection of objects and events than is appropriate. (375-376)

13. Children overextend many more words in (production/comprehension) than they do in (production/comprehension). (376)

14. To fill in for words they have not yet learned, young children _____ new words based on words they already know. (376)

15. Preschoolers also extend language through _____. (376)

Later Semantic Development

1. True or False: Although vocabulary continues to grow between the start of elementary school and young adulthood, children on average only increase their vocabularies by about 50 percent. (376)

2. Children's word definitions change with age. Five- and 6-year-olds give very concrete descriptions that refer to _____ or _____. By the end of elementary school, _____ and explanations of _____ relationships appear. (376-377)

3. What are some implications of school-age children's ability to appreciate the multiple meanings of words? (377)

_____

_____

4. Adolescents' capacity for _____ reasoning permits them to grasp words rarely used at younger ages and to understand _____ word meanings. As a result they become masters of _____ and _____. (377)

Ideas About How Semantic Development Takes Place

1. Research indicates that adult feedback (does/does not) facilitate semantic development. (377)

2. A special part of working memory, a _____ that permits retention of speech-based information, supports young children's fast mapping. (377)

3. True or False: The greater a 4-year-old's phonological memory skill, the greater their vocabulary growth over the following year. (377)

4. According to lexical contrast theory, what two principles govern vocabulary growth? (378)
A._____
B._____

5. According to Markman, in the early phases of vocabulary growth, children adopt a principle of _____ in which they assume that words refer to entirely separate categories. (378)

6. What do young children do when adults call a single object by more than one name? (378)

_____

_____

_____

200

7. For words other than object labels, children may deduce many word meanings by observing how words are used in syntax, or the structure of sentences--a hypothesis called _____. (378)

8. Children also rely on _____ cues to identify non-object words. (378)

Grammatical Development

First Word Combinations

1. Sometime between _____ and _____ years, first sentences appear when children combine two words in what is called _____ speech. (379)

2. Telegraphic speech characterizes children learning languages that emphasize _____. (379)

3. Researchers (do/do not) agree as to whether children's two-word sentences are based on a full adultlike grammar. (379)

From Two-Word Utterances to Complex Speech

1. Between ____ and ____ years of age, three-word sentences appear. In English-speaking children, they follow the _____ word order. This word order (is/is not) a universal grammatical structure. (380)

2. _____ are small markers that change the meaning of sentences. (381)

3. What two characteristics of morphemes play important roles in determining a regular sequence of acquisition by English-speaking 2- and 3-year-olds? (381-382)
A._____
_____
B._____
_____

4. Once children grasp a regular morphological rule, they extend it to words that are exceptions, a type of error called _____. This type of error occurs (frequently/occasionally). (382)

5. Why do children use some correct irregular forms before they start to overregularize? (382)

_____
_____

Development of Complex Grammatical Forms

1. Name the three types of negation in the order in which they develop. (382)
A._____ B._____ C._____

2. Why do children younger than age 3 use the "no + utterance" to express nonexistence and rejection, but not denial? (382)

_____

_____

3. When first creating questions using words such as "why," "what," and "where," English-speaking children cling to the _____ word order. A little later, they include the _____ without inverting. Finally, they apply all the rules. (383)

4. Between ages 3 and 6, children begin to use increasingly complex grammatical forms. First _____ appear. Later, children produce _____, _____, _____, and _____ _____. (383)

Later Grammatical Development

1. How does understanding and use of the passive voice change from the preschool years into the school years? (383)

_____

_____

_____

2. An improved ability to take the perspective of others may facilitate mastery of _____. (384)

Ideas About How Grammatical Development Takes Place

1. Evidence that grammatical development is an extended process (does/does not) conform with Chomsky's strict nativist account. (384)

2. According to one view of grammatical development, children rely on the semantic properties of words to figure out basic grammatical regularities--an approach called _____. (384)

3. Another view of grammatical development argues that children master grammar through _____ of the structure of the language. (384)

4. Slobin proposes that children (do/do not) start with an innate knowledge of grammatical rules. He believes that they have a special _____ _____--a set of procedures for analyzing the language they hear that supports the discovery of _____. (384)

5. Research indicates that adults (do/do not) correct children's semantics, and usually (do/do not) provide direct feedback about grammaticality. (385)

6. Name two techniques by which adults may offer subtle, indirect feedback about grammatical errors, and give an example of each. (385)
A._____
B._____

Pragmatic Development

1. For a conversation to go well, participants must adhere to these four pragmatics of language: (386)
A._____   B._____
C._____   D._____

Acquiring Conversational Skills

1. At the beginning of early childhood, children engage in the following conversational skills: (386)
A._____
B._____
C._____
D._____

2. A conversational strategy that increases over the preschool years is _____, in which the speaker not only comments on what has just been said but also adds a request to get the partner to respond again. (386)

3. Between ages 5 and 9, _____ appears, in which a change of topic is initiated gradually rather than abruptly by modifying the focus of discussion. (386)

4. Effective conversation depends on understanding the _____ of utterances--that is, what a speaker means to say, regardless of whether the form of the utterance is perfectly consistent with it. (386)

5. True or False: Opportunities for young children to converse with adults are consistently related to general measures of language progress. (386)

6. Research on the role of social interaction in language development indicate that the presence of another child (enhances/reduces) the quantity and quality of parent-child interaction. (387)

7. Why might mother-toddler-sibling interaction offer a unique context for acquiring the pragmatics of language? (387)

_____
_____
_____

Learning to Communicate Clearly

1. The term _____ refers to the ability to produce clear verbal messages, as well as recognize when messages received are unclear so that more information can be obtained. (388)

2. When preschoolers are given relatively simple communication tasks or engage in face-to-face interaction with familiar people, they (do/do not) adjust their speech to the needs of their listeners. (388)

3. Around age _____, preschoolers start to ask others to clarify ambiguous messages. (388)

Sociolinguistic Understanding

1. Language adaptations to social expectations are called _____. (388)

2. Speech adjustments based on _____ and _____ appear during the preschool and early elementary years. (389)

3. True or False: In some cultures, much greater emphasis is placed on tutoring young children in social routines than in language per se. (389)

Development of Metalinguistic Awareness

1. The ability to think about language as a system is called _____
_____. (389)

2. True or False: Most 4- and 5-year-old children believe that word labels are a part of the objects to which they refer. (389)

3. True or False: Early metalinguistic understanding is not a predictor of vocabulary development during the preschool years. (390)

4. Give four examples of the increased metalinguistic skills present in middle childhood. (390)
A._____
B._____
C._____
D._____

5. As early as the preschool years, _____, the ability to reflect on the sound structure of spoken language, predicts reading and spelling success. (391)

6. True or False: Training children in phonological awareness is a promising technique for encouraging early literacy development. (391)

Bilingualism: Learning Two Languages in Childhood

1. _____ American school-age children speak a language other than English at home. (392)

2. In what two ways can children become bilingual? (392)
A._____
B._____

3. Children of bilingual parents who teach them both languages in early childhood (do/do not) show special problems with language development. (392)

4. Until recently, how did Americans view childhood bilingualism? (392)
_____
_____

5. Research now shows that bilingualism has a (positive/negative) impact on development. (392)

6. Children who are fluent in two languages do better than their single-language agemates on tests of _____, _____, and _____. In addition, their _____ skills are particularly well developed. (392)

7. Educators committed to bilingual education believe that providing instruction in the native tongue lets minority children know that their heritage is respected and also prevents _____, or inadequate proficiency in both languages. (393)

8. Semilingualism is one factor believed to contribute to school failure and dropout among low-income _____ youngsters. (393)

9. What type of language instruction is best for bilingual children? Why? (393)
_____
_____
_____

10. English-only supporters often point to _____, which recognizes the linguistic rights of its French-speaking minority but where friction between English- and French-speaking groups is intense. (393)

ASK YOURSELF...

9.1 How does research on acquiring a second language support the existence of a sensitive period for language development? What practical implications do these findings have for teaching foreign languages in school? (p. 366)

9.2 Cite findings indicating that both infant capacities and the child's language environment contribute to prelinguistic development. (p. 370)

9.3 Eric's first words included "see," "give," and "thank you," and his vocabulary grew slowly during the second year. What style of early language learning did he display, and what factors might explain it? (p. 379)

9.4 One day, 3-year-old Jason's mother explained that the family would take a vacation in Miami. The next morning, Jason emerged from his room with belongings spilling out of a suitcase and remarked, "I gotted my bags packed. When are we going to Your-ami?" What do Jason's errors reveal about his approach to mastering grammar? (p. 385)

9.5 Return to the illustrations of children's language at the beginning of this chapter. What pragmatic skills are reflected in Susan's and Connie's utterances? How do the children's parents support their pragmatic development? (p. 389)

9.6 Explain why development of metalinguistic awareness expands greatly in middle childhood. What might foster more rapid metalinguistic progress in bilingual children? (p. 392)

CONNECTIONS

9.1 Cite research, in this chapter and in Chapter 5, supporting the conclusion that the brain is not fully specialized for language at birth. Instead, areas of the cortex become increasingly committed to language processing with age. Relate these findings to the concept of brain plasticity. (See pages 188-189.)

9.2 Explain how parents' use of child-directed speech fits with Vygotsky's concept of the zone of proximal development. (See Chapter 6, page 261.)

9.3 Research indicates that infants advanced in language development have mothers who often establish joint attention and comment on what the baby sees. How is this quality of interaction similar to parental behavior that fosters secure attachment? (See Chapter 10, pages 426-427.)

9.4 Toddlers experiment with sounds, sound patterns, and speech rhythms in trying to pronounce words. Explain how Siegler's model of strategy choice can help us understand why such experimentation is adaptive. (See Chapter 7, page 281.)

9.5 What cognitive advances during middle childhood probably support school-age children's astounding growth in vocabulary? (See Chapter 7, pages 294 and 301.)

9.6 Explain why connectionists, who compare children's mastery of grammatical structures to that of artificial neural networks, argue against a nativist, modular view of grammatical development like Chomsky's? (See Chapter 7, page 280.)

9.7 Do boys and girls acquire different speech registers for interacting with peers? Describe these registers, and explain why they contribute to children's preference for playmates of their own sex. (See Chapter 13, pages 536-537.)

9.8 How can bilingual education support the development of a healthy ethnic identity? (See Chapter 11, page 461.)

PUZZLE 9.1

Across

2 Feedback about grammatical errors through increasing the complexity of the child's statement
6 ___ store, part of working memory that retains speech-based information
8 Error where children extend a morphological rule to words that are exceptions
9 ___ speech perception, the tendency to perceive a range of sounds in a phonemic class as identical
11 Semantic ___, relying on words' semantic properties for grammatical regularities
13 ___'s area controls language production
15 ___ registers are language adaptations to social expectations
16 ___ bootstrapping, observing how words are used in sentence structure
18 Repetition of consonant-vowel combinations

Down

1 Encouraging a partner to respond again through a request
3 ___ intent, what a speaker means to say
4 Words that children understand
5 Style that uses language for naming objects
7 Principle of ___ exclusivity, which assumes words refer to entirely separate categories
10 Grammatical ___, small markers that change the meaning of sentences
12 The communicative side of language
14 ___ contrast theory, assumes conventionality and contrast govern vocabulary growth
15 Topic change initiated gradually
17 Language used by adults when speaking to infants

210

PUZZLE 9.2

Across

6 Proto___, a preverbal gesture that makes an assertion
8 Fast-___ quickly connects a word with a concept
11 Applies words too broadly
13 ___-making capacity supports discovery of grammatical regularities
15 Concerned with syntax and morphology
16 Applies word too narrowly
17 ___'s area interprets language
18 Proto___, used to get a person to act
19 Language children use

Down

1 Language component concerned with understanding and producing speech sounds
2 Responses that restructure incorrect speech into appropriate forms
3 Smallest speech unit that can be distinguished
4 ___ speech, which leaves out smaller words
5 Pleasant vowel-like noises made by infants
7 ___ communication skills, the ability to produce and recognize clear verbal messages
9 ___ awareness, the ability to think about language as a system
10 Style that uses language to talk about feelings and needs
12 Concerned with understanding meaning of words
14 Innate system for picking up language

PRACTICE TEST

1. Semantics involves: (358)
    A. application of an intricate set of rules to produce complicated sound patterns.
    B. sociolinguistic knowledge.
    C. the way underlying concepts are expressed in words.
    D. the rules by which words are arranged into sentences.

2. According to Skinner, language is acquired through: (359)
    A. classical conditioning.
    B. operant conditioning.
    C. symbolic communication.
    D. universal grammar.

3. Chomsky's nativist perspective argues that: (359)
    A. imitation and reinforcement promote language development.
    B. language is a biologically based, uniquely human accomplishment.
    C. adults must engage in intensive language tutoring of children.
    D. grammar is specific to a particular language.

4. Which of the following does NOT support Chomsky's nativist approach to language development? (361-363)
    A. Deaf preschoolers spontaneously produced a gestural communication system similar to verbal language.
    B. The structure of creole languages is similar around the world.
    C. Humans have evolved specialized regions in the brain that support language skills.
    D. Some languages have very different grammatical systems.

5. _____, located in the temporal lobe, is responsible for interpreting language. (362-363)
    A. Brady's area
    B. Broca's area
    C. Wernicke's area
    D. William's area

6. The case of Genie, a child reared in a linguistically and emotionally impoverished environment until she was 13 1/2 years old, supports the hypothesis that: (363)
    A. language learning is optimal during the period of brain lateralization.
    B. damage to Wernicke's area may occur if a child is reared in a poor environment.
    C. language development does not have unique biological properties.
    D. grammar is not an essential aspect of language.

7. The interactionist perspective on language development: (364, 366)
    A. reflects and continues the Skinner-Chomsky dichotomy.
    B. views the child as a passive recipient of communication.
    C. stresses the combination of innate abilities and social context in
       language learning.
    D. emphasizes classical conditioning as a determinant of language
       development.

8. The tendency to perceive as identical a range of sounds that belong to the same
phonemic class is called: (367)
    A. underextension.
    B. syntactic bootstrapping.
    C. lexical contrast.
    D. categorical speech perception.

9. Which of the following is NOT true of child-directed speech? (367)
    A. It is high-pitched and exaggerated.
    B. It is used by adults who are deliberately trying to teach infants to talk.
    C. It arises from an unconscious desire to keep a young child's attention.
    D. It contains distinct pauses between speech segments.

10. Around 2 months, babies begin to make _____ noises, called cooing, and
around 4 months, babbling appears in which infants repeat _____ in
long strings. (368)
    A. vowel-like/consonants
    B. consonant-like/consonants
    C. vowel-like/consonant-vowel combinations
    D. consonant-like/consonant-vowel combinations

11. One-year-old Gina just received a new doll before visiting her grandparents. She
catches their attention, repeatedly holds the doll up for her grandparents to see, and
vigorously points to it. This is an example of: (369)
    A. semantic bootstrapping.
    B. the protodeclarative.
    C. turnabout.
    D. the protoimperative.

12. Which of the following is NOT true of phonological development? (370-371)
    A. Children's phonological errors are very resistant to adult correction.
    B. Phonological development is largely complete by the time children
       begin school.
    C. Early phonological and semantic development are unrelated.
    D. Changes in syllabic stress after certain abstract words take on endings
       are not mastered until adolescence.

13. Which of the following statements is NOT true of semantic development? (372-374)
    A. On the average, children say their first word around 18 months of age.
    B. Comprehension develops ahead of production.
    C. Early language builds on sensorimotor foundations.
    D. Temperament can influence the rate of development.

14. The expressive style of language learning: (374)
    A. contains more pronouns and social formulas than the referential style.
    B. indicates that the child thinks words are for naming objects.
    C. results in faster vocabulary growth.
    D. is used by a greater number of children than is the receptive style.

15. When 2-year-old Jeremy and his parents boarded a train for the first time, he shouted, "Car! Car!" This is an example of: (376)
    A. fast mapping.
    B. overextension.
    C. lexical contrast.
    D. turnabout.

16. Lexical contrast theory: (378)
    A. assumes the principles of conventionality and contrast govern vocabulary growth.
    B. suggests that children adopt a principle of overregularization in early phases of vocabulary growth.
    C. assumes children use syntactic bootstrapping to deduce word meanings.
    D. assumes language production proceeds faster than language comprehension.

17. Two-year-old Jana says, "Mommy hand." This is an example of: (379)
    A. syntactic bootstrapping.
    B. overregularization.
    C. telegraphic speech.
    D. delayed development.

18. Grammatical morphemes: (381)
    A. are used consistently by children once they first appear.
    B. are acquired in a regular sequence by young English-speaking children.
    C. with regular forms are always acquired before those with irregular forms.
    D. with the same meaning are acquired in very different orders across languages.

19. Overregularization: (382)
    A. occurs in at least 25 percent of instances in which children use irregular forms.
    B. reflects a grammatical defect that must be unlearned.
    C. occurs when a regular morphological rule is extended to words that are exceptions.
    D. occurs because children hear adults overregularize.

20. In the development of complex grammatical forms: (383)
    A. connectives appear that join whole sentences before passive sentences are used.
    B. denial, as a type of negation, occurs before nonexistence.
    C. around age 2, children add auxiliary verbs to sentences.
    D. English-speaking children invert the subject and auxiliary verb from the time questions first appear.

21. Environmental support for grammatical development: (385)
    A. occurs continually as adults provide direct feedback to children about grammar.
    B. may occur as children frequently imitate adult repetitions of their correct speech.
    C. may occur indirectly in the form of expansions and recasts.
    D. occurs in the form of indirect feedback that is provided to all children in all cultures.

22. A(n) _____ is a conversational strategy in which the speaker adds a request to get the partner to respond again. (386)
    A. illocutionary intent
    B. utterance
    C. turnabout
    D. referent

23. Which of the following is NOT true of language learning in mother-toddler-sibling conversations? (387)
    A. Mothers of more than one child address each with fewer utterances.
    B. Mother-toddler-sibling interaction seems to offer a unique context for acquiring the pragmatics of language.
    C. Twins generally have slower early vocabulary growth.
    D. Mother-toddler-sibling conversations are shorter than mother-toddler conversations.

24. Which of the following is NOT true of metalinguistic awareness? (389-391)
    A. It is the ability to think about language as a system.
    B. It is present in early childhood.
    C. It is delayed in bilingual children.
    D. It is evident in school-age children's improved ability to appreciate the multiple meanings of words in puns and riddles.

25. Which of the following is NOT true of bilingual education? (393)
    A. It promotes semilingualism.
    B. It lets minority children know that their heritage is respected.
    C. It encourages minority children to be more involved in learning.
    D. It results in easier acquisition of the second language.

215

CHAPTER 10

EMOTIONAL DEVELOPMENT

SUMMARY

Although the emotional side of development was overshadowed by cognition for several decades, new excitement surrounds the study of emotions today. The functionalist approach emphasizes that the broad function of emotions is to prompt action in the service of personal goals. It regards emotions as central forces in all aspects of human activity--cognitive processing, social behavior, and even physical health--and as becoming increasingly voluntary and socialized with age.

The development of emotional expression is a gradual process that begins in infancy and continues into adolescence. Changes in happiness, anger, sadness, and fear reflect infants' developing cognitive capacities and serve social as well as survival functions. Signs of almost all the basic emotions are present in early infancy, and they soon become clear, well-organized signals. At the end of the second year, self-conscious emotions emerge. Emotional self-regulation begins in infancy, and during the preschool years, children start to conform to the emotional display rules of their culture. Parenting practices and the child's temperament affect the development of emotional self-regulation. The ability to meaningfully interpret others' emotional expressions emerges at the end of the first year. Around this time, infants start to engage in social referencing. Although the roots of empathy are present early in development, true empathy requires children to understand that the self is distinct from other people.

Heredity influences early temperament, but child-rearing experiences affect whether a child's emotional style is sustained or modified over time. According to ethological theory, infants are biologically prepared to contribute to the attachment bond with the caregiver, which evolved to promote survival. Caregiving that is responsive to babies' needs supports the development of secure attachment; insensitive caregiving is linked to attachment insecurity. Family conditions, parents' internal working models, and infants' health and temperament also contribute to quality of attachment. Although some findings indicate that secure attachment in infancy cases improved cognitive, emotional, and social competence during later years, continuity of caregiving may be responsible for these outcomes.

Today the majority of American mothers with children younger than age 2 are employed. Infant child care is associated with a slight risk of attachment insecurity. Quality of care is the determining factor in the effect of child care on young children's emotional security.

LEARNING OBJECTIVES

After reading this chapter, you should be able to:

10.1 Describe the functionalist approach to emotional development. (398-399)

10.2 Describe changes in the expression of happiness, anger, sadness, and fear during infancy. (401-403)

10.3 Discuss the development of self-conscious emotions, emotional self-regulation, and conformity to emotional display rules, including cognitive, temperamental, parenting, and cultural influences. (404-407)

10.4 Discuss changes in emotional understanding from infancy into adolescence, including the roles of cognitive development and social experience. (408-410)

10.5 Distinguish empathy and sympathy, and describe the development of empathy from infancy into adolescence, noting factors that influence individual differences. (410-412)

10.6 Discuss models of temperament, and explain how researchers measure temperament. (412-416)

10.7 Discuss the roles of heredity and environment in the stability of temperament, the relationship of temperament to cognitive and social functioning, and the goodness-of-fit model. (416-421)

10.8 Describe the unique features of ethological theory of attachment in comparison to psychoanalytic and drive-reduction (behaviorist) views. (421-423)

10.9 Cite the four attachment patterns assessed by the Strange Situation and the Attachment Q-Sort, and discuss factors that affect the development of attachment. (423-429)

10.10 Discuss fathers' attachment relationships with their infants and the role of early attachment quality in later development. (430-432)

10.11 Discuss the effects of maternal employment and child care on attachment security and psychological development. (432-435)

STUDY QUESTIONS

The Functions of Emotions

1. A(n) _____ expresses your readiness to establish, maintain, or change your relation to the environment on a matter of importance to you. (398)

2. The functionalist approach emphasizes that the broad function of emotions is to prompt _____ in the service of _____. (398)

Emotions and Cognitive Processing

1. True or False: Emotions have a profound impact on cognitive processing. (398)

2. (High/Moderate/Low) anxiety can facilitate performance on cognitive tasks. (398)

3. True or False: Although they affect many areas of cognitive processing, emotions do not influence memory. (398)

4. What evidence did Michael Lewis and his colleagues find to support the assumption of a bidirectional relationship between emotion and cognition? (398)

_____
_____
_____
_____

Emotions and Social Behavior

1. In studies in which the exchange of emotional signals between mother and infant is disrupted by having the mother assume an unreactive pose or a depressed emotional state, how does the infant react? (399)

_____
_____
_____

2. Approximately ____ to ____ percent of women experience chronic depression. In some cases, it emerges after childbirth--a form called _____. _____, _____, and _____ factors increase the risk of this illness. (400)

3. What factors may be responsible for the fact that children of depressed parents are two to five times more likely to develop behavior problems? (400)

_____
_____
_____
_____

4. Describe how a child of a depressed parent develops a negative world view? (400)

_____
_____

5. True or False: In most cases of postpartum depression, treatment is unsuccessful. (400)

Emotions and Physical Health

1. Describe how the results of Terman's longitudinal study illustrate the relationship of emotional stress to physical health. (399)

_____

_____

_____

Other Features of the Functionalist Approach

1. Name two roles of emotions besides their central role in cognitive, social, and physical experience. (399, 401)

A._____

B._____

Development of Emotional Expression

1. True or False: Cross-cultural research indicates that when looking at photographs of facial gestures, people around the world do not associate them with the same emotions. (401)

2. Discuss the controversy concerning whether infants come into the world with the ability to express a wide variety of emotions. (401)

_____

_____

_____

_____

3. True or False: By the middle of the first year, emotional expressions are well organized and specific. (401)

Happiness

1. During the early weeks, when do newborns smile? (402)

_____

_____

2. True or False: By the end of the first month, infants start to smile at dynamic, eye-catching events. (402)

3. Between 6 and 10 weeks, the human face evokes a broad grin from an infant called a(n) _____. (402)

4. By 3 months, infants smile most when _____. (402)

219

5. Laughter, which appears around _____ to _____ months, reflects (faster/slower) processing of information than does smiling. (402)

6. How do expressions of happiness change between early infancy and the middle of the first year? (402)

_____

_____

Anger and Sadness

1. To what types of experiences do newborn babies respond with generalized distress? (402)

_____

2. In what types of situations do babies display anger? (402)

_____

_____

3. Why do angry reactions increase with age? (402-403)

_____

_____

4. How is the rise in anger adaptive? (403)

_____

_____

5. Expressions of sadness are (more/less) frequent than expressions of anger. (403)

6. Sadness is common when _____. (403)

7. When is extreme sadness seen in infants? (403)

_____

Fear

1. Fear reactions are (common/rare) during early infancy. Why? (403)

_____

2. At what point in development does fear increase? (403)

_____

3. The most frequent expression of fear is toward unfamiliar adults, a reaction called _____. Factors that influence this reaction include _____, _____, and _____. (403)

4. True or False: To minimize stranger anxiety, an unfamiliar adult should immediately pick up the infant and talk to him or her. (403)

5. Once wariness develops, babies start to use the familiar caregiver as a(n) _____ from which to explore and a haven of safety. (403)

6. Encounters with strangers lead to two conflicting tendencies in the baby: _____ and _____. (403)

7. What factors influence the decline of fear reactions in toddlers? (403)

_____

_____

Self-Conscious Emotions

1. The higher-order set of emotions includes _____, _____, _____, _____, and _____. These are called _____. (404)

2. Self-conscious emotions first appear at _____, as the sense of _____ emerges. _____ and _____, the last to appear, are present by age 3. (404)

3. What ingredient besides self-awareness is required in order for children to experience self-conscious emotions? (404)

_____

4. True or False: The situations in which adults encourage children to feel self-conscious emotions are very similar across cultures. (404)

5. Self-conscious emotions of 3-year-olds (are/are not) linked to self-evaluation. (404)

6. Describe the conditions under which preschoolers experience self-conscious emotions. (404)

_____

_____

_____

7. As children develop guidelines for good behavior, the presence of others (will/will not) be necessary to evoke self-conscious emotions. (404)

Emotional Self-Regulation

1. _____ refers to the strategies we use to adjust our emotional state to a comfortable level of intensity so we can accomplish our goals. It requires attention _____ and _____, as well as the ability to _____. (404)

2. Babies depend on _____ for help in adjusting
their emotional reactions. (405)

3. Rapid development of the _____ increases the baby's
tolerance for stimulation. (405)

4. How do caregivers help babies increase their tolerance for stimulation? (405)
_____
_____

5. _____ and _____ enable infants to regulate feelings more
effectively by approaching or retreating from various stimuli. (405)

6. How do gains in representation and language lead to new ways of regulating emotion?
(405)
_____
_____
_____

7. List 3 ways children engage in active efforts to control their feelings. (405)
A._____
B._____
C._____

8. The _____ powerfully affects children's capacity to cope
with stress. They pick up strategies for regulating emotion by watching
_____ and having _____ conversations.
(405-406)

9. What additional strategies do children in middle childhood and adolescence use to
handle emotionally arousing situations? (406)
_____
_____
_____

10. When the development of emotional self-regulation has gone along well, young
people aquifer a sense of _____--a feeling of being in
control of their emotional experience. This fosters a(n)
_____ and _____. (406)

Acquiring Emotional Display Rules

1. _____ specify when, where, and how it is appropriate to
express emotions in a culture. (407)

2. Middle-SES mothers (frequently/rarely) imitate expressions of anger and sadness while playing with their infants. (407)

3. At older ages, children receive _____ in emotional display rules. (407)

4. Not until age _____ can children pose an expression they do not feel. These expressions are usually limited to (positive/negative) feelings. (407)

5. Societies that stress (individual/collective) needs place particular emphasis on emotional display rules. (407)

6. Conscious awareness and understanding of display rules emerges in _____. (407)

7. Older children justify display rules by referring to _____; younger children justify them as _____. (407)

Understanding and Responding to the Emotions of Others

1. Detecting others' emotions through emotional contagion suggests that babies are beginning to _____. (408)

2. Between 7 and 10 months, infants start to realize that an emotional expression not only has meaning, but is a(n) _____ _____. (408)

Social Referencing

1. _____ involves relying on another person's emotional reaction to appraise an uncertain situation. (408)

2. What two capacities lead to the emergence of social referencing? (408)
A._____
B._____

3. True or False: Mothers are much more effective sources of emotional information for babies than are fathers. (408)

4. True or False: A caregiver's emotional cues during moments of uncertainty may be a major reason that she serves as a secure base for exploration. (408)

Emotional Understanding in Childhood

1. During the preschool years, children's emotional understanding expands rapidly, and they refer to _____, _____, and _____ of emotion. (409)

2. Four- and 5-year-olds (can/cannot) correctly judge the causes of many basic emotional reactions. (409)

3. Four- and 5-year-olds tend to emphasize (external/internal) factors over (external/internal) states. (409)

4. An improved ability to consider multiple sources of information when explaining others' emotions develops during _____. (410)

5. True or False: Preschoolers understand that people can experience more than one emotion at a time. (410)

6. Both _____ and _____ fosters emotional understanding. (410)

7. What types of social experiences contribute to children's emotional understanding? (410)

_____
_____
_____

8. As early as 3 to 5 years, emotional knowledge is related to _____, _____, and _____. (410)

Empathy

1. In empathy, _____ and _____ of emotions are interwoven. (410)

2. What three factors combine to produce an empathic response? (410)
A._____
B._____
C._____

3. Beginning in the preschool years, empathy is an important motivator of _____, or _____, behavior. (411)

4. Empathy does not always give way to _____--feelings of concern or sorrow for another person's plight. (411)

5. True or False: The cries of newborns in response to the cry of another baby may be the beginnings of empathy. (411)

6. True empathy requires children to understand that the _____ is distinct from others. (411)

7. Empathic responding (increases/decreases) over the elementary school years. What factors contribute to this change? (411)

_____

8. What changes occur in empathic responding during late childhood and adolescence? (411)

_____

_____

9. In what ways can parents foster empathy in their children? (412)

_____

_____

10. Abused toddlers reacted to other children's distress with _____,
_____, and _____. (412)

11. Individual differences in children's dispositions are the combined result of
_____ and _____ influences. (412)

Temperament and Development

1. _____ refers to stable individual differences in quality and intensity of emotional reaction, activity level, attention, and emotional self-regulation. (412)

2. The _____, initiated in 1956 by Thomas and Chess, is the longest and most comprehensive study of temperament to date. Results showed that temperament (is/is not) a major factor in increasing the chances that a child will experience psychological problems. (412, 414)

3. Thomas and Chess found that temperament (is/is not) fixed and unchangeable. (414)

4. _____ can modify children's emotional styles considerably. (414)

The Structure of Temperament

1. Describe the three types of children identified by Thomas and Chess on the basis of their nine dimensions of temperament. (414-415)

A._____

_____

B._____

_____

C._____

_____

2. ____ percent of the children did not fit any of these categories. (415)

3. The _____ pattern places children at high risk for adjustment problems. In the New York Longitudinal Study, ____ percent of these children developed behavior problems by school age, whereas ____ percent of the easy children did. (415)

4. By middle childhood, 50 percent of _____ children begin to show adjustment difficulties. (415)

5. Describe Rothbart and Mauro's model of temperament. (414, 415)

_____

_____

_____

Measuring Temperament

1. Temperament is often assessed through _____ or _____ given to parents. In addition, _____ by pediatricians or teachers and _____ have also been used. (415)

2. Information from parents, often emphasized in assessments of behavior, has been criticized as _____ and _____. (415)

3. Prebirth expectations (do/do not) influence parents' reports of infant behavior. (415)

4. Mothers with certain psychological characteristics--_____, _____, and _____--tend to regard their babies as more difficult. (415)

5. Parental ratings are (strongly/moderately) related to observational measures of children's behavior. (415)

6. Why is it useful to know parents' perceptions of their child? (415)

_____

7. What are two advantages of psychophysiological measures of temperament? (415)

A._____

B._____

8. Most efforts on the exploration of the biological basis of temperament have focused on _____ children, who react negatively to and withdraw from novel stimuli, and _____ children, who display positive emotion to and approach novel stimuli. (416)

9. Kagan focused on two temperamental styles of infants--_____ and _____. He believes that individual differences in arousal of the _____ contribute to contrasting temperamental styles. (417)

10. The heart rates of many shy children (speed up/slow down) in response to unfamiliar events, and they produce (more/less) cortisol. (417)

11. Another physiological correlate of approach-withdrawal to people and objects is the _____ in the frontal region of the _____. (417)

12. Greater right than left frontal brain wave activity is shown by (shy/sociable) infants and preschoolers. (417)

13. Describe how child-rearing practices affect a child's temperament. (417)

_____

_____

_____

Stability of Temperament

1. An infant or young child who scores high or low on measures of temperament (is/is not) likely to respond in a similar way a few years later. However, temperamental stability from one age period to the next is generally _____. (416)

2. Long-term prediction from early temperament is best achieved from the _____ of life and after, when styles of responding are _____. (416)

Genetic and Environmental Influences

1. Many _____ have compared individuals of different degrees of genetic relationship to determine the extent to which temperament and personality are heritable. The most common approach has been to compare _____. (416)

2. (Identical/fraternal) twins are more similar than (identical/fraternal) twins across a wide range of temperamental traits and personality measures. These resemblances are (higher/lower) than for intelligence. (416, 418)

3. Adoption studies report (very low/modest/very high) correlations for temperament and personality for both biological and nonbiological siblings. This suggests that (shared/nonshared) environmental factors are especially salient in personality development. (418)

4. How might nonshared environmental influences on personality operate? (418)

_____

_____

5. Some shared factors, such as _____ and _____, may affect children's personalities. (418-419)

6. Consistent ethnic differences in infant temperament (do/do not) exist. (419)

7. How do Japanese and American mothers differ in their approach to child rearing? (419)

_____

_____

_____

8. Individual differences in personality result from complex interdependencies between _____ and _____ factors. (419)

Temperament as a Predictor of Children's Behavior

1. Temperamental characteristics of _____ and _____ are related to learning and cognitive performance almost as soon as they can be measured. (419)

2. _____ and _____ are associated with poor school achievement. (419)

3. How does the social behavior of highly active preschoolers differ from that of inhibited children? (419)

_____

_____

4. Arguments between siblings increase when one member is _____ or _____. (420)

Temperament and Child Rearing: The Goodness-of-Fit Model

1. Thomas and Chess proposed the goodness-of-fit model to describe how _____ and _____ work together to produce favorable outcomes. (420)

228

2. According to the goodness-of-fit model, why are Western middle-SES children with difficult temperaments at high risk for later behavior problems? (420)

_____

_____

_____

3. True or False: When parents are positive and involved with their babies, despite their child's negative behavior, infant difficultness declines with age. (420)

4. In low-SES Puerto Rican families, caregivers (are/are not) patient with difficult children. (420)

5. In Western nations, shy, withdrawn children are regarded as _____, but in China, adults regard such children as _____. (420)

6. What type of parenting is beneficial for difficult and shy children? (420)

_____

7. For reserved, inactive toddlers, what type of maternal behavior is helpful? (420)

_____

Development of Attachment

1. _____ is the strong, affectional tie we feel for special people in our lives that leads us to feel pleasure and joy when we interact with them and to be comforted by their nearness during times of stress. (421)

2. By _____, infants have become attached to familiar people who have responded to their need for physical care and stimulation. (421)

Early Theories of Attachment

1. _____ first suggested that the infant's emotional tie to the mother provides the foundation for all later relationships. (421)

2. Psychoanalytic theory regards _____ as the central context in which caregivers and babies build a close emotional bond. (421)

3. According to the drive-reduction explanation, as the caregiver satisfies the baby's hunger, the _____ drive, her presence becomes a(n) _____ or _____ drive because it is paired with tension relief. (421)

4. How did the research on rhesus monkeys challenge the idea that attachment depends on hunger satisfaction? (421)

_____

_____

5. Observations of human infants reveal that they (do/do not) become attached to family members who seldom feed them. (421-422)

Bowlby's Ethological Theory

1. Today, the _____ is the most widely accepted view of the infant's emotional tie to the caregiver. (422)

2. Bowlby believed that the quality of attachment to the caregiver has profound implications for the child's feelings of security and capacity to _____
_____. (422)

3. What did Lorenz's studies of imprinting in baby geese contribute to Bowlby's theory of attachment? (422)

_____

_____

_____

4. List and briefly explain each of Bowlby's four phases of attachment. (422-423)
A._____
_____

B._____
_____

C._____
_____

D._____
_____

5. According to Bowlby, out of their experiences during the four phases, children construct a(n) _____ to the caregiver that permits them to use the attachment figure as a secure base. This inner representation becomes a vital part of personality. It serves as a(n) _____ of the availability and support of attachment figures. (423)

Measuring the Security of Attachment

1. The _____, designed by _____, is the most widely used technique for measuring the quality of attachment between 1 and 2 years of age. (423)

2. What assumptions underlie the use of the Strange Situation? (423-424)

_____

_____

3. The Strange Situation takes the baby through _____ short episodes in which brief
_____ and _____ with the parent occur. (424)

4. Name and describe the four attachment patterns identified by researchers using the
Strange Situation. (424)

A._____

_____

B._____

_____

C._____

_____

D._____

_____

5. Describe the Attachment Q-sort. (424-425)

_____

_____

Stability of Attachment

1. Securely attached babies (more/less) often maintain their attachment status than do
insecure babies. (425)

2. What happens to the quality of attachment when families experience major life
changes? What besides family stress and major life changes may account for shifts in
attachment quality? (425)

_____

_____

Cultural Variations

1. German infants show considerably more _____ attachment than American
babies do, and an unusually high number of Japanese infants display a(n) _____
response. (425)

2. Despite cultural variations, the _____ pattern is the most common
attachment classification in all societies studied to date. (426)

3. What were the results when the Q-sort was used to assess conceptions of the ideal
child among mothers of diverse cultures? (426)

_____

Factors That Affect Attachment Security

1. Name four factors that would be expected to affect attachment security. (426)
A. _____
B. _____
C. _____
D. _____

2. In the studies by Spitz, what were the consequences of maternal deprivation? (426)
_____
_____

3. Research indicates that a first attachment bond can develop as late as ____ to ____ years. These youngsters were (more/less) likely to display emotional and social problems. (426)

4. Fully normal development may depend on establishing bonds with caregivers during the _____ . (426)

5. Describe differences in caregiving between securely attached and insecurely attached infants. (426)
A. Attached: _____
_____
B. Insecurely attached: _____
_____

6. _____ is a sensitively tuned "emotional dance" in which the caregiver responds to infant signals in a well-timed, appropriate fashion. In addition, both partners match emotional states, especially positive ones. (426)

7. True or False: Secure attachment's association with moment-by-moment contingent interaction occurs in all cultures. (427)

8. Avoidant babies tend to receive _____, _____ care. (427)

9. Resistant infants often experience _____ care. (427)

10. _____ and _____ are associated with all three forms of attachment insecurity. Among these infants, the _____ attachment classification is especially high. (427)

11. True or False: In poverty-stricken, stressed families, prematurity, birth complications, and newborn illness are linked to attachment insecurity. (427)

12. Discuss three findings that argue against the primacy of temperament in determining attachment security. (427)

A._____

_____

B._____

_____

C._____

_____

13. Results from studies involving infants with cleft lip and palate showed that by 1 year of age, rate of attachment security for infants with clefts is (not as high/just as high) as for other babies. (428)

14. A major reason that temperament and other child characteristics do not show strong relationships with attachment quality may be that their influence depends on _____. (428)

15. Home-visited babies scored higher than controls in _____ and were twice as likely to be _____. (429)

16. The Adult Attachment Interview asks adults about _____ experiences and for a(n) _____ of those events. (429)

17. Parents' interpretations of their childhood attachment experiences provide an overall impression of their _____. (429)

18. True or False: Quality of maternal working models shows little relationship with attachment to their infants and children. (429)

19. Autonomous/secure mothers typically have _____ infants, dismissing mothers have _____ infants, preoccupied mothers have _____ infants, and unresolved mothers have _____infants. (429)

20. Explain why adults with unhappy upbringings are not destined to become insensitive parents. (429)

_____

_____

Multiple Attachments: The Father's Special Role

1. _____ believed that infants are predisposed to direct their attachment behaviors to a single person, especially when they are distressed. A 1-year-old who is distressed usually chooses the _____ for comfort, but this preference declines until ____ months, when it is no longer present. (430)

2. True or False: Fathers touch, look at, talk to, and kiss their newborn babies much less than mothers do. (430)

3. Compare mothers' and fathers' different styles of relating to babies. (430)

_____
_____
_____

4. Employed mothers tend to engage in (more/less) playful stimulation of their babies than do unemployed mothers. (430)

5. List three characteristics of fathers who are the primary caregivers. (430)
A._____
B._____
C._____

6. Describe Aka fathers' involvement with their babies. (431)

_____
_____

Attachment and Later Development

1. According to _____ and _____ theories, a healthy attachment relationship supports all aspects of psychological development. (430)

2. What has research shown about the link between infant-mother attachment and cognitive, emotional, and social development? (430-431)

_____
_____
_____
_____

3. Lamb suggests that _____ determines whether attachment security is linked to later development. (431)

Attachment and Social Change:
Maternal Employment and Child Care

1. Today, over ____ percent of American mothers with a child under age 2 are employed. (432)

2. Name four reasons why we should be cautious about concluding that child care is harmful to infants. (433)
A._____
B._____
C._____
D._____

3. Children exposed to poor-quality child care score lower on measures of
_____ and _____. (432)

4. Swedish children who entered out-of-home child care before their second birthday scored (higher/lower) in cognitive, emotional, and social competence during middle childhood and adolescence than children who were reared fully at home. (432)

5. In a study of several hundred randomly selected child-care centers in four states, researchers judged that only _____ provided a level of care sufficient to promote healthy psychological development. (434)

6. Briefly describe eight signs of high-quality child care that can be used in choosing a program for an infant or toddler. (435)

A._____

B._____

C._____

D._____

E._____

F._____

G._____

H._____

7. Many parents think their children's child-care experiences are (higher/lower) in quality than they really are. (434)

ASK YOURSELF...

10.1 Dana is planning to meet her 10-month-old niece Laureen for the first time. How should Dana expect Laureen to react? How would you advise Dana to go about establishing a positive relationship with Laureen? (p. 408)

10.2 At age 14 months, Reggie danced joyfully to the nursery rhyme, "Old MacDonald," as his grandparents clapped and laughed. When asked to dance at 20 months, he showed signs of embarrassment--smiling, looking away, and covering his eyes with his hands. What explains this change in Reggie's emotional reaction? (p. 408)

10.3 As 4-year-old Tia attended a carnival with her mother, the heat of the afternoon caused her balloon to pop. When Tia started to cry, her mother said, "Oh, Tia, we'll get another balloon on a cooler day. If you cry, you'll mess up your beautiful face painting." What aspect of emotional development is Tia's mother trying to promote? Why might her intervention also foster the development of empathy? (p. 412)

10.4 Slow-to-warm-up children are at risk for becoming withdrawn and constricted, whereas difficult children are at risk for both anxious withdrawal and defiant, aggressive behavior. Explain these relationships by considering the characteristics of each temperamental style and the parenting practices it often evokes. (p. 421)

10.5 Fifteen-month-old Caleb's mother tends to overwhelm him with questions and instructions that are not related to his ongoing actions. How would you expect Caleb to respond in the Strange Situation? Explain. (p. 432)

10.6 Around Emily's first birthday, her father lost his job, and her parents argued constantly over how they would pay bills. To look for employment, several times Emily's mother left her with a familiar baby-sitter. Emily, who had previously taken such separations well, cried desperately when her mother left and both clung and pushed her mother away after she returned. Describe the change in Emily's attachment pattern, and explain what may have caused it. (p. 432)

10. 7 In view of evidence on the development of attachment security, explain why each of the following indicators of child-care quality is important: caregiver stability, generous caregiver-child ratio, small group size, and frequent caregiver-parent communication. (p. 435)

CONNECTIONS

10.1 Language and parent-child conversations about emotion play a central role in the development of emotional self-regulation. Are these findings consistent with Vygotsky's sociocultural theory? Explain. (See Chapter 6, pages 259-262.)

10.2 School-age children can take multiple cues into account in interpreting others' emotions and are aware that people do not always express their true feelings. Relate these advances to cognition and metacognition in middle childhood. (See Chapter 6, page 249, and Chapter 7, pages 277 and 301.)

10.3 About 35 percent of children with attention-deficit hyperactivity disorder (ADHD) become defiant and aggressive. Using your knowledge of temperament and child rearing, explain why these children often display antisocial behavior. (See Chapter 7, page 289.)

10.4 How does attachment security contribute to early peer sociability? (See Chapter 15, page 599.)

10.5 Explain the impact of cultural values on the status of child care in the United States compared with other Western nations. (See Chapter 1, page 36.)

PUZZLE 10

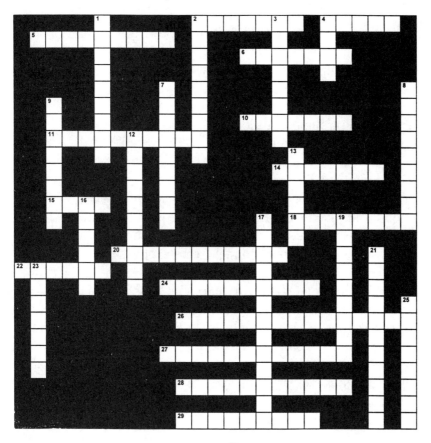

Across

2 ___ Situation assesses attachment security
4 Social ___ appears as infants' sensitivity to visual patterns improves
5 Benefits another without expected reward
6 Expresses readiness to establish or change relation to the environment on matter of personal significance
10 Emotional ___ rules tell when and where to express emotion
11 Self-___ adjusts emotions to a comfortable level
14 Inner representation of the parent-child bond serves as an internal ___ model
15 Child who is regular, adapts easily
18 Attachment in which infant seems unresponsive to parent
20 Stable individual differences in quality and intensity of emotional reaction
22 ___ base uses caregiver for emotional support
24 ___ anxiety, a distressed reaction to the departure of familiar caregiver
26 High-quality child care based on standards for ___ appropriate practice
27 Attachment pattern that reflects the greatest insecurity
28 Sociable child who displays positive emotion to novel stimuli
29 ___ caregiving, which is moderately related to secure attachment

Down

1 Self-___ emotions, which involve injury to or enhancement of the sense of self
2 Caregiver-infant interactional ___ is mutually rewarding
3 ___-of-fit model describes how temperament and environmental pressures work together to produce favorable outcomes
4 ___-to-warm-up child is inactive, adjusts slowly
7 About 10 to 15 percent of American infants show this attachment pattern
8 Child who is irregular, tends to react negatively
9 ___ anxiety, fear of unfamiliar adults
12 Strong affectional tie toward special people
13 ___ referencing relies on another's emotional reaction to appraise uncertain situations
16 Attachment pattern that uses parent as a secure base
17 Approach regards emotions as central forces
19 Child withdraws and displays negative emotion
21 Attachment theory that views emotional tie to the caregiver as promoting survival
23 Ability to understand and respond to others' emotions
25 Feelings of concern or sorrow for another's plight

PRACTICE TEST

1. According to functionalist theory, emotions: (398-399)
   A. are important in the emergence of self-awareness.
   B. have little impact on cognitive processing.
   C. are acquired through conditioning and modeling.
   D. do not influence children's health.

2. Research on happiness indicates that: (402)
   A. the social smile emerges at around 3 1/2 months of age.
   B. 3-month-old infants smile more at puppets than at people.
   C. smiling reflects faster processing of information than does laughter.
   D. infants smile and laugh when they achieve new skills.

3. Which of the following is NOT true of angry reactions in babies? (402-403)
   A. A 5-month old baby may display anger when her arms are restrained.
   B. Anger reactions in older infants are less intense when a familiar caregiver is responsible for blocking a goal.
   C. Anger is adaptive because it permits babies to overcome obstacles.
   D. Angry reactions increase with age because infants value control over their own actions.

4. Stranger anxiety: (403)
   A. is lessened if a strange adult immediately picks up the infant.
   B. should not be tolerated by parents.
   C. results in the use of the caregiver as a secure base.
   D. usually extends to unfamiliar small children as well as adults.

5. Self-conscious emotions: (404)
   A. do not require adult instruction as to when they should be felt.
   B. first appear around 6 months of age.
   C. in the form of envy and guilt emerge before pride.
   D. are linked to self-evaluation.

6. A child smiles and says "Thank you" when given a piece of chocolate cake at a birthday party, even though he does not like chocolate. This is an example of: (407)
   A. conforming to an emotional display rule.
   B. self-conscious emotions.
   C. social referencing.
   D. interactional synchrony.

7. An unfamiliar friend of his mother's offers 1-year-old Juan a bright toy. Juan hesitates and looks at his mother who smiles and nods. He then reaches out and grasps the toy. This is an example of: (408)
   A. interactional synchrony.
   B. social referencing.
   C. separation anxiety.
   D. a strange situation.

8. Which of the following is NOT true of emotional understanding? (410)
   A. Preschoolers recognize that people can experience more than one emotion at a time.
   B. It is stronger in preschoolers who frequently talk about feelings with their families.
   C. It is related to peer acceptance.
   D. Participation in make-believe play is related to advanced emotional understanding.

9. Empathic responses: (411-412)
   A. are more common in severely abused toddlers.
   B. require an understanding that the self is distinct from others.
   C. decrease over the elementary school years.
   D. are less likely if parents intervene when children display inappropriate emotions.

10. According to Thomas and Chess's model of temperament, a child who is inactive, shows mild, low-key reactions to environmental stimuli, and is negative in mood fits the _____ category. (415)
    A. slow-to-warm-up
    B. negative
    C. difficult
    D. lethargic

11. In the measurement of temperament: (415)
    A. parents' prebirth expectations for their infant's temperament have little impact on their reports.
    B. parental ratings are strongly related to observational measures of children's temperament.
    C. assessments should be made across different settings.
    D. assessment of physiological reactions has not proved helpful.

12. Which of the following is NOT true of physiological measures of temperament? (417)
- A. Individual differences in activity of the amygdala may contribute to uninhibited and inhibited styles.
- B. Pupil dilation is greater in sociable children.
- C. Shy babies show greater right than left frontal brain wave activity.
- D. Individual differences in heart rate and EEG patterns are proving to be useful markers of temperamental styles.

13. Research on genetic and environmental influences on temperament and personality show that: (418)
- A. twin resemblance for temperament and personality is higher than for intelligence.
- B. parents often look for and emphasize differences in their children's personalities.
- C. shared environmental influences have a strong impact on siblings' resemblance in temperament and personality.
- D. the more contact twins have with one another in adulthood, the more distinct in personality they become.

14. One way in which temperament predicts behavior is: (419-420)
- A. characteristics of interest and persistence are related to cognitive performance.
- B. uninhibited children tend to feel a greater sense of responsibility to others.
- C. arguments between siblings tend to decrease when one is highly active.
- D. 2- to 3-month-olds rated low in persistence show faster operant conditioning.

15. Which of the following is an example of a "good fit" between temperament and child rearing? (420)
- A. for difficult children, warm, accepting parenting
- B. for reserved, inactive toddlers, quiet, nonstimulating maternal behavior
- C. for very active toddlers, highly stimulating maternal behavior
- D. for children with difficult temperaments, punitive discipline

16. The most widely accepted view of attachment is the _____ theory. (422)
- A. behaviorist
- B. psychoanalytic
- C. ethological
- D. drive-reduction

17. A pattern of attachment in which the infant seeks closeness to the parent and fails to explore before separation, displays angry behavior when the parent returns, and cannot be comforted easily is _____ attachment. (424)
- A. secure
- B. avoidant
- C. resistant
- D. disorganized/disoriented

18. Research indicates that children who developed a first attachment bond between 4 to 6 years of age: (426)
    A. were unable to develop long-term emotional ties with their adoptive parents.
    B. enjoyed many friendships after adoption.
    C. had an excessive desire for adult attention.
    D. had difficulty sleeping.

19. Mothers of infants who are in the _____ attachment category tend to _____. (426)
    A. resistant/give overstimulating, intrusive care
    B. avoidant/be minimally involved in parenting and unresponsive
    C. secure/engage in interactional synchrony
    D. miscellaneous/neglect their infants

20. Research on attachment indicates that: (427)
    A. a substantial number of infants establish distinct attachment relationships with each parent.
    B. child problems such as serious physical disabilities have substantial impact on attachment quality.
    C. an intervention designed to promote sensitivity in mothers of irritable 6-month-olds did not lead to gains in attachment.
    D. a mother's mental illness is not associated with an increase in attachment insecurity.

21. The Adult Attachment Interview: (429)
    A. asks adults to evaluate childhood memories.
    B. asks couples who are parents how attached they are to each other.
    C. asks parents to determine their infant's category of attachment.
    D. asks adults if they agree with attachment theory.

22. Fathers: (430)
    A. touch, talk to, and kiss their newborns much less than mothers do.
    B. worry less about sending their child to day care than mothers do.
    C. tend to engage in more exciting, physical games with their infants than mothers do.
    D. are usually regarded as the preferred source of comfort by distressed 1-year-olds.

23. Research on attachment and later development indicates that: (431)
    A. the quality of attachment in infancy is not related to social development in early childhood.
    B. insecurely attached infants almost always develop into children with adjustment problems.
    C. at age 4, children who were resistantly attached were regarded as isolated and disconnected.
    D. at age 4, securely attached infants were rated as high in self-esteem and popular.

24. Among American infants placed in full-time child care: (433)
    A. most are securely attached.
    B. most are in good to excellent facilities.
    C. the rate of insecurity is much higher than that of home-reared infants.
    D. even those who enter poor-quality care during the first year and remain there until kindergarten have few difficulties.

25. Which of the following is NOT true of American child care? (434)
    A. Many parents view child-care settings as higher in quality than they really are.
    B. A large majority were either mediocre or poor.
    C. Caregivers always need special training in child development.
    D. Child care is affected by the macrosystem.

CHAPTER 11

SELF AND SOCIAL UNDERSTANDING

SUMMARY

The development of social cognition deals with how children's understanding of themselves, other people, and relationships between people changes with age. By the end of the second year, self-recognition is well established. The emergence of representational and language capacities permits toddlers to construct a categorical self as they classify themselves and others on the basis of salient characteristics. Early in the preschool years, children become aware of an inner self of private thoughts and imaginings. By age 4, they have formed a sophisticated theory of mind in which they understand the relationship of belief and desire to behavior.

Self-concept evolves from an appreciation of typical emotions, attitudes, and observable characteristics to an emphasis on personality traits. At the same time, self-esteem differentiates, becomes hierarchically organized, and declines in the early school years. From fourth grade on, it rises for the majority of young people. Adult communication patterns affect children's attributions for success and failure in achievement contexts and their willingness to persist at challenging tasks. Erikson first recognized identity--the construction of a solid self-definition consisting of self-chosen values and goals--as the major personality achievement of adolescence. Four identity statuses describe the degree of progress adolescents have made toward forming a mature identity. Around age 4, children move beyond a view of intention-in-action to appreciate intention as an internal mental state that guides but can be distinguished from action.

Like self-concept, person perception shifts in middle childhood from a focus on concrete activities and behaviors to an emphasis on personality traits. By the early school years, children absorb prevailing attitudes toward social groups and link physical characteristics with social status. During adolescence, inferences about others' psychological characteristics are drawn together into organized character sketches. Perspective taking begins with limited awareness of others' thoughts and feelings and evolves into advanced recursive and societal perspective-taking capacities.

Children's understanding of friendship evolves from a concrete relationship based on sharing activities and material goods to more abstract conceptions based on mutual trust and intimacy. With age, children become better at resolving conflict through social problem solving. Training in social problem solving leads to gains in psychological adjustment.

LEARNING OBJECTIVES

After reading this chapter, you should be able to:

11.1 Explain how social cognition differs from nonsocial cognition. (439-440)

11.2 Describe the development of self-awareness in infancy and toddlerhood and its consequences for young children's emotional and social capacities. (440-442)

11.3 Describe the development of the categorical, remembered, and inner selves and discuss factors that may contribute to preschoolers' belief-desire theory of mind. (442-445)

11.4 Discuss the development of self-concept from early childhood through adolescence, noting cognitive, social, and cultural influences. (445-448)

11.5 Discuss changes in self-esteem from early childhood through adolescence, including the role of social comparison, culture, and child-rearing practices. (448-452)

11.6 Discuss the development of achievement-related attributions, noting the influence of cognitive development and adults' messages to children, and suggest ways to prevent learned helplessness and foster a master-oriented style. (452-456)

11.7 Describe the quest for identity, the four identity statuses, and factors that influence identity development. (456-461)

11.8 Discuss gains in understanding intentions and in person perception, including children's appreciation of others' personalities, ethnicity, and social class. (462-464)

11.9 Cite major changes in perspective taking from early childhood into adolescence, and explain the role of perspective-taking skill in children's social behavior. (464-467)

11.10 Describe the development of friendship understanding, its implications for children's real friendships, and the benefits of close friendship ties. (468-472)

11.11 Describe the components of social problem solving, the development of social problem-solving skills, and ways to help children who are poor social problem solvers. (472-475)

STUDY QUESTIONS

1. The term _____ refers to the ability to understand the multifaceted social world, including the inner characteristics of the self and others. (439)

2. Social cognition develops from (concrete/abstract) to (concrete/abstract). (439)

3. True or False: Social cognition develops more slowly than nonsocial cognition. (440)

4. Name three features of social experience that probably help children make early sense of its complexity. (440)

A._____

B._____

C._____

5. The capacity for _____ permits children to imagine what another's thoughts and feelings might be. (440)

Thinking About the Self
---

1. Two distinct aspects of the self, identified by William James, emerge and become more refined with age. The _____ is a sense of self as _____, or _____, who is separate from but attends to and acts on objects and other people. The _____ is a _____ observer who treats the self as an object of knowledge and evaluation. (440)

2. What four realizations does the I-self include? (440)
A. _____
B. _____
C. _____
D. _____

3. What three types of qualities comprise the me-self? (440)
A. _____
B. _____
C. _____

Self-Awareness

1. How do researchers determine when infants discriminate themselves from others? (441)

_____
_____
_____

2. True or False: Many theorists believe that infants first grasp the notion of self as agent when they recognize that their own actions cause objects and people to react in unpredictable ways. (441)

3. During the second year, toddlers start to construct the _____-self; they become consciously aware of the self's _____ features. (441)

4. Describe the study that demonstrates toddlers' increasing awareness of their unique visual appearance. (441)

_____
_____
_____

5. _____ refers to perception of the self as a separate being, distinct from other people and objects. It is well established around age _____. (441)

247

6. True or False: Self-awareness leads to the child's first efforts to appreciate another's perspective. (441)

7. Research indicates that early struggles over objects are a sign of developing _____, an effort to clarify boundaries between self and other. (442)

The Categorical and Remembered Selves

1. Between 18 and 30 months, children develop a(n) _____ as they classify themselves and others according to salient ways people differ, such as _____, _____, _____, and even _____. (442)

2. An autobiographical memory grants the child a _____, which serves as a rich source of self-knowledge and a means through which the _____ is imbued with cultural values. (442)

3. Explain why the early me-selves of Chinese and Caucasian-American children are likely to differ? (442)

_____
_____
_____
_____

The Inner Self: Young Children's Theory of Mind

1. A theory of _____ is a coherent understanding of one's own and others' mental lives. (443)

2. True or False: Two-year-olds think that people always behave in ways consistent with their desires and do not understand that beliefs affect their actions. (443)

3. Preschoolers' more sophisticated view of the mind qualifies as a(n) _____ theory. At this age, children know that both _____ and _____ determine actions. (443)

4. A 4-year-old who listens to a story about a girl who really wants a new bicycle for her birthday (would/would not) be able to indicate how the girl would feel if she does not receive the present. (443)

5. By age 4, children realize that people can hold _____ that combine with desire to determine behavior. (443)

6. Preschoolers' mastery of false belief signals a major advance in representation--the ability to view beliefs as _____, not just reflections, of reality. (443)

7. Identify five social experiences and describe how each one is thought to contribute to children's developing theory of mind. (444-445)

A._____

_____

B._____

_____

C._____

_____

D._____

_____

E._____

_____

8. Many researchers believe children are _____ prepared to develop a theory of mind. (445)

9. Children with infantile autism are impaired in _____ and _____ behaviors required for successful social interaction. (446)

10. True or False: Evidence suggests that children with infantile autism have a severely deficient or absent theory of mind. (446)

11. Autistic children show deficits in capacities believed to contribute to an understanding of _____. For example, they less often establish _____, engage in _____, or imitate an adult's _____. (446)

12. Describe three hypotheses researchers use to explain the occurrence of infantile autism. (446)

A._____

_____

B._____

_____

C._____

_____

Self-Concept

1. _____ is the set of attributes, abilities, attitudes, and values that an individual believes defines who he or she is. (445)

2. Preschoolers' self-concepts are very concrete. Usually they mention _____ characteristics, such as their _____, _____, _____, and _____. (445)

3. True or False: By age 3 1/2, children have a beginning understanding of their unique psychological characteristics. (445)

4. Between ages 8 and 11, a major shift takes place in children's self-descriptions. They begin to mention _____. Instead of specific behaviors, they emphasize _____. (445, 447)

5. As adolescents' social world expands, contradictory self-descriptions (decrease/increase). Adolescents are often disturbed by these inconsistencies, and they usually (can/cannot) explain or resolve them. (447)

6. Teenagers place more emphasis on _____, which reflects their preoccupation with being liked and viewed positively by others. (447)

Cognitive, Social, and Cultural Influences on Self-Concept

1. How does cognitive development affect the changing structure of the self in school-age children? (447-448)

_____

_____

2. The changing _____ of the self is a product of both _____ capacities and feedback from others. Mead called the reflected self the _____ _____. (448)

3. Mead's ideas indicate that _____ are crucial in the development of a self-concept comprised of personality traits. (448)

4. How do children's sources of self-definition change as they move from middle childhood into adolescence? (448)

_____

_____

5. Evidence indicates that development of self-concept (does/does not) follow the same path in all societies. (448)

6. In characterizing themselves, children from individualistic cultures seem to be more _____ and _____, those from collectivist cultures more concerned with the _____. (448)

Self-Esteem: The Evaluative Side of Self-Concept

1. The judgments we make about our own worth and the feelings associated with those judgments are called _____. (448)

2. High self-esteem implies a realistic evaluation of the self's _____ and _____, coupled with an attitude of _____ and _____. (448)

3. How have researchers studied the multifaceted nature of self-esteem? (449)

_____

4. According to Harter, preschoolers distinguish _____
from _____. (449)

5. By 6 to 7 years, children have formed at least three separate self-esteems--
_____, _____, and _____ that become more
refined with age. (449)

6. With adolescence, several new dimensions of self-esteem are added--
_____, _____, and _____.
(449)

7. The hierarchical structure of self-esteem in adolescence is (similar/different) for
young people of different SES and ethnic groups. (449)

8. Self-esteem is (very high/moderate/very low) during early childhood. Then it
(increases/decreases) over the first few years of elementary school as children start to
make _____. (449-450)

9. Not until _____ grade do pupil self-ratings resemble the opinions of others. (450)

10. From fourth grade on, self-esteem (rises/falls) for the majority of young people.
(450)

11. A study of self-esteem in 10 industrialized countries showed that the majority of
teenagers had a(n) (optimistic/pessimistic) outlook on life. (450)

Influences on Self-Esteem

1. What does academic self-esteem predict? (451)

_____

2. Children with high social self-esteem (are/are not) better liked by their peers. (451)

3. What does positive overall self-esteem predict by adolescence? (451)

_____

4. Beginning in adolescence, cultural standards in the form of gender-stereotyped
expectations for _____ and _____ have an especially
detrimental effect on girls' self-esteem. (451)

5. Asian children (frequently/rarely) make statements referring to social comparisons.
(451)

6. What type of child-rearing practices result in high self-esteem for children? (451)

_____

7. When parental support is conditional, adolescents frequently display _____ behavior. Coercive parenting techniques communicate a sense of _____ to children, and overly tolerant, indulgent parenting creates a(n) _____
_____. (451)

8. Damon maintains that self-esteem (precedes/results from) accomplishment. (452)

9. Asian students (do/do not) attain their impressive levels of achievement at expense to their psychological well-being. (452)

Achievement-Related Attributions

1. _____ are our common, everyday explanations for the causes of behavior. There are two broad categories: _____, _____ causes and _____, _____ causes. (452)

2. The category of psychological causes is further divided into two types: _____ and _____. (452)

3. What are the rules we follow in assigning a cause? (452-453)

_____

_____

4. Differences among children in _____--the tendency to persist at challenging tasks--explain why some less intelligent pupils do better in school than their more intelligent classmates. (453)

5. What are the roots of achievement motivation? (453)

_____

_____

6. By the end of the second year, children turn to adults for evaluations of their accomplishments, picking up information about the meaning of _____in their culture. (453)

7. Around age 3, children begin making _____ about their successes and failures. (453)

8. Preschoolers are "learning optimists" who _____,
_____, and _____
_____. (453)

9. True or False: Young children believe that a person can succeed if she keeps trying. (453)

10. One reason that young children's attributions are usually optimistic is that cognitively, they cannot yet distinguish the precise cause of their _____ and _____. (453)

11. By age 4, some children give up easily when faced with a challenge. They conclude that they _____ and are _____ _____. (453)

12. True or False: When asked to act out an adult's reaction to failure, nonpersisters often respond, "He worked hard but just couldn't finish." (453)

13. How do nonpersisting 4- to 6-year-olds see themselves? (453)

_____

_____

14. During middle childhood, children distinguish _____, _____, and _____ in explaining their performance. (453)

15. Describe the mastery-oriented attributions of children who are high in achievement motivation. (453-454)

_____

_____

16. What explanations do children who develop learned helplessness give for their performance? (454)

_____

_____

17. Mastery-oriented children have a(n) _____--that ability can be altered. However, learned helpless children hold a(n) _____--that it is fixed and cannot be changed. (454)

18. Mastery-oriented children focus on _____ goals; learned-helpless children focus on _____ goals. (454)

19. Over time, the _____ of learned-helpless children no longer predicts their performance. They do not develop the _____ and _____ skills necessary for high achievement. (454)

20. True or False: In adolescence, young people realize that two people varying in ability can achieve the same outcome with different degrees of effort. (454)

21. What does research indicate about the impact of adult feedback on children's attributional styles? (454)

_____

_____

_____

_____

22. When pupils viewed their teachers as warm and consistent, this predicted classroom (engagement/disengagement) and (poor/better) academic performance. In contrast, when children experienced their teachers as unsupportive, this predicted classroom (engagement/disengagement) and (poor/better) achievement. (455)

23. (Girls/boys) more often blame their ability for poor performance, and (girls/boys) tend to receive messages from teachers and parents that their ability if at fault when they do not do well. (455)

24. True or False: African-American and Mexican-American children received less favorable feedback from teachers than did other children. (455)

25. Compared with Americans, Chinese and Japanese parents and teachers believe that success in school depends much more on (effort/ability). (455)

26. How is attribution retraining done? (455-456)

_____

_____

_____

_____

27. Describe four ways adults can foster a mastery-oriented approach to learning and thereby prevent children's learned helplessness. (456)
A._____
B._____
C._____
D._____

Constructing an Identity

1. According to Erikson, the major personality achievement of adolescence is the quest for _____. This involves _____, _____, and _____. (456)

2. According to Erikson, in complex societies, teenagers experience a(n) _____. Current theorists believe that _____ better describes the typical adolescent's experience. (456-457)

3. Explain what is meant by identity diffusion. (457)

_____

_____

4. Briefly describe the four identity statuses. (457-458)

A._____

_____

B._____

_____

C._____

_____

D._____

_____

5. In their search for identity, many young people start out as _____
and _____ and gradually move toward _____ and
_____. (457)

6. True or False: Adolescent girls tend to postpone the task of establishing an identity
and focus their energies on intimacy development. (457)

7. _____ and _____ are viewed as psychologically
healthy routes to a mature self-definition, whereas _____ and
_____ are maladaptive. (457)

8. What are the characteristics of young people who are identity achieved or actively
exploring? (457)

_____

_____

_____

9. Foreclosed individuals tend to be _____, _____, and
_____. Most are afraid of _____. A few who are alienated
from their families and society may join _____. (457-458)

10. Long-term diffused teenagers are the _____ mature in identity development.
They typically entrust themselves to _____ or _____. They are the most
likely to use _____, and many are at risk for _____ and _____.
(458)

11. The suicide rate (increases/decreases) over the life span. Among young people,
suicide is the _____ leading cause of death. (459)

12. (Boys/girls) show a higher rate of severe depression, but more (boys/girls) commit
suicide. (459)

13. Describe gender differences in suicide attempts. (459)

_____

_____

14. True or False: It is suggested that higher levels of support through extended families may be responsible for lower suicide rates among certain nonwhite ethnic minority teenagers. (459)

15. List five warning signs of suicide. (459)

A._____

B._____

C._____

D._____

E._____

16. In what two types of young people are warning signs of suicide likely to appear? (459)

A._____

B._____

17. _____, _____, and _____

_____ are common in the backgrounds of suicidal teenagers. (459)

18. Common circumstances just before a suicide include _____

_____ or _____. (459)

19. Why is suicide rare in childhood but on the rise in adolescence? (459)

_____

_____

20. Schools can help prevent suicide by _____,

_____, and _____.

(459)

21. What types of interventions are used with depressed and suicidal adolescents? (459)

_____

_____

22. Teenage suicides often take place in _____. (459)

23. List four factors that influence identity development. (458, 460)

A._____

B._____

C._____

D._____

24. What type of relationship with parents do foreclosed teenagers usually have? (460)

_____

25. Diffused young people report the (highest/lowest) levels of communication at home. (460)

26. For most Caucasian-American adolescents, their ethnicity (does/does not) prompt intense identity exploration. (461)

27. What challenges does ethnicity pose to the quest for identity of minority youths? (461)

_____
_____
_____
_____

28. Many minority high school students are _____ or _____ on ethnic identity issues. (461)

29. Society can help minority adolescents resolve identity conflicts by _____
_____, _____, _____
_____, and _____.
(461)

30. Biculturally identified adolescents tend to have _____,
_____, and _____
_____. (461)

Thinking About Other People

Understanding Intentions

1. As early as age _____, children talk about intentions. (462)

2. True or False: A 3-year-old believes that if statements and actions do not match, then the behavior was not intended. (462)

3. Describe Astington's bread crumb study, and note how the responses of 3-year-olds differ from those of 4- and 5-year-olds. (462)

_____
_____
_____
_____

4. To judge intentionality, 5-year-olds note whether a person is _____, whether the action leads to _____ or _____ outcomes, whether the person looks _____ at an outcome, and whether some _____ cause can account for behavior. (462)

5. Between ages 5 and 9, children rely increasingly on a(n) _____ _____ to evaluate the sincerity of others' statements about intentions. (462)

6. The mother of a 4-year-old tells her, "Yes, I really like your combination of plaids and stripes," but looks unhappy. The child (is/is not) likely to understand that her mother is probably not telling the truth. (462)

7. Highly aggressive children show striking _____ in inferring intentions. They often see _____ where it does not exist. (462)

Person Perception

1. _____ concerns how we size up people with whom we are familiar in everyday life. (462)

2. Like their self-descriptions, below age 8, children's descriptions of others focus on _____, _____, and _____. (463)

3. How do children's descriptions of others change with age? (463)

_____
_____
_____

4. During adolescence, inferences about others' personalities are drawn together into _____. (463)

5. By age 3 or 4, most children have formed basic concepts of _____ and _____. However, indicators of _____ are not accessible to children this age. (463)

6. Children are more likely to hold (positive/negative) attitudes toward groups to which they do not belong. However, school-age children's capacity to classify the social world in multiple ways tends to result in an (increase/decrease) in prejudice in middle childhood. (463)

7. List three factors that appear to influence childhood prejudice. (463-464)
   A._____
   B._____
   C._____

Perspective Taking

1. Perspective taking is important for a wide variety of social-cognitive achievements, including _____, _____, _____ and _____, _____, and _____. (464)

2. To develop his five-stage model of perspective taking, Selman asked children to respond to _____. (464)

3. Briefly describe Selman's five stages of perspective taking. (465)

A. _____

_____

B. _____

_____

C. _____

_____

D. _____

_____

E. _____

_____

4. Cross-sectional and longitudinal research (does/does not) provide support for Selman's stages. (465)

5. Individuals who fail Piaget's concrete operational tasks tend to be at Selman's Level _____; those who pass concrete but not formal operational tasks tend to be at Levels _____ and _____; and those who are increasingly formal operational tend to be at Levels _____ and _____. (465-466)

6. Each set of Piagetian tasks tends to be mastered somewhat (earlier/later) than its related perspective-taking level. (466)

7. Preschoolers' limited perspective-taking skills are largely due to their _____ view of the mind, their assumption that what a person knows is the result of _____ _____rather than actively _____ experience. (466)

8. In the experimental studies, 4-year-olds (did/did not) think a baby would be able to recognize pictures as easily as an older child, even when the objects were unfamiliar to the baby. (466)

9. What do children age 6 and older realize about interpreting a picture? (466)

_____

10. _____, the self-embedded form of perspective taking that involves thinking about what another person is thinking, improves over the _____ years. (466)

11. Recursive thought makes human interaction truly _____. (466)

12. Name two instances in which people use recursive thinking. (466)
A._____
B._____

13. Recursive thinking contributes to the _____ and concern with the _____ typical of early adolescence. (466)

14. In what ways are perspective-taking skills helpful in social relationships? (466)
_____
_____
_____

15. True or False: Good perspective taking always results in prosocial behavior. (466)

16. Interventions that provide coaching and practice in perspective taking are helpful in reducing _____ behavior and increasing _____.
(467)

Thinking About Relations Between People

Understanding Friendship

1. All theories of the development of friendship emphasize that friendship begins as a _____ relationship based on _____ activity and evolves into a more _____ relationship based on _____ and _____. (468)

2. In Damon's three-stage sequence of friendship understanding, a Level 1 friend is viewed as _____. (468)

3. Describe a Level 2 friendship. (468-469)
_____
_____
_____

4. In Level 2, once a friendship is formed, _____ becomes its defining feature. (468)

5. Level 3 friendships stress two characteristics: _____ and _____.
Level 3 friendships (are/are not) easily dissolved. (469)

6. After a psychological appreciation of friendship emerges, early concepts, such as sharing common activities, (are/are not) abandoned. (469)

7. Friendship reasoning is related to advances in _____. (469)

8. What do we know about the stability of friendships? (469)

_____
_____
_____

9. How do preschoolers interact with friends? (470)

_____
_____

10. Prosocial behavior toward friends (increases/decreases) with age. (470)

11. True or False: School-age friends compete with each other much less than they compete with nonfriends. (470)

12. Children who bring kindness to their friendships (lessen/strengthen) prosocial tendencies. In contrast, aggressive children who make friends tend to (lessen/strengthen) antisocial acts. (470)

13. The attributes on which friends are most alike throughout childhood and adolescence are _____, _____, _____, and _____. Friends also resemble one another in _____, _____, and _____. (470)

14. By adolescence, friends tend to be alike in _____, _____ _____, and _____. (470)

15. _____ and _____ are more common in girls' talk about friends than in boys'. Boys who identify strongly with the traditional masculine role are (more/less) likely to form close friendships than those who are more flexible. (471)

16. List three reasons why friendships further emotional and social development. (471)
A._____
B._____
C._____

261

Understanding Conflict: Social Problem Solving

1. Social conflicts offer children invaluable learning opportunities in _____ _____. (472)

2. List the steps into which Dodge organizes social problem solving. (472-473)
A. _____
B. _____
C. _____
D. _____
E. _____
F. _____

3. Dodge takes a(n) _____ approach to social cognition. (472)

4. Social problem solving has a profound impact on _____. (473)

5. True or False: There is no difference between children with poor peer relations and children with good peer relations in terms of quantity and quality of social problem-solving strategies. (473)

6. Dodge and his collaborators assessed school-age children's ability to _____ _____ cues by using a videotape dramatizing children playing a board game. (474)

7. Participants in Dodge's research also generated strategies for joining the game. The types of strategies included _____, _____, _____, _____, _____. (474)

8. List three ways that intervention with children who are poor social problem solvers can enhance development. (474)
A. _____
B. _____
C. _____

9. Describe Spivak and Shure's social problem-solving training program. (474)

_____
_____
_____

10. Evidence suggests that _____ training must be accompanied by practice in _____. (474)

ASK YOURSELF...

11.1 At age 13 Jeremy described himself as both "cheerful" and "glum." At age 16, he said, "Sometimes I'm cheerful, at other times I'm glum, so I guess I'm kind of moody." What accounts for this change in Jeremy's self-concept? (p. 460)

11.2 Several parents want to know what they can do to promote their child's self-esteem. What advice would you give them, and why? (p. 460)

11.3 Ten-year-old Marla is convinced that her classmate, Bernadette, who often doesn't turn in her homework, is lazy and will never be any good at her studies. Jane thinks that Bernadette tries but can't concentrate because her parents are getting a divorce. Why is Marla more likely than Jane to harbor social prejudices? (p. 467)

11.4 Review the sections on interaction between friends and benefits of friendships on pages 469 and 471. Cite ways that warm, gratifying friendships can serve as contexts for development of effective social problem-solving skills. (p. 474)

CONNECTIONS

11.1 Recall from Chapter 6 (see page 244) that between 4 and 8 years, children figure out who is really behind the activities of Santa Claus and the Tooth Fairy, and they realize that magicians use trickery. How might these understandings relate to the development of a theory of mind?

11.2 During middle childhood, children emphasize personality traits in their self-descriptions and distinguish ability, effort, and external factors in their causal explanations of behavior. What cognitive changes underlie these capacities? (See Chapter 6, page 249, and Chapter 7, page 277.)

11.3 Review the section on children's understanding of emotion in Chapter 10 (pages 408-411). List examples of age-related changes in the ability to take the emotional perspective of another and relate them to Selman's stages of perspective taking.

11.4 How are advances in perspective taking related to the emergence of the imaginary audience and personal fable in early adolescence? (See Chapter 6, page 255.)

11.5 How do the family experiences of aggressive children promote poor social problem solving? (See Chapter 12, page 514.)

11.6 Does temperament contribute to children's social problem solving? Explain, using examples. (See Chapter 10, pages 414-420.)

PUZZLE 11

Across

1 Identity ___, no firm commitment to values and goals
4 Self-___, or definition of the self
9 Perspective ___, capacity to imagine others' thoughts and feelings
10 Identity status of individuals who are exploring alternatives
11 Attribution ___ modifies attributions of learned-helpless children
14 Social ___, judgments of abilities, behavior, and appearance, in relation to others
18 Self-___, judgments about self-worth
19 ___ motivation, tendency to persist at challenging tasks
21 ___ helplessness, attributions that credit success to luck and failure to low ability
23 Common explanations for the causes of behavior
24 ___ perception, sizing up familiar people
27 ___ self, or early classification of the self
28 Identity ___, or commitment without exploration

Down

2 Well-organized conception of the self made up of values and goals to which one is committed
3 ___-self, the self as an object of knowledge and evaluation
5 Social ___, thinking about self, others, and social relationships
6 Social ___ solving, resolving conflicts in ways that are acceptable to others and help the self
7 ___ thought, or thinking about another's thought
8 Adolescents combine subcultural and dominant cultural values into a ___ identity
12 ___ self, one's life-story narrative
13 ___-oriented attributions credit success to ability and failure to insufficient effort
15 Identity ___, commitment to self-chosen values and goals
16 ___ other, blend of what we imagine important people in our lives think of us
17 Self-___, or perception of the self as a separate being
20 ___ view of ability, or belief that ability can be improved through trying hard
22 ___ self, awareness of the self's private thoughts and imaginings
25 ___ view of ability, or belief that competence is fixed and cannot be changed
26 ___-desire theory of mind emerges around age 4

PRACTICE TEST

1. Toddlers show that they can recognize the self's physical features when they: (441)
   A. smile at themselves in a mirror.
   B. touch a mirror image of their nose with red dye on it.
   C. rub their own nose when they see it with a red mark in the mirror.
   D. point to a mirror image of themselves.

2. A 2-year-old clutches her doll and shouts, "Mine!" at another child. This behavior indicates that: (442)
   A. she needs counseling.
   B. she is developing a strong self-definition.
   C. she is selfish.
   D. she has a hostile bias.

3. When asked to describe himself, Josh, a 2-year-old, says, "I am a big boy." What form of self has developed? (442)
   A. categorical
   B. recognizable
   C. gender-biased
   D. social

4. Which of the following is NOT true of young children's theory of mind? (443, 445)
   A. 6-year-olds understand the role of false belief in guiding behavior.
   B. Preschoolers with older siblings are advanced in performance on false belief tasks.
   C. 2-year-olds believe that people always behave in ways consistent with their desires.
   D. 4-year-olds do not understand that a person's beliefs affect his actions.

5. Research on children with infantile autism indicates that: (446)
   A. the disorder is not highly heritable.
   B. they are overly sensitive to a speaker's gaze.
   C. they never speak.
   D. most cannot attribute mental states to others or themselves.

6. Which of the following is NOT true of children's developing self-concepts? (445, 447)
   A. Preschoolers' self-concepts usually mention observable characteristics.
   B. Between ages 8 and 11, children begin to mention personality traits in their self-descriptions.
   C. Compared with adolescents, school-age children tend to place more emphasis on social virtues.
   D. By age 3 1/2, children often respond consistently when asked whether statements are true of themselves.

7. Research on self-esteem indicates that: (449)
   A. preschoolers have a general sense of self-worth.
   B. before age 7, children distinguish social acceptance from competence.
   C. in adolescence, self-esteem loses its hierarchical structure.
   D. by age 8, children have a maximum of two separate self-esteems.

8. Which of the following is NOT true of factors that influence self-esteem? (451)
   A. Gender-typed expectations have a detrimental effect on the self-esteem of adolescent girls.
   B. Overly tolerant parenting creates a false sense of self-esteem.
   C. Highly coercive parenting communicates a sense of inadequacy to children.
   D. Higher academic performance causes Japanese students to score higher in self-esteem than do American students.

9. A preschooler: (453)
   A. is likely to overestimate task difficulty.
   B. is a learning pessimist.
   C. separates effort and ability in explaining successes and failures.
   D. rates his or her own ability as very high.

10. Research on attribution indicates that: (453-454)
    A. mastery-oriented children believe that ability can be improved through increased effort.
    B. learned-helpless children attribute their failures to bad luck.
    C. over time, the ability of learned-helpless children continues to predict their performance.
    D. mastery-oriented children focus on performance goals.

11. Attribution retraining: (455)
    A. works better after children have had several years of experience in school.
    B. encourages learned-helpless children to believe effort can overcome failure.
    C. encourages learned-helpless children to focus more on grades.
    D. gives children easy tasks to prevent failure and negative attributions.

12. Research on identity construction indicates that: (457)
    A. most teenagers experience a serious identity crisis.
    B. adolescents seldom move from their initial identity status.
    C. girls show more sophisticated reasoning than boys in areas related to intimacy.
    D. most working youths settle on an identity later than do those in college.

13. When asked if she had ever thought about going to college instead of working on her parents' farm, Marie said, "No, we Smiths stay with the land." This is an example of: (457-458)
    A. identity diffusion.
    B. identity achievement.
    C. moratorium.
    D. identity foreclosure.

14. Which of the following is NOT true of identity status and personality? (457-458)
    A. Foreclosed teenagers typically entrust themselves to luck or fate.
    B. Long-term diffused teenagers are the most likely to abuse drugs.
    C. Those who are identity achieved or exploring are advanced in moral reasoning.
    D. Foreclosed individuals are afraid of rejection.

15. Among suicidal adolescents: (459)
    A. boys show a higher rate of severe depression.
    B. boys make more unsuccessful suicide attempts.
    C. belief in the personal fable can lead to isolation and despair.
    D. most successful suicides are sudden and impulsive.

16. Positive influences on identity development include: (460)
    A. the realization that we never know anything with certainty.
    B. classrooms that promote community activities.
    C. the belief that absolute truth is always attainable.
    D. unquestioning acceptance of parents' opinions.

17. Which of the following is NOT true of identity development among ethnic minority adolescents? (461)
    A. Many are diffused or foreclosed with regard to ethnic identity issues.
    B. Many try to conceal their abilities or accomplishments in order to conform with ethnic-group values.
    C. Those who are biculturally identified tend to have lower self-esteem.
    D. Many feel caught between the standards of the larger society and their ethnic traditions.

18. In understanding intentions: (462)
    A. 3-year-olds believe that if statements and actions do not match, the person was trying to deceive them.
    B. 5-year-olds believe negative outcomes are usually not intended.
    C. 4-year-olds understand that if someone says they like something but look unhappy, they are probably not telling the truth.
    D. highly aggressive children interpret others' intentions with great accuracy.

19. Which of the following is NOT true of the development of children's person perception? (463)
   A. By the early school years, children link physical characteristics with social status.
   B. Adolescents are able to create character sketches about others' personalities that combine physical traits, typical behaviors, and inner dispositions.
   C. Children begin to make comparisons between people before they begin comparing themselves to others.
   D. Children's person perception begin as comparisons of behavior.

20. Which of the following factors does NOT influence childhood prejudice? (463-464)
   A. children who have a fixed view of personality traits
   B. children with a high self-esteem
   C. children who are from high SES backgrounds
   D. a social world in which there are obvious group distinctions

21. Research on Selman's developmental sequence indicates: (465-466)
   A. rapid movement from one stage to the next.
   B. that gifted individuals skip stages.
   C. that each set of Piagetian tasks tends to be mastered somewhat later than its related perspective-taking level.
   D. that individuals who fail Piaget's concrete operational tasks tend to be at Selman's Level 0.

22. Perspective taking: (466)
   A. in the form of recursive thinking contributes to the concern of adolescents with the imaginary audience.
   B. in the form of two-loop recursions is mastered by sixth grade.
   C. always results in prosocial acts.
   D. makes social relationships more confusing and unpredictable.

23. Children's concepts of friendship are: (468)
   A. limited to a relationship based on pleasurable activity.
   B. defined by trust during the preschool years.
   C. not related to advances in perspective taking.
   D. more complex and psychologically based during middle childhood.

24. Research on friendship indicates that: (470)
   A. school-age friends compete less with each other than they do with nonfriends.
   B. boys typically demand greater emotional closeness than girls do.
   C. friends are less likely to voice differing opinions than are nonfriends.
   D. by adolescence, friends tend to be alike in educational aspirations.

25. Which of the following is NOT true of research on social conflict? (472-473)
   A. Improvement in social problem-solving skills does not seem to result in gains in other areas.
   B. Preschoolers seem to handle most of their quarrels constructively.
   C. Social problem solving has a profound effect on social competence.
   D. Highly aggressive children form biased expectations.

CHAPTER 12

MORAL DEVELOPMENT

SUMMARY

Accompanying the emergence of new representational capacities and self-awareness in the second year is another crowning achievement: the child becomes a moral being. What accounts for the early emergence of morality and children's expanding appreciation of standards of conduct with age? According to sociobiology, morality is grounded in our genetic heritage through prewired emotional reactions. Although psychoanalytic and social learning theories offer different accounts of moral development, both emphasize internalization--the adoption of preexisting standards of behavior as one's own.

Contrary to predictions from Freudian theory, emphasizing power assertion or love withdrawal does not promote conscience formation. Instead, induction, against a backdrop of nurturance, is far more effective. Social learning theorists have shown that modeling combined with reinforcement is effective in encouraging prosocial acts. In contrast, harsh punishment promotes only temporary compliance, not lasting changes in children's behavior.

The cognitive-developmental perspective regards construction--actively attending to and weighing multiple aspects of situations in which social conflicts arise and deriving new moral insights--as central to moral development. Piaget's work was the original inspiration for this perspective.

Kohlberg offers a three-level, six-stage theory of how morality changes from concrete, externally oriented reasoning to more abstract, principled justifications for moral choices. Moral reasoning is influenced by environmental factors such as peer interaction, child-rearing practices, schooling, and aspects of culture. The emergence of self-control is supported by self-awareness and representational and memory capacities.

Aggression, which first appears in late infancy, takes the form of either instrumental or hostile aggression. Whereas boys tend to express overt aggression, girls display more relational aggression. The incidence of delinquent acts rises in the teenage years, but few adolescents become recurrent offenders. Conduct problems that began in childhood are far more likely to persist than are those that first appear in adolescence. Although impulsive, overactive children are at risk for high aggression, whether they become so depends on child-rearing conditions. Among interventions designed to reduce aggression, procedures based on social learning theory and on social-cognitive theory are beneficial.

LEARNING OBJECTIVES

After reading this chapter, you should be able to:

12.1 Describe and evaluate the biological perspective on morality advanced by sociobiologists. (480-481)

12.2 Describe and evaluate the psychoanalytic perspective on moral development. (481-484)

12.3 Describe and evaluate the social learning perspective on moral development, including the importance of modeling, the effects of punishment, and alternatives to harsh discipline. (484-488)

12.4 Describe and evaluate Piaget's theory of moral development, paying special attention to recent evidence on children's reasoning about authority. (488-491)

12.5 Describe and evaluate Kohlberg's extension of Piaget's theory. (491-495)

12.6 Evaluate claims that Kohlberg's theory does not represent morality in all cultures and underestimates the moral maturity of females, and describe the relationship of moral reasoning to moral behavior. (497-500)

12.7 Explain how children separate moral imperatives from social conventions and matters of personal choice, and trace changes in their understanding from childhood into adolescence. (500-503)

12.8 Describe the development of children's distributive justice and prosocial moral reasoning, noting factors that foster mature understandings. (503-505)

12.9 Trace the development of self-control from early childhood and adolescence, noting the implications of individual differences for cognitive and social competencies. (506-509)

12.10 Trace the development of aggression from infancy into adolescence, noting individual, family, community, and cultural influences. (509, 511-515)

12.11 Describe successful interventions for aggressive children and adolescents. (515-517)

STUDY QUESTIONS

1. During _____, toddlers start to show concern with deviations from the way people should behave. (479)

2. By age ____, language includes references to standards of conduct and evaluations of behavior as "good" or "bad." (479)

3. The three facets of morality include a(n) _____ component, a(n) _____ component, and a(n) _____ component. (479)

4. Traditionally, these facets have been studied separately: biological and psychoanalytic theories focused on _____, cognitive-developmental theory on _____, and social learning theory on _____ _____. (479-480)

Morality as Rooted in Human Nature

1. The field of _____ suggests that many morally relevant prosocial behaviors are rooted in the genetic heritage of our species. (480)

2. What are some examples of prosocial behaviors among animals? (480)

_____

_____

3. Many sociobiologists believe that prewired _____ are involved in human prosocial behaviors. (480)

4. Morality cannot be fully explained by its biological foundations because morally relevant emotions, such as empathy, require strong _____ supports to develop, and their mature expression depends on _____ development. (480)

5. Following sympathetic feelings (is/is not) always moral. (480)

Morality as the Adoption of Societal Norms

1. Both psychoanalytic and social learning theory regard moral development as a matter of _____: adopting societal standards for right action as one's own. (481)

2. List four factors that jointly affect the child's willingness to adopt parental standards. (481)
A._____
B._____
C._____
D._____

Psychoanalytic Theory

1. According to Freud, morality emerges between ages ____ and ____. (481)

2. Psychoanalytic theory states that to master the anxiety associated with the Oedipus and Electra conflicts, to avoid punishment, and to maintain the affection of parents, the child forms a(n) _____ through identification with the same-sex parent. (481)

3. Freud believed that morality is transferred from _____ to _____ and that moral development was largely completed by age _____ or _____. (481)

4. Discuss two reasons why most child development researchers disagree with Freud's account of conscience development. (481-482)

A._____

_____

B._____

_____

5. A special type of discipline called _____ does support conscience formation. It can be effective as early as _____ years of age. (482)

6. List three reasons why induction is so effective. (482)

A._____

_____

B._____

_____

C._____

_____

7. Why is discipline that relies too heavily on threats of punishment not as effective as induction? (482)

_____

8. Kochanska points out that children's _____ affect the parenting practices that best promote responsibility and concern for others. (483)

9. For temperamentally inhibited 2- and 3-year-olds, _____ predicted conscience development; for relatively fearless, impulsive children, mild disciplinary tactics showed (some/no) relationship to moral internalization. (483)

10. For fearless, impulsive children, what predicts compliance? Why? (483)

_____

_____

11. Why does Freud's theory place a heavy burden on parents? (482)

_____

12. Freud (was/was not) correct that guilt is an important motivator of moral action. (482)

13. True or False: In older children, guilt may contribute to moral behavior by triggering a general motive to act morally that goes well beyond the immediate situation. (483)

14. According to Emde, sensitive emotional exchanges between caregiver and infant that support the _____ serve as a vital foundation for acquiring moral standards. (483)

15. Current psychoanalytic theorists believe that the superego children build from parental teachings consists not just of prohibitions but also of _____. (484)

16. How does the positive side of conscience develop? (484)
_____

17. Toddlers use their capacity for _____ to check back with the parent, searching for emotional information that can serve as a guide for moral conduct. (484)

18. Around age _____, guilt reactions are clearly evident. (484)

Social Learning Theory

1. Social learning theory (does/does not) consider morality to be a special form of human activity that follows a unique course of development. (484)

2. Social learning theorists believe children learn to behave morally largely through _____. Once children acquire a moral response, _____ and _____ increase its frequency. (484)

3. What are three characteristics of a model that influence children's willingness to imitate behavior? (484-485)
A._____
B._____
C._____

4. Models exert their strongest influence on prosocial development during the _____. (485)

5. Research on modeling indicates that it can help children learn how to inhibit unfavorable acts if the model _____. (485)

6. When is the use of sharp reprimands or physical force sometimes justified? (485)
_____

7. Research shows that punishment promotes (long-term/momentary) compliance. (485)

8. What are three undesirable side effects of harsh punishment? (485)
A._____
B._____
C._____

9. List two alternatives to harsh punishment. What are the advantages of each? (486)

A._____

B._____

10. Cite three ways to increase the effectiveness of punishment. (486-487)

A._____

B._____

C._____

11. What parenting practices are the most effective forms of discipline? (487)

_____

_____

Limitations of "Morality as the Adoption of Societal Norms" Perspective

1. Cite a major criticism of theories that treat morality as entirely a matter of internalization of societal norms. (487)

_____

2. The cognitive-developmental perspective assumes that individuals develop morally through _____--actively attending to and interrelating multiple aspects of situations in which social conflicts arise and deriving new moral understandings. (488)

3. How does the cognitive-developmental perspective view the child? (488)

_____

Morality as Social Understanding

1. According to the cognitive-developmental perspective, _____ and _____ lead to advances in moral understanding. (488)

Piaget's Theory of Moral Development

1. Piaget relied on _____ to study children's ideas about morality. In addition, he gave children _____. (488-489)

2. The period of _____ morality extends from about ___ to ____ years. Children of this stage view rules as _____, _____, _____, and _____. (489)

3. According to Piaget, what two factors limit children's moral understanding during the period of heteronomous morality? (489)

A._____

B._____

4. During the period of heteronomous morality, children's moral understanding is characterized by _____. That is, they regard rules as external features of reality. (489)

5. True or False: During the period of heteronomous morality, children focus on the intent to do harm rather than on objective consequences. (489)

6. _____, _____, and _____ lead children to make the transition to _____ morality. (489)

7. Why did Piaget regard disagreements between peers as especially facilitating? (489)

_____
_____

8. Gradually, children start to use a standard of fairness called _____, in which they express the same concern for the welfare of others as they do for themselves. (489)

9. What are the effects of reciprocity on children's understanding of rules and punishment? (489)

_____
_____
_____

Evaluation of Piaget's Theory

1. Piaget's method yields a(n) _____ picture of young children's ability to make moral judgments. (490)

2. When questioned about moral issues in a way that makes a person's intent stand out as strongly as the harm they do, preschool and early school-age children (are/are not) capable of judging ill-intentioned people as naughtier than well-intentioned ones. (490)

3. How does the morality of intentions change from early elementary school children to ages 9 or 10? (490)

_____
_____

4. Describe children's views of authority during the preschool and school years. (490)

_____
_____
_____
_____

5. The characteristics associated with each of Piaget's two broad stages of moral understanding (do/do not) correlate very highly. (491)

279

6. Moral development is currently regarded as a (more/less) extended process than Piaget believed. (491)

Kohlberg's Extension of Piaget's Theory

1. Like Piaget, Kohlberg used a(n) _____ procedure to study moral development. (491)

2. Kohlberg presented people with _____ and asked them to decide both what the main character should do and why. (491)

3. What types of dilemmas are examined by Kohlberg to determine the structure of a person's moral reasoning? (491)

_____

4. Kohlberg emphasized that it is the _____ of the answer--the way an individual reasons about the dilemma--and not the _____ of the response that determines moral maturity. (491)

5. According to Kohlberg, at the highest two stages of morality, both _____ and _____ are relevant. (491)

6. True or False: According to Kohlberg, given a choice between obeying the law and preserving individual rights, the most advanced moral thinkers support individual rights. (491)

7. The most recently devised questionnaire instrument for assessing moral understanding is the _____. (492)

8. Explain how the SRM-SF works. (492)

_____

_____

9. Scores on the SRM-SF correlate (poorly/moderately/well) with those obtained from clinical interviews. (492)

10. Kohlberg organized his ____ stages into ____ general levels. (492)

11. What were three beliefs of Kohlberg about the properties of his sequence of stages? (492)
A._____
B._____
C._____

12. Kohlberg believed that moral understanding is promoted by _____ and _____. (492)

13. At the _____ level of Kohlberg's developmental sequence, morality is externally controlled. Children accept the rules of authority figures, and actions are judged by their _____. (492)

14. Describe Stage 1 and Stage 2. (492-493)
Stage 1:_____

_____
Stage 2: _____

_____

15. At the _____ level, individuals believe that actively maintaining the current social system is important for ensuring _____ and _____. (493)

16. Describe Stage 3 and Stage 4. (493)
Stage 3:_____

_____
Stage 4:_____

_____

17. Individuals at the _____ level define morality in terms of _____. (493-494)

18. Describe Stage 5 and Stage 6. (494)
Stage 5:_____

_____
Stage 6:_____

_____

Research on Kohlberg's Stages

1. Both longitudinal and cross-sectional research reveals that progress through Kohlberg's stages (is/is not) related to age. In addition, longitudinal research determined that the stages form a(n) _____. (494)

2. Describe the age trends in moral reasoning (494)

_____

_____

3. When people generate real-life moral problems of their own, they tend to fall at a (higher/lower) stage than on hypothetical situations. Why might this occur? (495)

_____

4. Kohlberg's moral stages are best viewed as a (strict/loose) concept of a stage. (495)

5. Moral maturity is positively correlated with _____, _____ _____, and _____. Kohlberg argued that these are necessary but not sufficient conditions because in addition, _____ is necessary. (495)

6. Moral reasoning (can/cannot) be stimulated beyond the stage for which an individual has the appropriate cognitive prerequisites. (495)

7. Match each of Kohlberg's moral stages with its parallel cognitive and perspective-taking stages. (496)

Kohlberg's Moral Stage

1. Punishment and obedience
2. Instrumental purpose
3. "Good boy-good girl"
4. Social-order maintaining
5. Social-contract
6. Universal ethical principle

Piaget's Cognitive Stage

___ Formal operational
___ Concrete operational
___ Early formal operational
___ Preoperational, early
    concrete operational

Selman's Perspective-Taking Stage

___ Societal
___ Self-reflective
___ Third-party
___ Social-informational

Environmental Influences on Moral Reasoning

1. Maturity of moral reasoning is correlated with _____, _____, and _____. (496)

2. What did the study by Blatt and Kohlberg conclude about the effects of participation in classroom discussion of moral dilemmas? (497)

_____

_____

3. Studies have found that _____, _____ exchanges between peers are especially effective in stimulating moral understanding. It usually takes (many/only a few) peer interaction sessions to produce moral change. (497)

4. Walker and Taylor found that parents who created a supportive atmosphere when they discussed moral dilemmas by _____, _____ _____, _____, and _____ _____ had children who gained most in moral understanding when interviewed 2 years later. (497)

5. Parents who use low levels of _____ and high levels of _____ and _____ and who _____ have morally mature children. (497)

6. Years of schooling completed (is/is not) a powerful predictor of moral understanding. (497)

7. True or False: Moral reasoning advances in late adolescence and young adulthood only as long as a person remains in school. (497)

8. Why does schooling make a difference in moral maturity? (497)

_____

_____

9. True or False: Cross-cultural research indicates that there are no cultural differences in the stage of moral reasoning reached by an individual. (497)

10. Give two possible reasons for cultural variation in moral understanding. (497-498)
A._____

_____

B._____

_____

11. East Indians often explain behaviors in _____ rather than _____ terms. (498)

Are There Sex-Related Differences in Moral Reasoning?

1. Gilligan believes that Kohlberg's theory does not adequately represent the morality of _____. (498-499)

2. What are the results of research on Gilligan's claims? (499)

_____

_____

3. Some evidence shows that females tend to stress _____, whereas males either stress _____ or use _____ and _____ equally. (499)

Moral Reasoning and Behavior

1. A central assumption of the cognitive-developmental perspective is that moral _____ should affect moral _____. _____ predicted that the two should come closer together as individuals move toward the higher stages of moral understanding. (499)

2. A (strong/moderate/weak) connection exists between moral thought and action. (499)

Further Questions About Kohlberg's Theory

1. Kohlberg believes that moral maturity is not achieved until the _____ level. Gibbs finds maturity in the ethically ideal aspects of Stages ____ and ____. (500)

2. Kohlberg's stages tell us little about moral understanding in _____ and _____. (500)

1. Describe the three facets of children's moral understanding. (500-501)
A._____
B._____
C._____

Distinguishing Moral, Social-Conventional, and Personal Domains

1. Preschool and young grade school children distinguish _____ from _____ and _____. (501)

2. In one study, by 34 months, children viewed moral transgressions as _____ _____, and by 42 months, they indicated that moral (but not social-conventional) violations would still be wrong if _____ and _____ _____. (501)

3. Briefly describe the three forms of children's environmental moral reasoning. (502)
A._____
B._____
C._____

4. Children's environmental moral reasoning (was/was not) similar across cultures. (502)

5. How do young children come to make the distinctions between moral and social-conventional transgressions? (501)

_____

_____

_____

6. Justice considerations (do/do not) appear to be a universal feature of moral thought. (503)

7. When is moral understanding enhanced in adolescents? (503)

_____

Distributive Justice

1. _____ involves beliefs about how to divide up resources fairly. (503)

2. Four-year-olds recognize the importance of sharing, but their reasons for doing so often seem _____ and _____. (504)

3. As children enter middle school, their ideas of fairness are based on _____ at first. Later, children start to view fairness in terms of _____ (504)

4. Around 8 years, children can reason on the basis of _____. They recognize that special consideration should be given to those at a(n) _____. (504)

5. According to Damon, parental _____ and _____ support these developing standards of justice, but _____ is especially important. (504)

6. Advanced distributive justice reasoning is associated with more effective _____ and a greater willingness to _____. (504)

Prosocial Moral Reasoning

1. Eisenberg asked preschoolers through twelfth-graders to respond to prosocial dilemmas in which the primary sacrifice in aiding another person is _____. (504)

2. Briefly name and describe Eisenberg's levels of prosocial reasoning. (505)

A. _____

B. _____

C. _____

D. _____

E. _____

3. Eisenberg found that punishment- and authority-oriented reasoning was (common/rare) in children's responses, and that children's prosocial understanding was (advanced/delayed) when compared to the timing of Kohlberg's stages. (505)

4. According to Eisenberg, prosocial dilemmas bring out a form of moral reasoning called _____. (505)

Development of Self-Control

1. Whether children and adults act in accord with their beliefs depends in part on _____. Sometimes it is called _____. (506)

Beginnings of Self-Control

1. Name two prerequisites for self-control. (506)
A._____
B._____

2. The first glimmerings of self-control appear in the form of _____.
Between ____ and ____ months, children start to show clear awareness of caregivers'
wishes and expectations and can voluntarily obey requests. (506)

3. For most toddlers, resistance is gradually transformed into _____
and _____ with parents over the preschool
years. (506)

4. Control of the child's actions during the second year depends heavily on
_____ from caregivers. (507)

5. According to Vygotsky, children cannot guide their own behavior until they develop
_____. (507)

6. Researchers typically study self-control by creating situations that call for
_____--waiting for a more appropriate time and place to
engage in a tempting act or obtain a desired object. (507)

7. Research indicates that the ability to delay gratification increases substantially
between ____ and ____ months. (507)

8. Gralinski and Kopp's research showed that caregiver rules for children expanded from
an initial focus on _____, _____, and
_____ to a broader emphasis on issues related to
_____, _____, and _____. (507-508)

Development of Self-Control in Childhood and Adolescence

1. Gains in _____ and _____ permit children to
use a variety of effective self-instructional strategies to resist temptation. (508)

2. In his research on strategies for self-control, Mischel found that
_____ was especially important in the ability to delay
gratification. (508)

3. Mischel found that teaching children to transform the stimulus in ways that
_____ is highly effective in promoting delay of
gratification. (508)

4. When an adult refrains from giving preschoolers instructions in how to resist temptation, their ability to wait in delay-of-gratification tasks declines (slightly/considerably). (508)

5. In early elementary school, self-control is transformed into a flexible capacity for _____ --the ability to monitor one's own conduct, constantly adjusting it as circumstances present opportunities to violate inner standards. (508)

6. _____ knowledge plays an important role in the development of self-regulation. (508)

7. How does knowledge of strategies for self-regulation change from age 3 to age 11? (508)

_____
_____
_____

8. Why does awareness of the importance of transforming ideation appear so late in development? (508)

_____

9. Longitudinal research reveals (strong/modest/weak) stability in children's capacity to manage their behavior in a morally relevant fashion. (508)

10. Researchers believe that enduring individual differences in self-regulation are the combined results of _____ and _____. (509)

The Other Side of Self-Control: Development of Aggression

---

1. Conflicts between young children are (more/less) frequent than friendly, cooperative interaction. (509)

2. As early as the _____, some children show abnormally high rates of hostility. (509)

Emergence of Aggression

1. During the second half of the first year, two types of aggression emerge. The most common is _____ aggression; the other type is _____ aggression. (509)

2. List and describe the two varieties of hostile aggression. (509)
A._____
B._____

Aggression in Early and Middle Childhood

1. _____ aggression declines during the preschool years, but _____ increase. (511)

2. (Boys/Girls) are more physically aggressive, whereas (boys/girls) are more likely to resort to relational aggression. (511)

Aggression and Delinquency in Adolescence

1. Adolescents under the age of 21 account for about ____ percent of police arrests in the United States. (511)

2. Both police arrests and self-reports show that delinquency (rises/stays the same/ falls) over the early teenage years, (rises/ stays the same/falls) during middle adolescence, and then (rises/stays the same/falls) into young adulthood. (511)

3. The desire for peer approval (decreases/increases) antisocial behavior among young teenagers. (511)

Stability of Aggression

1. From middle childhood on, aggression is a (highly stable/somewhat stable) personality characteristic. (512)

2. Longitudinal research on adolescent delinquency reveals that the (early-onset/late-onset) type is far more likely to lead to a life-course pattern of aggression and criminality. (513)

3. Briefly describe why many youths become delinquent around the time of puberty. (513)

_____

_____

4. There (is/is not) strong continuity in aggression across generations. (512)

5. Children who are _____ and _____ are clearly at risk for high aggression, but _____ influence the outcome. (512)

6. _____, _____, _____, and _____ are strongly linked to children's antisocial acts. (512)

The Family as Training Ground for Aggressive Behavior

1. _____, _____, _____, and _____ are linked to antisocial behavior from early childhood through adolescence for children of both sexes. (512)

2. Describe the pattern of conflict in homes of aggressive children. (512)

_____

_____

_____

3. Parents can also encourage aggression indirectly through _____ _____. (514)

Social-Cognitive Deficits and Distortions

1. Aggressive children often see _____ where it does not exist. They also fall behind their agemates in _____ skill and in _____ _____. (514)

2. When tempted to aggress, aggressive children are more concerned about _____, less concerned about _____ or _____, and less likely to _____. (514)

3. Antisocial children may retain a basic tendency to respond empathically but may neutralize it by using cognitive-distortion techniques such as _____. (514)

Community and Cultural Influences

1. When peer group atmospheres are _____ and _____, hostility is more likely. These group characteristics are more common in _____ neighborhoods with stressors such as _____, _____ _____, and _____. (515)

2. The United States ranks _____ in the industrialized world in interpersonal violence and homicides. (515)

3. List five outcomes common for children of war. (516)

A._____

B._____

C._____

D._____

E._____

4. The best safeguard against lasting problems for children of war is
_____. (516)

Helping Children and Parents Control Aggression

1. Interventions with _____ and _____ children have been most successful. (515)

2. Describe Patterson's parent-training program, which is designed to interrupt destructive family interaction. (515)

_____

_____

_____

3. What programs for children are helpful in reducing aggression? (515)

_____

_____

4. Once aggressive children begin to change, parents must give them _____ and _____ for their prosocial acts. (515)

5. In one program, directly teaching aggressive children empathy by having them practice identifying others' feelings and expressing their own reduced _____ _____ and increased _____, _____, and _____. (516-517)

6. In a program designed to remediate social-problem solving deficits, adolescents were taught to _____; _____ _____; and _____. (517)

7. According to some researchers, effective treatment for antisocial children and adolescents needs to be multifaceted, encompassing _____, _____, _____, and _____. (517)

8. One comprehensive approach to treatment of antisocial children, _____, served as the basis for treatment. It was supplemented with _____, _____, _____, and _____. (517)

9. To ensure optimal development of all children, intensive efforts to create _____ environments are needed. (517)

290

ASK YOURSELF...

12.1 Alice and Wayne want their two young children to develop a strong, internalized conscience and to become generous, caring individuals. List as many parenting practices as you can that would promote these goals. (p. 488)

12.2 Nanette told her 3-year-old son, Darren, not to go into the front yard without asking, since the house faces a busy street. An impulsive child, Darren disobeyed several times. How would you recommend that Nanette discipline Darren, and why? Considering Darren's temperament, what kind of parent-child relationship is likely to help him internalize parental standards? (p. 488)

12.3 Tam grew up in a small village culture, Lydia in a large industrialized city. At age 15, Tam reasons at Kohlberg's Stage 2, Lydia at Stage 4. What factors might account for the difference? (p. 500)

12.4 At preschool, 3-year-old Dahlia noticed that her classmate, Claude, reacted angrily when another child snatched his toy. Later, at the snack table, Dahlia watched the teacher tell Claude to use his napkin. Claude complied unemotionally. During outdoor play, Dahlia listened as Claude asked to play on the jungle gym. "You can do whatever you like," the teacher responded. Explain how these events help Dahlia and Claude differentiate moral imperatives, social conventions, and matters of personal choice. (p. 506)

12.5 Throughout his school years, Mac had difficulty learning, was disobedient, and picked fights with peers. At age 16, he was arrested for burglary. Zeke had been a well-behaved child in elementary school, but around age 13, he started spending time with the "wrong crowd." At age 16, he was arrested for property damage. Which boy is more likely to become a long-term offender, and why?
(p. 517)

CONNECTIONS

12.1 What social-cognitive capacities are probably fostered by inductive discipline? (See Chapter 11, pages 445 and 465.)

12.2 In Chapter 11 (page 447), we noted that compared to school-age children, adolescents place more emphasis in their self-descriptions on social virtues, such as being friendly, considerate, kind, and cooperative. They also stress personal moral values as key themes. How do these changes in self-concept relate to stagewise advances in moral reasoning, described on page 493?

12.3 Older school-age children's grasp of the relation between emotion and moral transgression includes the realization that a victim's unhappiness can affect the perpetrator, producing a mixture of positive and negative emotion. How is this finding related to changes in emotional understanding in middle childhood? (See Chapter 10, page 410.)

12.4 Read the section on teenage pregnancy in Chapter 5 (page 214), adolescent suicide in Chapter 11 (page 459), and substance abuse in Chapter 15 (page 614). What factors do these problems have in common with delinquency? How would you explain the finding that teenagers who experience one of these difficulties are likely to display others?

PUZZLE 12

Across

4 ___ conventional level bases morality on consequences
7 Matters of ___ choice are up to the individual
8 Self-___ inhibits behavior violating moral rules
9 Morality is defined by abstract principles and at the ___ conventional level
11 Voluntary obedience to requests and commands
14 ___ out is mild punishment
15 Process in which children weigh multiple aspects and derive new moral understandings
17 Kohlberg's second level, based on conformity to social rules
19 Aggression that harms others through physical injury or threat of such injury
22 Process of moral development in which children adopt preexisting standards
23 ___ imperatives protect people's rights and welfare
24 Assumes genetically influenced social behaviors
25 Views rules as permanent at the ___ stage.

Down

1 Distributive ___ involves fair division
2 Moral ___, or conflict situation used to assess development of moral reasoning
3 Views rules as flexible at the ___ stage
5 Rules viewed as external features of reality
6 Communicates the effect of misbehavior on others
10 ___ conventions, or customs determined solely by consensus
12 ___ aggression does not intend deliberate harm
13 Delay of ___, waiting for a more appropriate time and place to engage in tempting acts
16 Aggression that damages another's peer relationships
18 Standard of fairness in which individuals express the same concern for others as for selves
20 Questionnaire assessing moral understanding
21 ___ aggression, intended to harm another

PRACTICE TEST

1. Sociobiologists believe that morality is: (480)
    A. rooted in genetics.
    B. internalized standards.
    C. obtained directly from parents.
    D. learned from social norms.

2. Both psychoanalytic and social learning theory regard moral development as a matter of: (481)
    A. construction.
    B. realism.
    C. internalization.
    D. reciprocity.

3. Which of the following is NOT a reason why induction supports conscience formation? (482)
    A. It tells children how to behave so they can refer to it in the future.
    B. It recruits children into the family structure.
    C. It encourages children to empathize.
    D. It points out the effects of misbehavior on others.

4. Jason, an active, impulsive child, ignores his mother's patient instruction not to kick the wall. In fact, he regularly ignores his mother's requests. His mother should: (483)
    A. spank him.
    B. use polite requests.
    C. build a warm, caring relationship with him when he is behaving well.
    D. allow him to express his hostility without intervening.

5. Models: (484)
    A. exert their most powerful effect on prosocial development during the early school years.
    B. are equally effective no matter what their characteristics.
    C. who are strict and demanding are more effective.
    D. who are warm and responsive are more effective.

6. Punishment: (486)
    A. is regarded by some social learning theorists as playing a valuable role in moral development.
    B. is never justified.
    C. promotes lasting changes in behavior.
    D. tends to be used with decreasing frequency over time by punitive adults.

7. Which of the following is NOT a parenting practice that tends to reduce the need for punishment? (487)
    A. encouraging and rewarding good conduct
    B. making punishment unpredictable
    C. letting children know ahead of time how to act
    D. finding alternative activities for children to reduce temptations

8. During the period of heteronomous morality: (489)
    A. children believe that punishment should be rationally related to the offense.
    B. children believe that there may be a good reason to break a rule.
    C. children focus on objective consequences rather than intent to do harm in judging an act's wrongness
    D. children use the standard of reciprocity.

9. Research on Piaget's theory of morality: (489)
    A. supports his conclusion that gradual release from adult control increases moral understanding.
    B. does not support his emphasis on peer interaction as a means to moral understanding.
    C. indicates that Piaget's method yields an overoptimistic picture of children's ability to make moral judgments.
    D. supports his assumption that young children regard adults with unquestioning respect.

10. A child who, when asked about the proper actions to take in the "Heinz Dilemma," says that Heinz should not steal the drug because the police will put him in jail is in Kohlberg's Stage _____ of the _____ level. (492-493)
    A. 2/preconventional
    B. 1/preconventional
    C. 4/conventional
    D. 3/conventional

11. A child who says that Heinz should not steal the drug because everyone, including his family, will think he is a criminal is in Stage _____ of the _____ level. (493)
    A. 2/preconventional
    B. 1/preconventional
    C. 4/conventional
    D. 3/conventional

12. Research on Kohlberg's stages indicates that: (494)
    A. progress through the stages is not strongly related to age.
    B. for many people, progress through the stages is rapid.
    C. most people reach Stage 5.
    D. Stage 3 increases through mid adolescence and then declines.

13. Research on Kohlberg's dilemmas indicates that: (495)
   A. Kohlberg's scoring procedure maximizes variability in responses.
   B. when people generate real-life moral problems, they tend to fall at a lower stage than on the dilemmas.
   C. moral responses do not change, even when the possibility of punishment is highlighted.
   D. people tend to feel more confused by hypothetical situations than real-life moral dilemmas.

14. Which of the following is NOT positively correlated with moral maturity? (495)
   A. performance on Piagetian cognitive tasks
   B. perspective-taking skill
   C. IQ
   D. unquestioning respect for authority

15. An aspect of peer discussion that appears to simulate moral development includes: (497)
   A. making assertions about one's beliefs.
   B. telling personal anecdotes.
   C. clarifying and critiquing one another's statements.
   D. unemotional discussions of issues.

16. Research on the relationship between schooling and moral development indicates that: (497)
   A. lecture-style classes in college tend to advance moral reasoning more than open discussion.
   B. advances in moral maturity were the same in just community and traditional high school settings.
   C. years of schooling completed is a weak predictor of moral development.
   D. moral reasoning advances in late adolescence and young adulthood only as long as a person stays in school.

17. Research on Gilligan's claim that Kohlberg's approach underestimates the moral maturity of females indicates that: (499)
   A. Kohlberg's system usually scores adolescent and adult females as behind males in moral development.
   B. themes of justice and caring appear in the responses of both sexes.
   C. when girls raise interpersonal concerns, they are downscored in Kohlberg's system.
   D. Kohlberg's system emphasizes caring as the highest of moral ideals.

18. Which of the following is NOT true of the relationship between moral reasoning and behavior? (499)
   A. Higher-stage individuals more often engage in prosocial acts.
   B. The connection between moral thought and action is moderate.
   C. There is no difference in demonstrated honesty among the various stages.
   D. Moral behavior is influenced by noncognitive as well as cognitive factors.

19. Distinctions between moral rules and social conventions: (501)
   A. are drawn by children on the basis of their observations of people's responses to each type of violation.
   B. occur when children are taught them in school.
   C. occur as a result of direct parental instruction.
   D. are very different cross-culturally.

20. Children's distributive justice reasoning: (504)
   A. at first emphasizes merit.
   B. around 8 years of age is based on equality.
   C. develops partly as a result of the give-and-take of peer interaction.
   D. occurs much later than Piaget and Kohlberg believed.

21. Erin asks Jessica if she can borrow her umbrella. Jessica gives it to Erin "because she needs it." According to Eisenberg's developmental levels, Jessica's level of prosocial reasoning is the: (505)
   A. hedonistic, pragmatic orientation.
   B. "needs of others" orientation.
   C. stereotyped, approval-focused orientation.
   D. empathic orientation.

22. According to Vygotsky, children cannot guide their own behavior until they acquire: (507)
   A. a superego.
   B. private speech.
   C. realism.
   D. reciprocity.

23. Which of the following is NOT shown by research on delay of gratification? (507-508)
   A. The single best predictor of individual differences in the capacity for self-control is motor ability.
   B. The ability to delay gratification increases substantially between 18 and 30 months.
   C. Delay of gratification improves during childhood and adolescence.
   D. Deemphasizing the arousing qualities of a stimulus promotes delay of gratification.

24. Research on aggression shows that: (512)
    A. the hostile form is more common among toddlers.
    B. boys and girls are equally aggressive.
    C. from middle childhood on, aggression is a highly stable personality characteristic.
    D. there is little continuity across generations.

25. Research on juvenile delinquency indicates that: (511)
    A. teenagers who have many encounters with the police are usually not serious offenders.
    B. young people under the age of 21 account for about 10 percent of arrests.
    C. among teenagers, the desire for peer approval increases antisocial behavior.
    D. most families of delinquent youths use consistent discipline.

CHAPTER 13

DEVELOPMENT OF SEX-RELATED
DIFFERENCES AND GENDER ROLES

SUMMARY

Perhaps more than any other area of child development, the study of gender typing has responded to societal change; hence, theoretical revision marks the study of gender typing. At one time, psychoanalytic theory offered an influential account of how children acquired "masculine" and "feminine" traits. Social learning theory, with its emphasis on modeling and reinforcement, and cognitive-developmental theory, with its focus on children as active thinkers about their social world, are major current approaches to gender typing. A recent information-processing view, gender schema theory, combines elements of both theories to explain how children acquire gender-typed knowledge and behavior.

According to Maccoby, early on, hormones affect play styles, leading to rough, noisy movements among boys and calm, gentle actions among girls. Then, as children begin to interact with peers, they choose partners whose interests and behaviors are compatible with their own. During the preschool years, children acquire a wide variety of gender stereotypes about activities, behaviors, and occupations. Stereotypes involving personality traits and achievement areas are added in middle childhood. At the same time, a more flexible view of what males and females can do emerges.

Cross-cultural similarities in gender typing are not consistent enough to support a strong role for biology. Powerful environmental influences on gender typing exist. Beginning in infancy, adults view boys and girls differently, and they treat them differently. According to social learning theory, behavior precedes self-perceptions in the development of gender identity. In contrast, cognitive- developmental theory assumes that self-perceptions emerge first and guide children's behavior. In fact, gender-typed behavior is present so early in development that modeling and reinforcement must account for its initial appearance.

Biological, social, and cognitive factors combine to make early adolescence a period of gender intensification. Girls are advanced in early language development and in reading achievement and are more emotionally sensitive, compliant, and dependent. Boys do better at spatial and mathematical skills and are more aggressive.

The developmental challenges of adolescence combined with gender-typed coping styles seem to be responsible for the higher rate of depression among adolescent girls. Parents and teachers can counteract young children's readiness to absorb gender-linked associations by delaying access to gender stereotypes and pointing out exceptions as well as the arbitrariness of many gender inequalities in society.

LEARNING OBJECTIVES

After reading this chapter, you should be able to:

13.1 Explain how the study of gender typing has responded to societal change, noting the development of new theories and the use of new terms. (521-523)

13.2 Cite examples of gender stereotypes, and describe the development of gender stereotyping from early childhood into adolescence. (523-527)

13.3 Discuss the role of biology in gender stereotyping and gender-role adoption, including cross-cultural evidence and the influence of sex hormones. (527-531)

13.4 Discuss environmental influences on gender stereotyping and gender-role adoption, including expectations and treatment by parents, teachers, and peers; observational learning; and the impact of siblings. (531-537)

13.5 Explain the meaning of androgyny, and describe and evaluate the accuracy of social learning and cognitive-developmental views of the development of gender identity in early childhood. (538-540)

13.6 Describe the development of gender identity in middle childhood and adolescence. (540-541)

13.7 Explain how gender schema theory accounts for the persistence of gender stereotypes and gender-role preferences. (541-543)

13.8 Describe sex-related differences in mental abilities and personality attributes, noting factors that contribute to those differences. (544-552)

13.9 Cite ways to reduce gender stereotyping in children. (552, 554)

STUDY QUESTIONS

1. What changes have occurred in the way sex-related differences are regarded? (522)

_____

_____

2. According to Freud, gender-typed attitudes and behaviors are acquired by children as a result of _____ with the _____. (522)

3. List three reasons why most researchers have abandoned the psychoanalytic approach to gender typing in favor of other perspectives. (522)

A._____

B._____

C._____

4. Define the following terms: (522)

A. Sex-related:_____

B. Gender:_____

C. Gender stereotype:_____

D. Gender role:_____

E. Gender identity:_____

F. Gender typing:_____

Gender Stereotypes and Gender Roles

---

1. When researchers in the 1960s asked people what personality characteristics they considered typical of men and women, widespread agreement (was/was not) found. (523)

2. _____ traits, reflecting _____, _____, and _____, were regarded as masculine; _____ traits, emphasizing _____, _____, and _____ were viewed as feminine. (523)

3. True or False: When undergraduate students were asked how typical personality traits of boys and girls were, they did not distinguish the sexes. (523)

4. The instrumental-expressive dichotomy (is/is not) a widely held stereotype around the world. (523)

5. Besides personality traits, other gender stereotypes include _____, _____, and _____ or _____. (523)

Gender Stereotyping in Early Childhood

1. Around age _____, children label their own sex and that of other people. (523)

2. True or False: Even before children can label their own sex, they prefer "gender-appropriate" activities. (524)

3. By age _____, gender-stereotyped preferences become highly consistent for both boys and girls. (524)

4. Preschoolers' gender stereotypes (are/are not) flexible. (524)

5. What two factors may account for the rigidity of preschoolers' gender stereotypes? (524)

A._____

B._____

6. Most preschoolers do not yet realize that characteristics _____ with one's gender do not _____ whether a person is male or female. (524)

Gender Stereotyping in Middle Childhood and Adolescence

1. By age ____, gender stereotyping of activities and occupations is well established. (524)

2. How do researchers assess stereotyping of personality traits? (524)

_____

3. Research in many countries reveals that stereotyping of personality traits increases steadily in _____, becoming adultlike around age ____. (524)

4. Describe the pattern of children's trait learning. (524-525)

_____
_____

5. Throughout the school years, children regard the subjects of _____, _____, and _____ as more for girls and _____, _____, and _____ as more for boys. (525)

6. By the mid-elementary school years, children have acquired a general stereotype of _____ as a "masculine" pursuit. (525)

7. From kindergarten to sixth grade, gender-stereotype flexibility (increases/stays the same/decreases). (525)

8. Gender stereotypes become more flexible as children develop the capacity to integrate conflicting _____ and consider the individual's unique _____. (525)

9. True or False: Accompanying gender-stereotype flexibility is an increased trend to view gender differences as primarily biologically influenced. (525)

10. How do children and adults evaluate violations of gender-role expectations for behavior? (526)

_____
_____

Individual, Sex-Related, and Ethnic Differences in Gender Stereotyping

1. The various components of gender stereotyping--_____,
_____, _____, and _____
_____ -- (do/do not) correlate highly during the years when children are
developing knowledge of gender stereotypes. (526)

2. (Boys/Girls) hold more rigid gender-stereotyped views throughout childhood and
adolescence. (526)

3. (Boys/Girls) are more likely to devalue the achievements of (males/females).
(526)

4. True or False: A few recent studies indicate that boys' views of gender roles may be
growing more flexible. (526)

5. Black children hold (more/less) stereotyped views of females than do white children.
What factor may account for this difference? (526)

_____

6. SES differences in gender stereotyping (are/are not) present in childhood. In
adolescence and adulthood, higher-SES individuals tend to hold (more/less) flexible
views than lower-SES individuals. (526)

Gender Stereotyping and Gender-Role Adoption

1. Do children's gender-stereotyped patterns of thinking influence their gender-role
adoption? (527)

_____

_____

2. Give three reasons why gender-related expectations may not always be reflected in
gender-typed behavior. (527)
A._____
B._____
C._____

3. Stereotype (knowledge/flexibility) is a good predictor of gender-role adoption during
the school years. (527)

Influences on Gender Stereotyping and Gender-Role Adoption

1. According to _____ theorists, direct teaching is the way gender-
stereotyped knowledge and behaviors are transmitted to children. (527)

The Case for Biology

1. What two sources of evidence support the role of biological influences on gender typing? (528)

A._____

B._____

2. Most societies promote _____ traits in males and _____ traits in females, but great diversity exists in the magnitude of this difference. (528)

3. Why is there less diversity in personality traits and behaviors between girls and boys in Nyansongo than in other villages? (528)

_____

_____

_____

4. How has Sweden's progressive family policy affected the gender beliefs and behaviors of its youths? (529)

_____

_____

_____

_____

5. True or False: Cultural reversals of traditional gender typing do not exist. (528)

6. What effect does exposure to sex hormones during certain sensitive periods have on animals? (528-529)

_____

_____

7. Maccoby argues that hormonal effects (do/do not) extend to humans. As early as the preschool years, children prefer _____ playmates, and this preference continues until adolescence. (529)

8. According to Maccoby, why is sex segregation among young children so widespread and persistent? (529-530)

_____

_____

_____

9. Play-style preferences are especially powerful in (girls'/boys') choice of playmates. (530)

10. What factors other than sex hormones contribute to gender segregation? (530)

_____

11. Describe the behavior of boys and girls with congenital adrenal hyperplasia (CAH). (530)

_____

_____

_____

12. According to Money and Ehrhardt, _____
supports "masculine" gender-role behavior. (530)

13. What environmental factors could account for the behavior of girls with CAH? (531)

_____

_____

14. Research on individuals reared as members of the other sex because they had ambiguous genitals indicates that in most cases, gender typing is consistent with (genetic sex/sex of rearing). (531)

15. Research on the impact of sex hormones on gender typing indicates that they affect _____ and _____. (531)

16. How can biological factors be modified by experience? (531)

_____

The Case for Environment

1. What happens when adults are asked to observe a neutrally dressed infant who is labeled as either a boy or a girl? (531)

_____

2. True or False: Among new parents, gender-biased perceptions of infants are much weaker than among adults in general. (531)

3. List three ways that parents continue to hold different perceptions and expectations of their sons and daughters. (532)
A._____
B._____
C._____

4. Parents emphasize the child-rearing values of _____, _____, and _____ as important for sons. They regard _____, _____, and _____ as important for daughters. (532)

5. A combined analysis of 172 studies reported that, on the whole, differences in the way parents socialize boys and girls (are/are not) large. (532)

6. (Younger/Older) children receive more direct training in gender roles from parents. (532)

7. How do parents encourage "gender-appropriate" play activities and behaviors in infancy and early childhood? (532)

_____

_____

_____

8. Early in development, parents provide experiences that encourage _____,

_____, _____,

and _____ in boys. They promote _____,

_____, and _____ in girls. (532)

9. In teaching situations, parents demand greater _____ from boys and behave in a more _____ fashion with sons. (532-533)

10. In a longitudinal study, parents rated daughters as more competent in _____ and rated sons as more competent in _____ and _____. (533)

11. What influences parents' judgments about the relative competencies of daughters and sons? What impact do these judgments have on the children's perceptions? (533)

_____

_____

_____

12. Women's progress in entering and excelling at male-dominated professions has been (rapid/slow). In virtually all fields, women's achievements (lag behind/exceed) those of men, who _____, _____

_____, _____, and _____

_____ (534)

13. _____ messages play a role in gender differences in achievement. Although girls' grades are (lower/higher) than those of boys', they reach adolescence (more/less) confident of their abilities and more likely to (overestimate/underestimate) their achievement. (534)

14. True or False: Even though female valedictorians outperformed their male counterparts in college courses, they achieved at lower levels after career entry. (534)

15. What four experiences do academically talented girls who continue to achieve have in common? (534)

A._____

B._____

C._____

D._____

16. How does differential treatment by parents extend to the freedom granted children in their everyday lives? (533)

_____

_____

17. What are three possible consequences of sons' engaging in "feminine" housework when fathers hold stereotypical views? (535)

A._____

B._____

C._____

18. How do children growing up in countercultural families committed to gender equality differ from those in other families? (535)

_____

_____

19. In most aspects of differential treatment of boys and girls, (fathers/mothers) are the ones who discriminate the most. (535)

20. The same-sex-child bias is more pronounced for (fathers/mothers). (535)

21. In what ways do teachers reinforce pupils of both sexes for "feminine" rather than "masculine" behavior? (535)

_____

22. In what ways do teachers maintain or extend gender roles taught at home? (535)

_____

_____

23. At older ages, teachers praise boys for their _____ and girls for their _____. (535)

24. How can teachers promote gender equality? (536)

_____

_____

25. When teachers intervene to promote gender equality, (boys/girls) are more responsive, and the changes in children's behavior are (long lived/short lived). (536)

26. In what ways are children exposed to gender-typed models? (536)

_____

_____

_____

27. Children who often see their parents cross traditional gender lines (less/more) often endorse gender stereotypes. (536)

28. List three ways that girls with career-oriented mothers show special benefits of being exposed to nonstereotyped models. (536)

A._____

B._____

C._____

29. Children of divorced parents, in homes without a same-sex parent, are (less/more) gender typed. (536)

30. By age ____, same-sex peers positively reinforce one another for "gender-appropriate" play by _____, _____, _____, or _____ in the activity of an agemate. When preschoolers display "gender-inappropriate" play, they are _____ and _____. (536)

31. Peer rejection is greater for (girls/boys) who frequently engage in "cross-gender" behavior. (536)

32. To get their way with male peers, boys more often rely on _____, _____, and _____. Girls learn to emphasize _____ and _____ with female peers. (536-537)

33. Boys _____ girls' gentle communication tactics. (537)

34. How can teachers promote mixed-sex interaction? (537)

_____

_____

35. What is a possible negative consequence of mixed-sex interaction? (537)

_____

36. Growing up with siblings also affects gender typing, but the effects are complex because their impact depends on _____ and _____. (537)

37. In an observational study, the play behaviors of same-sex siblings in their homes were _____. Among mixed-sex siblings, play choices were determined by the _____. (537)

38. In a laboratory setting, preference for "other-gender" toys was (more/less) common among children whose siblings were all of their own sex. (537)

39. Individuals with same-sex siblings are (more/less) stereotyped in their interests and personality characteristics than are those from mixed-sex families. (537)

40. Studies reporting a modeling and reinforcement effect were limited to children from _____ families. Those reporting a differentiation effect included children from _____ families. (537)

41. In what ways may families in which siblings are all of the same sex provide opportunities to step out of traditional gender roles? (537)

_____

_____

Gender Identity

1. _____ is a person's perception of the self as relatively masculine or feminine in characteristics. (538)

2. How do researchers measure children's gender identity? (538)

_____

_____

3. Although the majority of individuals view themselves in gender-typed terms, a substantial minority have a type of gender identity called _____. They score high on both masculine and feminine personality characteristics. (538)

4. Gender identity (is/is not) a good predictor of psychological adjustment. (538)

5. Masculine and androgynous children have a (lower/higher) sense of self-esteem, whereas feminine individuals often have (low/high) self-esteem. (538)

6. Androgynous individuals are more _____ in behavior and show greater maturity of _____. (538)

7. The _____ component of androgyny is largely responsible for the superior psychology health of androgynous women. (538)

Emergence of Gender Identity

1. How do children develop gender-role identities? According to social learning theory, _____ comes before _____. Preschoolers first acquire gender-typed responses through _____ and _____. (539)

2. Cognitive-developmental theory emphasizes that _____ come before _____. Children first develop _____ _____, the understanding that sex remains the same even if clothing, hairstyle, and play activities change. Then children use this idea to guide their actions. (539)

3. _____ first proposed that before age 6 or 7, children cannot maintain the constancy of their gender. (539)

4. Name and describe the three stages of development of gender constancy, as proposed by Kohlberg. (539)

A._____

_____

B._____

_____

C._____

_____

5. Mastery of gender constancy is associated with attainment of _____, as Kohlberg assumed. (539)

6. Poor performance on gender constancy tasks results both from cognitive immaturity and _____. (539)

7. True or False: Children as young as 3 who are aware of genital characteristics usually answer gender-constancy questions correctly. (539)

8. Is gender constancy responsible for children's gender-typed behavior? Why or why not? (540)

_____

_____

_____

9. How does a cross-sectional study support the assumptions of social learning theory about gender-role adoption? (540)

_____

_____

_____

10. True or False: Preschoolers who reach the stage of gender labeling early show especially rapid development of "gender-appropriate" play preferences and are more knowledgeable about gender stereotypes than are their late-labeling peers. (540)

11. Some studies report that gender constancy leads to a rise in _____ activity. Others find that it predicts _____. (540)

12. The impact of gender constancy on gender typing (is/is not) great. (540)

Gender Identity During Middle Childhood

1. Describe the development of gender identity for boys and girls during middle childhood. (540)

_____

_____

_____

2. Girls (do/do not) increase their preference for gender-typed activities in middle childhood. (540)

3. What cognitive and social forces promote the changes in gender identity and behavior? (540-541)

_____

_____

_____

Gender Identity During Adolescence

1. Describe the development of gender identity for boys and girls during adolescence. (541)

_____

_____

_____

2. How do the following factors account for a period of gender intensification? (541)
A. Biological:_____
B. Social:_____
C. Cognitive:_____

3. As young people move toward a mature personal identity, they become (more/less) concerned with others' opinions of them and (more/less) involved in finding meaningful values to include in their self-definitions. This results in a(n) (increase/decrease) in stereotypic self-perceptions. (541)

Individual Differences

1. A more (masculine/feminine) and less (masculine/feminine) identity is associated with a higher sense of overall _____ as well as better performance on _____ and _____ tasks. (541)

2. Girls with (feminine/masculine) orientations are more popular with agemates. (541)

3. A gender identity that leans toward the (feminine/masculine) side seems to be the key factor in the majority of positive outcomes. (541)

4. According to recent theory and research, masculine and feminine self-perceptions arise from _____ and _____. (541)

Gender Schema Theory

1. Gender schema theory is a(n) _____ to gender typing that combines _____ and _____ features. (541)

2. Discuss how self-perceptions become gender typed and serve as additional gender schemas. (541-542)

_____
_____
_____

3. According to gender schema theory, gender stereotypes and gender-role preferences are self-perpetuating, because children _____ and _____ schema-consistent information, whereas they _____, _____, or _____ schema-inconsistent information. (542)

4. True or False: Among children with strong stereotypical beliefs, self- perceptions, and activity preferences, gender-schematic thinking is especially extreme. (543)

5. In an experiment, the impact of "gender classrooms" was largely limited to _____, children who had trouble understanding that a person can belong to more than one social category at once. (543)

6. When 5- to 10-year-olds were taught that ability and interest, not gender, determine whether a person can do a job well, they gained in _____ and memory for _____. (543)

To What Extent Do Boys and Girls *Really* Differ in Gender-Stereotyped Attributes?

1. Describe how boys and girls differ in three mental abilities. (544)
A._____
B._____
C._____

2. Describe how boys and girls differ in three personality traits. (544)
A._____
B._____
C._____

3. Sex usually accounts for about _____ to _____ percent of individual differences. (544)

4. During the past several decades, the gender gap has (widened/narrowed) in all areas of mental ability for which differences have been identified except _____ _____. (544)

Mental Abilities

1. True or False: Boys and girls do not vary in specific mental abilities; however, they do differ in intelligence. (544)

2. In what ways are girls ahead in language progress early in development? (545)

_____

_____

3. True or False: Currently, girls' advantage on tests of general verbal ability is substantial compared to boys. (545)

4. Girls' early advantage in language skills may be fostered by their faster rate of _____, believed to promote earlier development of the (right/left) cerebral hemisphere, where _____ functions are often housed. (545)

5. In what ways could experience contribute to girls' superior language and reading performance? (545-546)

_____

_____

6. The male advantage in mathematics is clearly evident among highly gifted students by age ____. Among all students, the size of the difference is (large/small), but among the most capable, the gender gap is (insignificant/considerable). (546)

7. Sex-related differences in mathematics (are/are not) present on all test items. The difference appears on tests of _____. (546-547)

8. One common assumption is that sex-related differences in mathematical ability are rooted in boys' superior _____. (547)

9. Describe two spatial tasks where the gender gap favors males. (546)
A._____
B._____

10. Sex differences on _____, involving analysis of complex visual forms, are weak or nonexistent. (546)

11. Discuss a hypothesis that seeks to explain why sex differences in spatial abilities emerge by middle childhood and persist throughout the life span. (546)

_____

_____

_____

314

12. How might experience contribute to males' superior spatial performance? (547)

_____

_____

13. Boys are advantaged not only in mental rotation but in math _____.
When their grades are poorer than girls', boys judge themselves to be (worse/better) at math. (547)

14. What types of social pressures contribute to girls' underrepresentation among the mathematically talented? (547)

_____

_____

15. When parents hold nonstereotyped gender-role values, daughters are (less/more) likely to show (gains/declines) in math and science achievement at adolescence. (548)

16. What is the evidence on girls' math and science achievement in single-sex secondary schools? (548)

_____

_____

Personality Traits

1. Beginning in the preschool years, girls perform slightly better than boys when asked to make judgments of others' emotional states using _____.
Except for _____, girls also express feelings more freely. (548)

2. True or False: Preschool and adolescent girls display greater empathy than do boys. (548)

3. True or False: Research suggests that girls are naturally more nurturant. (548)

4. Girls are given far (less/more) encouragement to express and reflect on feelings than are boys. (549)

5. Why is it likely that activity environments play a major role in girls' greater compliance and dependency? (549)

_____

_____

_____

6. In one study, the assertive and compliant tendencies of preschoolers of both sexes (were/were not) easily modified by assigning them to classroom activities that differed in degree of adult structure. (549)

7. The most common psychological problem of adolescence is _____.
About ___ to ___ percent of adolescents have had one or more _____
_____. (549)

8. True or False: Depressive symptoms occur twice as often in adolescent boys as girls. (549)

9. Describe how the developmental changes of adolescence combined with gender-typed coping styles seem to be responsible for girls being more prone to depression. (550)

_____
_____
_____

10. Teachers and parents tend to (overlook/recognize) teenagers' depressive symptoms; 70 to 80 percent (do not/do) receive treatment. (550)

11. When is the gender gap in aggression likely to appear in childhood? (550)

_____
_____

12. Although boys are more _____ aggressive than girls, girls exceed boys in another form of hostility--_____. (550)

13. The percentage of girls who use relational aggression is (smaller than/ the same as/larger than) the percentage of boys who frequently engage in direct attacks. (550)

14. Why do almost all researchers agree that biology must be involved in male aggression? (551)

_____

15. It is likely that in humans, only a(n) _____ for aggression results from androgen exposure. (551)

16. Adolescence is a phase in which _____ have implications for aggressive behavior. Adolescent boys who are high in androgens are more _____, and they display (less/more) aggression with peers. (551)

17. Higher _____ and _____ were linked to more frequent expressions of anger by adolescent girls. (551)

18. Why are boys more likely to exhibit aggressive behavior as the result of coercive child-rearing practices and strife-ridden families? (551-552)

_____
_____
_____
_____

Developing Non-Gender-Stereotyped Children

1. Bem suggests that parents and teachers make a special effort to delay young children's learning of gender-stereotyped messages. What are some ways to do this? (552)

_____
_____
_____

2. Once children notice the wide array of gender stereotypes, parents and teachers can _____ and can explain that _____ and _____ should determine a person's occupation. (552)

ASK YOURSELF...

13.1 Four-year-old Trixie announced to her 8-year-old sister, Natasha, that girls can't drive police cars. Natasha responded, "Yes they can. If mom can drive our car, she can drive a police car." Explain how cognitive development supports Natasha's flexible view of gender stereotypes. (p. 527)

13.2 Dennis discovered that he was the only boy in a home economics cooking class. "How are we supposed to be your friends if that's where you spend your time?" Tom and Bill complained at lunchtime. Cite research that sheds light on Tom and Bill's negative reaction to Dennis's "cross-gender" behavior. (p. 527)

13.3 One day, Pat and Chris each announced to their mothers that they had to do a science project. Pat's mother said, "Perhaps you'd like to go to the library tonight to choose your topic." Chris's mother said, "You'd better get started right away. We already have some books on whales, so you can do it on that." Is Pat more likely to be a boy or a girl? How about Chris? Explain, using research findings. (p. 538)

13.4 Geraldine cut her 3-year-old daughter Fern's hair very short for the summer. When Fern looked in the mirror, she said, "I don't wanna be a boy," and began to cry. Why is Fern upset about her short hairstyle, and what can Geraldine do to help? (p. 544)

13.5 When 4-year-old Roger was in the hospital, he was cared for by a male nurse named Jared. After Roger recovered, he told his friends about Dr. Jared. Using gender schema theory, explain why Roger remembered Jared as a doctor, not a nurse. (p. 544)

13.6 Thirteen-year-old Donna reached puberty early and feels negatively about her physical appearance. She also has a feminine gender identity. Explain why Donna is at risk for depression. (p. 552)

CONNECTIONS

13.1 Cite parallels between the development of gender stereotyping and children's understanding of ethnicity and social class. (See Chapter 11, page 463.)

13.2 Girls are more susceptible than boys to learned helplessness in achievement situations. Explain why this is so, using research in this chapter (see page 533) and in Chapter 11 (see page 455).

13.3 Describe gender-stereotyped messages conveyed to children on television. (See Chapter 15, page 619.)

13.4 Describe gains in perspective taking that lead young teenagers to be very concerned with what others think, thereby contributing to gender intensification. (See Chapter 11, page 466.)

13.5 Return to Chapter 11, page 471, and review sex-related differences in children's friendships. Can the nature of girls' friendships shed light on why they tend to express hostility through relational aggression? (Hint: Consult Chapter 12, page 511.)

13.6 Describe the consequences of overt and relational aggression for children's peer acceptance. (See Chapter 15, page 606.)

PUZZLE 13

Across

1 Gender ___, the reflection of gender stereotypes in everyday behavior
5 Gender-stereotype ___, the belief that both genders can display gender-stereotyped personality traits
8 Gender ___, when gender constancy is mastered
11 Gender ___, view of the self as relatively masculine or feminine
15 Gender ___, when gender identities of both sexes become more traditional
16 ___-related refers to comparisons without specifying the source of those differences

Down

2 Gender ___, or first stage of gender constancy
3 Gender identity of a person who scores high on both masculine and feminine characteristics
4 Involves judgments about biological or environmental influences, or both
6 Masculine-stereotyped personality traits
7 Gender ___ theory, an information-processing approach to gender typing
9 Feminine-stereotyped personality traits
10 Gender ___, or beliefs about characteristics appropriate for males and females
12 Gender ___, the process of developing gender-linked beliefs, gender roles, and identity
13 Gender ___, the understanding that sex remains the same even if clothing or hairstyle changes
14 Gender ___, the stage at which preschoolers have a partial understanding of the permanence of their sex

PRACTICE TEST

1. _____ is the process of developing gender-linked beliefs, gender roles, and gender identity. (522)
   A. Gender stereotypes
   B. Gender assessment
   C. Gender formation
   D. Gender typing

2. Gender stereotypes: (523)
   A. have been largely erased by the political activism of the 1970s and 1980s.
   B. in the form of the instrumental-expressive dichotomy are limited to Western nations.
   C. show little consistency or stability.
   D. are deeply ingrained patterns of thinking.

3. Research on gender stereotyping in early childhood indicates that: (524)
   A. preschoolers use gender stereotypes as flexible guidelines.
   B. most preschoolers believe that characteristics associated with sex determine it.
   C. children learn to label their own sex and that of others around age 4.
   D. children do not prefer "gender-appropriate" activities until the school years.

4. Research on gender stereotyping indicates that: (524)
   A. 5-year-olds have not yet established any gender stereotypes of activities and occupations.
   B. as children move through middle school, stereotypes become more rigid.
   C. the first stereotypes of traits reflect own-sex favoritism.
   D. once trait stereotyping is well under way, elementary school pupils are most familiar with negative feminine and positive masculine traits.

5. Gender stereotyping in achievement areas: (525)
   A. does not occur among school-age children.
   B. occurs only in the United States.
   C. suggests that by the mid-elementary school years, children regard achievement as a "masculine" pursuit.
   D. occurs when male failures are interpreted as due to lack of ability.

6. Research on gender stereotypes indicates that: (525)
   A. accompanying gender-stereotype flexibility is a trend to view gender differences as socially influenced.
   B. gender-stereotype flexibility decreases from kindergarten to sixth grade.
   C. children and adults are fairly tolerant of male violations of gender-role expectations for behavior.
   D. there is greater social pressure on girls and woman to conform to gender roles.

323

7. Research indicates that: (526)
    A. the various components of gender stereotyping correlate highly.
    B. girls hold more gender-stereotyped views throughout childhood and adolescence.
    C. black children hold more stereotyped views of females.
    D. higher-SES individuals tend to hold more flexible gender-stereotyped views than their lower-SES counterparts.

8. Which of the following does NOT support the argument that biological influences on gender typing are substantial? (528-530)
    A. The instrumental-expressive dichotomy is reflected in the gender stereotyping of many national groups.
    B. Preschool and school-age children prefer to play with children of their own sex.
    C. Girls with CAH display "masculine" gender-role behavior.
    D. Cultural reversals of traditional gender typing exist.

9. Play preferences: (530)
    A. for same-sex peers do not occur until age 6.
    B. for same-sex peers decline by third grade.
    C. for boys are based more on play style rather than gender.
    D. are not influenced by hormones.

10. Research examining environmental factors influences on gender-role development indicates that: (532)
    A. age effects emerge in the way parents socialize boys and girls.
    B. older children receive more direct training in gender roles than do younger children.
    C. parents perceive male and female newborns similarly.
    D. parents seldom interpret children's behavior in stereotyped ways.

11. In teaching situations with their school-age children, parents: (532)
    A. demand greater independence from girls.
    B. more often ignore a son's request for help.
    C. behave in a more mastery-oriented fashion with daughters.
    D. frequently stray from task goals to play with sons.

12. Which of the following is NOT true of sex-related differences in vocational development? (534)
    A. Adolescent girls are more likely than boys to underestimate their achievement.
    B. High school teachers tend to view bright female students as more capable than their male counterparts.
    C. Educational aspirations of mathematically talented females decline considerably during college.
    D. The proportion of girls in gifted programs continues to drop during high school.

13. Research on differential treatment of boys and girls indicates that: (535)
    A. mothers are the ones who discriminate the most.
    B. parents seem especially committed to ensuring the gender typing of children of the opposite sex.
    C. mothers more than fathers encourage "gender-appropriate" behavior in childhood.
    D. the same-sex-child bias is more pronounced for fathers.

14. Teachers: (535)
    A. often reinforce pupils of both sexes for "feminine" rather than "masculine" behavior.
    B. interrupt boys more often than girls during conversation.
    C. usually reprimand boys for giving a wrong answer rather than for misbehavior.
    D. tend to praise boys for obedience, girls for knowledge.

15. Traditional gender-role beliefs and behaviors: (536)
    A. are positively reinforced by same-sex peers.
    B. are increased when a child lives in a household without a same-sex parent.
    C. are stronger when children have parents who cross traditional gender lines.
    D. are especially strong when girls have career-oriented mothers.

16. Which of the following is NOT found when observing peer interactions? (536-537)
    A. Male peers ignore boys who frequently engage in "cross-gender" behavior, even when they enter "masculine" activities.
    B. Fostering mixed-sex interaction always reduces gender stereotypes.
    C. Boys ignore girls' gentle social influence tactics.
    D. Girls and boys develop different styles of social influence in gender-segregated groups.

17. Children with siblings: (537)
    A. of the same sex in small, two-child families often experience a differentiation effect.
    B. all of the same sex in large families tend to be more gender typed.
    C. all of the same sex are more likely to be assigned "cross-gender" chores.
    D. tend to model the behavior of the sibling closest in age.

18. Research on gender identity indicates that: (538)
    A. it is not a good predictor of psychological adjustment.
    B. masculine and androgynous children have higher self-esteem.
    C. androgynous individuals tend to have the lowest self-esteem.
    D. individuals with a "feminine" identity show greater maturity of moral judgment than those with other orientations.

19. Anne knows that boys grow up to be men and girls grow up to be women. Nevertheless, she also thinks that if a boy has long hair, he becomes a girl. She is in the _____ stage of development. (539)
    A. gender constancy
    B. gender stability
    C. gender consistency
    D. gender permanence

20. Which of the following is NOT true of gender constancy? (539-540)
    A. Cognitive immaturity is the sole reason for preschoolers' poor performance on gender constancy tasks.
    B. Mastery of gender constancy is associated with attainment of conservation.
    C. Children as young as 3 who are aware of genital characteristics usually answer gender constancy questions correctly.
    D. Gender constancy does not initiate gender-role conformity.

21. During middle childhood: (540)
    A. girls' identification with feminine characteristics increases.
    B. boys are the more androgynous of the sexes.
    C. girls increase their preference for gender-typed activities.
    D. boys strengthen their identification with the "masculine" role.

22. Research on gender identity indicates that: (541)
    A. androgynous children are advantaged in both academic and social domains.
    B. girls with masculine orientations are more popular with agemates.
    C. Gender identities that lean toward the masculine side are associated with more positive outcomes.
    D. individual differences in gender identity are strongly related to gender-role behavior.

23. Sex-related differences in spatial abilities: (546)
    A. are especially large on spatial visualization tasks.
    B. emerge in middle childhood but then decline and disappear in adulthood.
    C. on mental rotation tasks are not decreased when females are trained in the tasks.
    D. may be caused at least in part by prenatal exposure to androgen hormones.

24. Which of the following is NOT true of sex-related differences in personality traits? (548-549)
    A. Girls are naturally more nurturant than boys.
    B. Girls' tendency in the preschool years to be more compliant than boys is largely a learned pattern of behavior.
    C. Girls are given much more encouragement to express and reflect on feelings than are boys.
    D. Activity environments of boys and girls differ and influence their social behaviors.

25. Research indicates that: (551)
   A. gender-atypical aggressive children have less severe emotional and behavior problems.
   B. in adolescence, girls start to display more overt forms of hostility.
   C. arguing between husband and wife is more likely to promote hostility in boys.
   D. lower estrogens and androgens are linked to more frequent expressions of anger by adolescent girls.

CHAPTER 14

THE FAMILY

SUMMARY

The family is the child's first and longest-lasting context for development. Although other social settings also mold children's development, in power and breadth of influence none equals the family. The human family originated with our hunting-and-gathering ancestors, for whom it was uniquely suited to promote survival. Important functions of the modern family include reproduction, socialization, and emotional support.

According to the social systems perspective, the family consists of a complex network of bidirectional relationships that continually readjust as family members change over time. The quality of these relationships, and therefore children's development, depends in part on links established with formal and informal social supports in the surrounding community.

Child-rearing practices can be organized along two dimensions: demandingness and responsiveness. When combined, these characteristics yield four parenting styles: authoritative, authoritarian, permissive, and uninvolved. Consistent SES differences in child rearing exist, and ethnic variations in child rearing can be understood in terms of cultural values and the context in which families live.

Rapid changes in family life have taken place in Western industrialized nations. The recent trend toward a smaller family size is associated with more favorable child development. Most children grow up with at least one sibling. Parents' early differential treatment of siblings has a powerful influence on children's personality development. Only children are just as well adjusted and socially competent as other children and advantaged in some respects. Adopted children and adolescents have more learning and emotional difficulties than do their nonadopted agemates. Transracially and transculturally adopted young people typically develop identities that are healthy blends of their birth and rearing backgrounds.

Children of never-married mothers show slightly better academic performance and emotional adjustment than do children of divorced or remarried mothers but not as good as children in first-marriage families. Large numbers of American children experience the divorce of their parents. Although divorce is painful for children, evidence shows that remaining in a high-conflict intact family is much worse than making the transition to a low-conflict, single-parent household. Effective parenting is the most important factor in helping children adapt to life in a single-parent or a blended family.

Maternal employment is related to positive outcomes in children, although these vary depending on the children's sex and SES, the demands of the mother's job, and the father's participation in child rearing. High-quality child care fosters cognitive, language, and social development. Unfortunately, much child care in the United States is substandard and poses serious risks to children's development. Self-care children who have a history of authoritative child rearing, are monitored from a distance by telephone calls, and have regular after-school chores appear responsible and well adjusted.

Child maltreatment is related to factors within the family, community, and larger culture, and efforts to prevent it must be directed at each of these levels. Child and parent characteristics often feed on one another to produce abusive behavior. A society that approves of force and violence as appropriate means for solving problems promotes child abuse.

LEARNING OBJECTIVES

After reading this chapter, you should be able to:

14.1 Discuss the evolutionary origins and adaptive value of the family among our hunting-and-gathering ancestors. (557-558)

14.2 Name five functions that must be carried out for a society to survive, and indicate which ones remain primarily the province of the family. (558-559)

14.3 Describe the social systems perspective on family functioning, including its view of family interaction and the influence of surrounding social contexts. (559-562)

14.4 Discuss the influence of four child-rearing styles on development, and explain how effective parents adapt child rearing to children's growing competence during middle childhood and adolescence. (563-568)

14.5 Describe socioeconomic and ethnic variations in child rearing, including the impact of poverty. (568-571)

14.6 Describe the influence of family size on child rearing, and explain how sibling relationships change with age and how they affect development. (571-575)

14.7 Discuss children's development and adjustment in adoptive families, gay and lesbian families, and never-married single-parent families. (575-577)

14.8 Discuss factors that influence children's adjustment to divorce and blended families. (577-583)

14.9 Describe the influence of maternal employment and life in dual-earner families on children's development. (583-585)

14.10 Discuss the influence of child-care quality on preschoolers' development, the status of child care in the United States compared to other industrialized nations, and the impact of self-care on school-age children's adjustment. (585-587)

14.11 Discuss the multiple origins of child maltreatment, its consequences for development, and prevention strategies. (588-593)

STUDY QUESTIONS

Evolutionary Origins

1. The family in its most common form--a lifelong commitment between a man and woman who feed, shelter, and nurture their children until they reach maturity--arose _____ years ago among our _____ . (558)

2. Anthropologists believe that _____--the ability to walk upright on two legs--was an important evolutionary step that led to the human family unit. (558)

3. _____ percent of the history of our species was spent in the hunting-and-gathering stage. (558)

Functions of the Family

1. List five functions that must be carried out for a society to survive. (558)
A. _____
B. _____
C. _____
D. _____
E. _____

2. Of the five functions above, list the four that have been assumed partly or completely by institutions other than the family, and indicate the institutions involved. (558)
A. _____
B. _____
D. _____

3. In today's modern family, children are economic (contributors/liabilities)--one factor that has contributed to the (increasing/declining) birth rate in modern industrialized nations. (559)

4. Three important functions--_____, _____, and _____--remain primarily the province of the family. (559)

5. The _____ perspective views the family as a complex set of interacting relationships influenced by the larger social context. (559)

The Family as a Social System

1. Today, family systems theorists recognize that _____ exist in which the behaviors of each family member affect those of others. (559)

Direct Influences

1. Many studies show that when parents are firm but patient, children tend to _____, whereas parents who discipline with harshness and impatience, children _____. (560)

Indirect Influences

1. Interaction between any two members in a family is affected by others present in the setting. Bronfenbrenner called these indirect influences the effect of _____. (560)

2. List three reasons why a couple's marital happiness declines in the early weeks after a new baby's arrival. (561)
A._____
B._____
C._____

3. Women expect (more/less) help than they will get with their new baby from their partners. (561)

4. Explain why postponing childbearing until the late twenties or thirties eases the transition to parenthood. (561)
_____
_____
_____

5. Third parties can serve as effective _____ for children's development, or they can _____ children's well-being. (560)

6. What type of dispute is particularly harmful to children? (560)
_____

7. Describe an example of how a third party can help restore effective interaction in a family. (560)
_____

Adapting to Change

1. The interplay of forces within the family must (remain static/constantly adapt to changes in its members). (560)

The Family System in Context

1. Connections to formal organizations in the community influence parent-child relationships. Examples of these organizations include: (562)
_____

2. _____ of relatives, friends, and neighbors influence parent-child relationships. (562)

3. List four reasons why ties to the community reduce family stress and foster child development. (562)

A._____

B._____

C._____

D._____

Socialization Within the Family

1. Socialization begins in earnest during the _____ year, once children are first able to comply with parental directives. (563)

Styles of Child Rearing

1. List and define the two broad dimensions of parenting that emerged from Baumrind's observations of parents' interactions with their preschool children. (563)

A._____

_____

B._____

_____

2. Define the authoritative style of child rearing, and note its relationship to child outcomes. (563-564)

_____

_____

_____

_____

3. At older ages, authoritative child rearing is linked to _____,

_____, _____,

_____, and _____. (564)

4. Parents who use a(n) _____ are also demanding, but they place such a high value on _____ that they are _____ when children are unwilling to obey. If the child does not accept an adult's word in a(n) _____ manner, _____ are used. (564)

5. The authoritarian style is biased in favor of (children's/parents') needs. (564)

6. Describe child outcomes associated with authoritarian child rearing. (564)

_____

_____

7. In adolescence, young people with authoritarian parents are (better/less well) adjusted than are those with authoritative parents, but do better in school and are less likely to engage in antisocial acts than are those with _____ parents. (564)

8. Describe the permissive style of parenting and indicate the type of child it produces. (564)

_____
_____
_____

9. The link between permissive parenting and dependent, nonachieving behavior is especially strong for (girls/boys). (564)

10. In adolescence, parental indulgence is related to _____. Permissively reared teenagers are less involved in _____ and use _____ more frequently. (564)

11. Describe uninvolved parenting. (564-565)

_____
_____
_____

12. At its extreme, uninvolved parenting is _____. (565)

What Makes the Authoritative Style So Effective?

1. Baumrind emphasizes that not just firm control, but _____ and _____ use of firm control, facilitates development. (565)

2. Children of parents who go back and forth between _____ and _____ styles are especially aggressive and irresponsible and do very poorly in school. (565)

3. Child-rearing practices can either _____ or _____ difficult behavior. (565)

4. List five reasons authoritative child rearing supports children's competence and helps bring children's recalcitrant behavior under control. (565-566)
A._____
B._____
C._____
D._____
E._____

Adapting Child Rearing to Children's Development

1. During middle childhood, the amount of time children spend with parents declines (slightly/dramatically). (566)

2. What are some effective child-rearing strategies parents use with school-age children? (566)

_____

_____

3. Coercive discipline (increases/declines) during middle childhood. (566)

4. Effective parents of school-age children engage in _____, a transitional form of supervision in which they exercise general oversight while permitting children to be in charge of moment-to-moment decision making. (566)

5. Cite three parental tasks and one child task involved in a cooperative, coregulatory relationship. (566-567)
A. Parental:_____
B. Parental:_____
C. Parental:_____
D. Child:_____

6. During adolescence, young people in complex societies deal with the need to choose from many options by seeking _____, establishing themselves as separate, self-governing individuals. (567)

7. Autonomy has a vital _____ component, and it also has an important _____ component. It is closely related to the quest for _____. (567)

8. What changes within the adolescent support autonomy? (567)

_____

_____

9. Autonomy is a central task of _____, and it resurfaces at _____. (567)

10. Adolescents in troubled homes (do/do not) benefit when they can separate themselves emotionally from stressful parent-child interaction. (567)

11. Overall, autonomy achieved in the context of warm, supportive parent-child ties is most adaptive. It predicts _____, _____, _____, and _____. (567)

12. True or False: The primary task for parents and teenagers is simply to separate. (568)

Socioeconomic and Ethnic Variations in Child Rearing

1. A parenting style that is _____ but moderately _____ is the most common pattern around the world. (568)

2. Parents who work in skilled and semiskilled manual occupations place a high value on _____ characteristics, such as _____, _____, and _____. (568)

3. Parents in white-collar and professional occupations tend to emphasize _____ traits, such as _____, _____, and _____. (568)

4. The values and behaviors required for success in the work world are believed to affect parents' ideas about traits important to train in their children. Low-SES parents often feel a sense of _____ and a lack of _____ in relationships beyond the home. Higher-SES parents have a greater sense of _____ over their lives and are used to making _____ _____ and convincing others of their point of view. (568)

5. How do education and economic security contribute to SES differences in child rearing? (568)

_____

_____

_____

_____

6. Describe how constant stresses that accompany poverty weaken the family system. (569)

_____

_____

7. Compared to Caucasian-Americans, Chinese adults describe their own parenting techniques and those they experienced as children as _____. (569)

8. In Hispanic and Asian Pacific Island families, firm insistence on respect for _____ is paired with unusually high _____. This combination is believed to promote _____, _____ and _____. (569)

9. African-American mothers tend to rely on a(n) _____ in which they expect _____ from children. Forceful discipline may be necessary to protect children when parents have few _____ and live in _____. (570)

10. The African cultural tradition of _____, in which one or more adult relatives live with the parent-child _____, is a vital feature of black family life. (570)

11. How does the African-American extended family help reduce the stress of poverty and single parenthood? (571)

_____
_____
_____
_____

12. In families rearing adolescents, kinship support increases the likelihood of _____. (571)

13. Compared with African-American nuclear families, extended-family arrangements place more emphasis on _____ and _____ and _____ values. (571)

14. Older black adults are more likely to possess a strong _____ and to regard _____ as an important part of socialization. (571)

Family Lifestyles and Transitions

1. Rapid transitions in family life over the past several decades--a dramatic rise in _____, _____, and _____-- have reshaped the family system. (572)

From Large to Small Families

1. In the mid-1950s, the average number of children in an American family was ____. Today, it is ____. (572)

2. List four reasons why family size has declined. (572)
A._____
B._____
C._____
D._____

3. Overall, a smaller family size has (negative/positive) effects on parent-child interaction. (572)

4. Parents who have fewer children are more _____ and are less _____. They have more _____ to devote to each child. (572)

5. Anxiety is (less/more) common in small families. (572)

6. _____ and _____ probably contribute to higher rates of antisocial behavior and delinquency in families with many children. (572)

7. What other factors may be responsible for the negative relationship between family size and children's well-being? (572)

_____

8. ____ percent of American children grow up with at least one sibling. (572)

9. The common assumption that _____ is a key element in sibling interaction originated with _____ theory. (573)

10. A drop in maternal involvement with the older preschool child (does/does not) occur after the birth of a baby. (573)

11. Describe early ties between preschool children and their infant siblings. (573)

_____

_____

12. How do mothers' statements differ from those of siblings? (573)

_____

_____

13. The skills acquired during sibling interaction probably contribute to _____, _____, and _____. (573)

14. True or False: Positive sibling ties predict favorable adjustment, even among hostile children at risk for social difficulties. (573)

15. Children's _____ affects how positive or conflict ridden sibling interaction will be. (573)

16. In what ways are sibling relationships influenced by parental behavior? (573)

_____

_____

_____

17. Cold, intrusive child rearing is associated with sibling _____. When parents are hostile and coercive, _____ is promoted among all family members. (573-574)

18. During middle childhood, sibling conflict tends to (increase/decrease). (574)

19. What actions by parents tend to increase sibling conflict in middle childhood? (574)

_____

_____

20. Unequal treatment by (mothers/fathers) tends to result in greater sibling conflict. (574)

21. What are some positive aspects of sibling relationships during the school years? (574)

_____

_____

22. Older siblings' influence (increases/declines) during the teenage years, and sibling interaction becomes (more/less) intense during adolescence. (574)

One-Child Families

1. True or False: Research indicates that sibling relationships are essential for healthy development. (574)

2. Only children (are/are not) as socially competent as other children. (574)

3. True or False: Only children do not achieve as much in school as do children with siblings. (574)

4. Chinese only children (do/do not) differ from children with siblings in social skills and peer acceptance. (575)

5. List two disadvantages of a one-child family mentioned by parents. (575)
   A._____
   B._____

Adoptive Families

1. True or False: The availability of healthy babies for adoption has increased in recent years. (575)

2. What types of challenges do adoptive families face? (575)

_____

_____

_____

3. True or False: In a Swedish longitudinal study, researchers found that adoptees developed much more favorably than children reared in foster families or returned to their birth mothers. (575-576)

4. From _____ to _____ percent of parents who adopt children with special needs report high satisfaction with the adoptive experience. (576)

5. By adolescence, adoptees' lives are often complicated by unresolved curiosity about their _____. (576)

6. Most adoptees (are/are not) well adjusted as adults. (576)

Gay and Lesbian Families

1. Gay and lesbian parents (are/are not) as committed to and effective at the parental role as are heterosexual parents. (576)

2. What does research indicate about the effectiveness of gay fathers? (576)

_____

3. Children of gay and lesbian parents (are/are not) as well adjusted as other children, and the large majority are (heterosexual/homosexual). (576)

4. With time, interactions of homosexual parents with their families of origin become (less/more) positive. (576)

5. Under what circumstances do partners of homosexual parents tend to be more involved with children? (576-577)

_____

Never-Married Single-Parent Families

1. Children of never-married parents make up _____ percent of the child population in the United States. (577)

2. African-American women postpone marriage (less/more) and childbirth (less/more) than do all other American ethnic groups. (577)

3. Children of never-married mothers show slightly (worse/better) academic performance and emotional adjustment than do children of divorced or remarried mothers. (577)

Divorce

1. Between 1960 and 1985, the divorce rate in the United States _____. (577)

2. True or False: Currently, the divorce rate in the United States is the highest in the world. (577)

3. About _____ of divorced parents marry a second time, and _____ of these marriages end. (578)

4. Name three factors that make a difference in how children respond to divorce. (578)

A._____

B._____

C._____

5. Why is the period surrounding divorce often accompanied by a rise in family conflict? (578)

_____

_____

_____

_____

6. Describe the highly disorganized family situation called "minimal parenting." (578-579)

_____

_____

_____

7. The _____ immaturity of preschool and early school-age children makes it difficult for them to grasp the reasons behind their parents' separation. They tend to _____ and fear _____ by both parents. (579)

8. Younger children are often (mildly/profoundly) upset by divorce. They may _____ _____, displaying intense _____. Preschoolers are especially likely to _____. (579)

9. Older children's ability to _____ may reduce some of the pain of divorce. (579)

10. For older children, undesirable peer activities such as _____, _____, _____, and _____, are common. (579)

11. For some--especially the oldest child in the family--divorce can trigger _____ _____. (579)

12. True or False: Temperament can either reduce or increase children's risk for maladjustment. (579)

13. Girls sometimes respond to divorce with _____, _____, and _____. At other times, they show _____ behavior. (579)

14. True or False: Boys of divorcing parents tend to receive more emotional support and to be viewed more positively by mothers, teachers, and peers. (579)

15. The _____ cycles of interaction that boys often establish with their divorced mothers soon spread to _____. (579)

16. School problems after divorce are greater for (boys/girls). (579)

17. The majority of children show improved adjustment by ____ years after divorce. (579)

18. Which children are especially likely to experience lasting behavior problems after divorce? Why? (580)

_____

19. Among girls of divorced parents, the most consistent long-term effects involve _____ --a rise in _____, _____ _____, and _____. (580)

20. What is the overriding factor in positive adjustment following divorce? (580)

_____

_____

21. For girls, a good father-child relationship appears to contribute to _____ _____. For boys, it seems to affect _____ _____. (580)

22. Outcomes for sons are (better/worse) when the father is the custodial parent. (580)

23. How does contact with their father help boys? (580)

_____

_____

24. True or False: Divorce can ultimately result in better outcomes for children than does living in a high-conflict, intact family. (580)

25. Cognitive and social outcomes are improved if preschool and school-age children attend classrooms in which teachers create a(n) _____ atmosphere in which _____ is combined with _____. (580)

26. _____ is a national organization that provides _____ _____, _____, and _____ designed to relieve the problems of single parents. (580)

27. _____ for children are also available to help them through divorce. (580)

28. _____ consists of a series of meetings between divorcing adults and a trained professional, who tries to help them settle disputes. Research reveals that it increases _____, _____, and _____ among divorcing parents. (580)

29. In _____, the court grants the mother and father equal say in important decisions about the child's upbringing. (581)

30. What types of living arrangements for the children result from joint custody? (581)
_____
_____

31. The success of joint custody requires _____
_____. (581)

32. Today, _____ U.S. states permit grandparents to seek legal visitation judgments. This new policy is motivated by _____
_____. (581)

33. Research suggests that the courts are wise to _____ in awarding grandparent visitation privileges in divorce cases. (581)

34. Many single-parent families depend on _____ from the absent parent to relieve financial strain. A noncustodial father (is/is not) more likely to maintain contact with his children if he pays child support. (581)

Blended Families

1. If single parents remarry or cohabit, parent, stepparent, and children form a new family structure called the _____, or _____, family. (581)

2. List two aspects of blended families that make adjustment difficult for children. (581)
A._____
B._____

3. The most frequent form of blended family is a(n) _____ arrangement. (Girls/Boys) usually adjust quickly. (581)

4. Boys welcome a stepfather who is _____, _____
_____, and who _____
_____. (581)

5. After remarriage, mothers' friction with sons tends to decline due to _____
_____, _____, and
_____. (581)

6. Girls adapt (more/less) favorably when custodial mothers find new partners. Why? (581)

_____

7. Early adolescents of both sexes find it (harder/easier) to adjust to blended families. (581)

8. About _____ of adolescent boys and _____ of adolescent girls disengage from their stepfamilies. (582)

9. Remarriage for noncustodial fathers often leads to _____. They tend to withdraw from their "previous" families, more so if they have (daughters/sons). (582)

10. Give two reasons why children who have custodial fathers might react negatively to remarriage. (582)
A._____
B._____

11. Give two reasons why girls, especially, have a hard time getting along with their stepmothers. (582)
A._____
B._____

12. _____ and _____ can help parents and children adapt to the complexities of living in a blended family. (582)

13. The divorce rate for second marriages (is/is not) higher than for first marriages. (583)

14. True or False: A study of fourth-grade boys indicated that the number of marital transitions experienced had little impact on their adjustment. (583)

15. Two percent of the child population live with grandparents but apart from parents in _____. (584)

16. List two reasons why grandparents would assume custody of their grandchildren. (584)
A._____
B._____

17. Compared with children in divorced, single-parent families and in blended families, children reared by grandparents were _____, _____ _____, and _____. (584)

Maternal Employment and Dual-Earner Families

1. For children of any age, over _____ percent of their mothers are employed. (583)

2. Children of mothers who enjoy working and remain committed to parenting show _____ adjustment--_____,
_____, _____, and _____
_____. (583)

3. Employed mothers who value their parenting role are more likely to use _____
_____. (583)

4. Maternal employment (does/does not) reduce the total amount of time school-age children and adolescents spend with their mothers. It results in (more/less) time with their fathers. (583-584)

5. _____ and _____ are associated with less favorable outcomes. _____ employment seems to have benefits for children of all ages. (584)

6. _____ and _____ when children are ill would help many women juggle the demands of work and child rearing. At present, only _____ is mandated by U.S. federal law. (585)

Child Care

1. The tremendous shortage of affordable child care in the United States is reflected by the fact that _____ percent of employed mothers of 3- and 4-year-olds and _____ percent of mothers of school-age children get by without any child-care arrangements. (585)

2. Preschoolers in poor-quality child care score lower on measures of _____
and _____ skills. (585)

3. List some ingredients of high quality child care. (585-586)

_____
_____
_____

4. In the United States, from _____ to _____ percent of child-care homes are unlicensed and therefore not monitored for quality. (586)

5. Over _____ percent of caregivers leave their jobs annually. (586)

6. Describe child care in Australia and Western Europe. (587)

_____
_____
_____

7. True or False: The United States has a national child care policy and is at approximately the same level as other industrialized nations in supply, quality, and affordability of child care. (587)

Self-Care

1. An estimated ____ million 5- to 12-year-olds in the United States regularly look after themselves during after-school hours. (587)

2. Self-care children who have a history of _____, are _____
_____, and have _____ _____
appear responsible and well adjusted. Those who are _____ are
more likely to bend to peer pressures and engage in antisocial behavior. (587)

3. Before age ____ or ____, children should not be left unsupervised. (587)

4. After-school programs for 6- to 13-year-olds are (common/rare) in American communities. Enrolling children in poor-quality after-school care can _____
_____. High-quality after-school care results in _____
_____, _____, and _____.
(587)

Vulnerable Families: Child Maltreatment

Incidence and Definitions

1. Child maltreatment (is/is not) especially common in large industrialized nations. (588)

2. True or False: Child maltreatment occurs so often in the United States that a recent government committee called it a "national emergency." (588)

3. A total of _____ cases of child maltreatment were reported to juvenile authorities in 1997, an increase of ____ percent over the previous decade. (588)

4. List and define five forms of child maltreatment. (588-589)
A._____
B._____
C._____
D._____
E._____

5. Although all experts recognize that these five types exist, they do not agree on how _____ and _____ an adult's actions must be to be called maltreatment. (589)

6. Why is consensus on a definition of child maltreatment important? (589)

_____

7. Some investigators regard _____ abuse as the most destructive form of child maltreatment. (589)

8. What problems occur if definitions of psychological abuse are too narrow or too lenient? (589)
Too narrow:_____
Too lenient:_____

9. Until recently, child sexual abuse was viewed as a (frequent/rare) occurrence. (590)

10. Over _____ cases of child sexual abuse are reported each year. (590)

11. Sexual abuse is committed more often against (boys/girls). Its incidence is highest in _____ childhood. (590)

12. What are the characteristics of child abusers? (590)

_____

_____

13. Reported cases of child sexual abuse are strongly linked to _____, _____, and _____. (590)

14. Adjustment problems of child sexual abuse victims include _____, _____, _____, _____, and _____. Younger children react with _____, _____ _____, and _____. (590)

15. Adolescent victims may _____ or show _____, _____, and _____. (590)

16. Sexually abused children frequently display _____ and _____ _____ beyond their years. (590)

17. In treatment of child sexual abuse, _____ with both children and parents is usually necessary. (591)

18. What are some ways to prevent child sexual abuse from continuing. (591)

_____

_____

Origins of Child Maltreatment

1. When child maltreatment first became a topic of research in the early 1960s, it was viewed as rooted in _____. (589)

2. True or False: A single "abusive personality type" exists among adults who maltreat their children. (589)

3. Describe characteristics that make certain children more likely to become targets of abuse. (589)

_____

_____

4. Describe personal and situational conditions that increase the chances that parents will maltreat their children. (590-591)

_____

_____

_____

5. List two reasons why the majority of abusive parents are isolated from both formal and informal social supports in their communities. (591)

A._____

_____

B._____

_____

6. _____, _____, and _____ profoundly affect the chances that child maltreatment will occur when parents feel overburdened. (592)

7. True or False: In the United States, strong support still exists for the use of violence as an appropriate way to solve problems. (592)

8. Over ____ percent of American parents report using slaps and spankings to discipline their children. (592)

Consequences of Child Maltreatment

1. The family circumstances of maltreated children impair the development of

_____, _____, _____

_____, and _____. (592)

2. Describe the consequences of maltreatment for children. (592)

_____

_____

3. A family characteristic strongly associated with child abuse is _____
_____. (592)

4. At school, maltreated children are _____, and their
noncompliance, poor motivation, and cognitive immaturity interfere with _____
_____. (592-593)

Preventing Child Maltreatment

1. Providing social supports to families (does/does not) sharply reduce child
maltreatment. (593)

2. What is the most important factor in preventing mothers with childhood histories of
abuse from repeating the cycle with their own youngsters? (593)

_____

3. An organization that provides social supports to families is _____
_____. Its main goal is to help child-abusing parents learn _____
_____. (593)

4. Many experts believe that child maltreatment cannot be eliminated as long as _____
_____ is widespread and _____ is regarded as an acceptable
child-rearing alternative. (593)

5. List three reasons why judges hesitate to permanently remove maltreated children
from the family. (593)
A._____
B._____
C._____

ASK YOURSELF...

14.1 On one of your trips to a local shopping center, you see a father getting very angry at his young son. Using the social systems perspective on family functioning, list as many factors as you can that might account for the father's behavior. (p. 563)

14.2 Don teaches in a school district serving many ethnic minority families. He notices that the parents are very strict, insisting that children comply with adult directives immediately. Why should Don ask the parents to explain their approach to child rearing rather than simply concluding that they are authoritarian? (p. 570)

14.3 "How come you don't study hard and get good grades like your sister?" a mother exclaimed in exasperation after seeing her son's poor report card. What impact do remarks like this have on sibling interaction, and why? (p. 588)

14.4 What advice would you give divorcing parents of two school-age sons about how to help their children adapt to life in a single-parent family? (p. 588)

14.5 Eight-year-old Bobby's mother has just found employment, so Bobby takes care of himself after school. What factors are likely to affect Bobby's adjustment to this arrangement? (p. 588)

14.6 Chandra heard a news report that ten severely neglected children, living in squalor in an inner-city tenement, were discovered by Chicago police. Chandra thought to herself, "What could possibly lead parents to mistreat their children so badly?" How would you answer Chandra's question? (p. 593)

CONNECTIONS

14.1 Review research on the goodness-of-fit model (see Chapter 10, page 420). How does it illustrate bidirectional influences between parent and child?

14.2 Explain how disintegration of family ties to neighborhood and community promotes delinquency in adolescence. (See Chapter 12, page 515.)

14.3 How might adolescents' view of personal versus social-conventional issues contribute to parent-child conflict? (See Chapter 12, page 503.)

14.4 Review Figure 11.8 on page 470. What might explain the decline in self-disclosure to parents in early adolescence, followed by the rise from tenth grade through college?

14.5 Review research on resilient children in Chapter 1 (see page 10). Are factors that foster resiliency similar to those that promote favorable adjustment to divorce and remarriage? Explain.

14.6 Can the U.N. Convention on the Rights of the Child help prevent child maltreatment? Explain, drawing on the concept of the macrosystem in Bronfenbrenner's ecological model. (See Chapter 1, pages 29 and 39.)

14.7 After reviewing factors linked to teenage parenthood, explain why it places children at risk for child abuse and neglect. (See Chapter 5, pages 214-216.)

PUZZLE 14

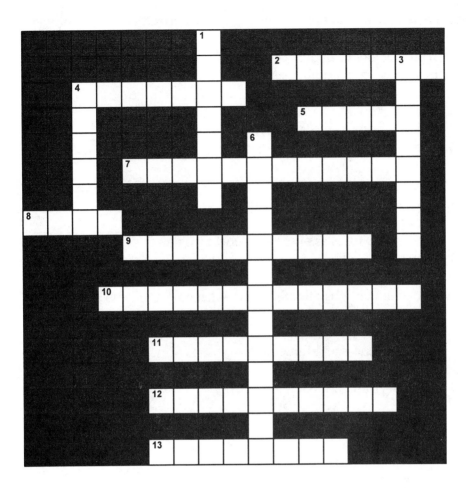

Across

2 Family unit that consists of parents and their children
4 In ___-generation family, children live with grandparents but apart from parents
5 Custody arrangement in which both parents have equal say in important decisions
7 Transitional form of supervision in which the child is in charge of immediate decisions
8 ___-care children look after themselves
9 Child-rearing style that is undemanding and unresponsive
10 Child-rearing style that is demanding and responsive
11 Series of settlement meetings between divorcing adults and a trained professional
12 Child-rearing style that is responsive but undemanding
13 Household in which parent and child live with one or more adult relatives

Down

1 Family structure resulting from cohabitation or remarriage
3 Sense of self as a separate and self-governing individual
4 ___ systems perspective views the family as complex set of relationships influenced by larger context
6 Parenting style that is demanding but low in responsiveness

PRACTICE TEST

1. Of the five historical functions of the family, the three that remain primarily the province of the family are: (559)
  A. reproduction, economic services, and social order.
  B. reproduction, economic services, and socialization.
  C. reproduction, social order, and emotional support.
  D. reproduction, socialization, and emotional support.

2. In explaining the *complex* patterns of interaction among family members, researchers: (560)
  A. focus on one-way effects of children's behavior on parents.
  B. emphasize that interaction between any two members is affected by third parties.
  C. view third parties as always supporting children's development.
  D. view the interplay of forces within the family system as static.

3. The two broad dimensions of child rearing that emerged from Baumrind's observations of parents' interactions with preschool children are: (563)
  A. maturity and immaturity.
  B. cooperativeness and forcefulness.
  C. demandingness and responsiveness.
  D. dominance and affection.

4. Which style of child rearing places a very high value on conformity? (564)
  A. authoritative
  B. permissive
  C. authoritarian
  D. uninvolved

5. Baumrind found that children of _____ parents were very immature, had difficulty controlling their impulses, and were overly demanding and dependent on adults. (564)
  A. authoritative
  B. permissive
  C. authoritarian
  D. uninvolved

6. Which of the following is NOT true of child-rearing styles? (565)
  A. Children whose parents alternate between authoritative and permissive styles are especially aggressive.
  B. Rational and reasonable use of firm control facilitates development.
  C. Research findings are correlational and open to different interpretations.
  D. Temperamentally difficult children are more likely to receive coercive discipline.

7. Coregulation: (566-567)
    A. is the type of supervision used by effective parents of preschoolers.
    B. requires that children be willing to inform parents of their whereabouts and problems.
    C. means that children are separate, self-governing individuals.
    D. should not be attempted until children are in high school.

8. Research indicates that, when rearing children: (568)
    A. parents who work in semiskilled manual occupations tend to emphasize traits such as curiosity and self-control.
    B. middle- and high-SES parents are more likely to be restrictive and worry about spoiling children.
    C. parents in white-collar occupations tend to emphasize obedience and cleanliness.
    D. low-SES parents rely more on criticism and physical punishment.

9. Research on the child-rearing beliefs and practices of particular ethnic groups indicates that: (569)
    A. Chinese parents tend to emphasize control.
    B. Hispanic mothers tend to be emotionally detached and remote.
    C. African-American mothers tend to be permissive.
    D. there are no distinct ethnic child-rearing practices and beliefs.

10. Which of the following is NOT true of the African-American extended family? (571)
    A. It increases the likelihood of authoritarian parenting of adolescents.
    B. Black adolescent mothers living in extended families are more likely to complete high school.
    C. Black grandmothers displayed more sensitive interaction with the babies of their teenage mothers.
    D. It assists in transmitting black cultural values to children.

11. Family size: (572)
    A. is currently increasing.
    B. has no effects on parent-child interaction.
    C. has increased partly because of marital instability.
    D. has effects on anxiety levels of its members.

12. Which of the following is NOT true of sibling interaction? (573)
    A. Cold, intrusive child rearing is associated with sibling bonding.
    B. It contributes to perspective-taking skills.
    C. Positive sibling ties predict favorable adjustment, even among hostile children.
    D. It is affected by children's temperaments.

13. Only children: (574)
    A. do not tend to be as socially competent as children with siblings.
    B. attain higher levels of education.
    C. have distant relationships with their parents.
    D. in China report more emotional distress than do children with siblings.

14. Children: (575)
    A. who are adopted have more emotional and learning difficulties in childhood.
    B. who are adopted are generally poorly adjusted as adults.
    C. in gay and lesbian families are mostly homosexual.
    D. in gay and lesbian families are not as well adjusted as other children.

15. Divorce: (579)
    A. may trigger more mature behavior in older children.
    B. is relatively infrequent in the United States.
    C. has a minimal impact on preschool-age children.
    D. results in more serious emotional and behavioral difficulties for girls than for boys.

16. In families of divorce: (579)
    A. girls receive less emotional support and are viewed more negatively by mothers, teachers, and peers.
    B. boys often establish coercive cycles of interaction with their mother.
    C. only boys show declines in school achievement.
    D. boys tend to improve their relationships with siblings.

17. Which of the following is NOT true of father-child relationships in divorce? (580)
    A. For girls, a good father-child relationship contributes to healthy heterosexual development.
    B. For boys, outcomes are better when the mother is the custodial parent.
    C. Fathers are more likely than mothers to praise a boy's good behavior.
    D. Fathers are less likely than mothers to ignore a boy's disruptiveness.

18. The mother-stepfather arrangement: (581)
    A. usually results in rapid adjustment on the part of girls.
    B. usually results in difficult adjustment for boys.
    C. often results in a decline in friction between mothers and sons.
    D. often results in even closer ties between mothers and daughters.

19. The father-stepmother arrangement: (582)
    A. often leads to withdrawal of a noncustodial father from the children of his previous marriage.
    B. often leads to closer ties between a noncustodial father and his daughters.
    C. often leads to positive reactions from children when fathers have custody.
    D. results in increasingly negative interactions between the stepmother and girls.

20. Maternal employment: (583-584)
    A. does not reduce the total amount of time school-age children spend with their mothers.
    B. results in children spending less time with fathers.
    C. results in more positive outcomes for sons than daughters.
    D. results in a decrease in fathers' involvement in child-care and household duties.

21. Child care: (585)
    A. in centers is not common during the preschool years.
    B. which is of poor-quality is associated with lower scores on measures of cognitive and social skills.
    C. is generally of high quality in the United States.
    D. in the United States has low turnover of caregivers.

22. Self-care children: (587)
    A. almost always suffer from low self-esteem.
    B. should be at least 6 years old before being left unsupervised.
    C. are few in number in the United States.
    D. should be given after-school chores and monitored by telephone.

23. Child maltreatment: (589)
    A. involving psychological and sexual abuse is regarded by some investigators as the most destructive form.
    B. is committed by individuals with a particular, identifiable abusive personality type.
    C. is rare in large industrialized nations.
    D. is easily defined in terms of the range and intensity of adult behaviors.

24. Child sexual abuse: (590)
    A. is rare and generally not a problem in the United States.
    B. is committed more often against boys.
    C. often results in severe adjustment problems for victims.
    D. is committed equally often by males and females.

25. Which of the following is NOT a reason why judges are reluctant to permanently remove a maltreated child from the family? (593)
    A. Family members prefer to stay together.
    B. Government intervention into family life is viewed as a last resort.
    C. Maltreated children and their parents are usually attached to each other.
    D. The American legal system tends to regard children as human beings in their own right.

CHAPTER 15

PEERS, MEDIA, AND SCHOOLING

SUMMARY

Beginning at an early age, socialization in the family is supplemented by experiences in the wider world of peers, media, and school. In all human societies, children spend many hours in one another's company. Experiments with rhesus monkeys reveal that peer interaction is a vital source of social competence.

Peer sociability begins in infancy as isolated smiles, gestures, and babbles evolve into coordinated interaction. During the preschool years, cooperative play increases. In middle childhood and adolescence, gains in communication skills and greater awareness of social norms contribute to advances in peer interaction. Parents influence young children's peer relations by arranging peer-play activities and teaching and modeling effective social skills. Cultural values and beliefs about the importance of play influence children's interaction and play activities.

Peer acceptance is a powerful predictor of long-term psychological adjustment. Children's social behavior is a major determinant of peer acceptance. A particularly destructive form of interaction that emerges during middle childhood is peer victimization. By the end of middle childhood, peer groups form, through which children and adolescents learn about the functioning of social organizations. Children socialize one another through reinforcement, modeling, and direct pressures to conform to peer expectations.

American children spend more time watching TV than they do in any other waking activity. Heavy TV viewing promotes aggressive behavior, indifference to real-life violence, a fearful view of the world, ethnic and gender stereotypes, and a naive belief in the truthfulness of advertising.

Computers have become increasingly common in the lives of children. Computer-assisted instruction, word processing, programming, and electronic communications each offer unique educational benefits. Although speed-and-action videogames foster attentional and spatial skills, violent videogames promote aggression and desensitize children to violence. The Internet may enhance understanding of other cultures, but excessive home use negatively affects emotional and social adjustment.

Schools are powerful forces in children's development. Pupils in traditional classrooms are slightly advantaged in achievement; those in open classrooms are more independent, tolerant of individual differences, and excited about learning. Teachers who are effective classroom managers and who provide cognitively stimulating activities enhance children's involvement and academic performance. Educational self-fulfilling prophecies are likely to occur when teachers emphasize competition and comparisons between pupils, have difficulty controlling the class, and engage in ability grouping. To be effective, mainstreaming must be carefully tailored to meet the academic and social needs of children with learning disabilities. Largely due to pressure from parents, some schools have extended mainstreaming to full inclusion.

Regardless of students' abilities, parent involvement in education is crucial for children's optimum learning. Cross-national comparisons of mathematics and science achievement reveal that students in Asian nations are consistently among the top performers, whereas Americans score no better than average and often below it; these differences become greater with increasing grade. American adolescents have no widespread vocational training system to assist them in preparing for challenging, well-paid careers.

LEARNING OBJECTIVES

After reading this chapter, you should be able to:

15.1 Discuss evidence indicating that both parental and peer relationships are vital for children's development. (598)

15.2 Trace the development of peer sociability from infancy into adolescence. (598-601)

15.3 Discuss how parental encouragement, play materials, age mix of children, and cultural values influence peer sociability. (602-604)

15.4 Describe major categories of peer acceptance, the relationship of physical appearance and social behavior to likeability, and ways to help rejected children. (604-608)

15.5 Describe peer group formation in middle childhood and adolescence, including factors that influence group norms and social structures. (608-612)

15.6 Discuss techniques peers use to socialize with one another, including reinforcement, modeling, and direct pressures to conform. (612-615)

15.7 Cite factors that influence how much time children devote to TV viewing, and describe the development of television literacy. (617-618)

15.8 Discuss the influence of television on children's development, including aggression; ethnic and gender stereotypes; consumerism; prosocial behavior; and academic learning and imagination. (618-621)

15.9 Discuss children's classroom and home-based computer use, noting benefits and concerns. (621-625)

15.10 Discuss the influence of class and student body size and teachers' educational philosophies on academic and social development. (626-629)

15.11 Cite factors that affect adjustment to school transitions in early childhood and adolescence, and describe interventions that help children adjust favorably. (629-632)

15.12 Discuss the role of teacher-pupil interaction and grouping practices in academic achievement. (632-634)

15.13 Cite conditions in which placement of mildly mentally retarded and learning disabled children in regular classrooms is successful, and explain how schools can foster parent involvement in education. (634-636)

15.14 Describe the findings of cross-national research on academic achievement, and cite factors that may contribute to the poor performance of American students in relation to students in Asian nations. (637-639)

15.15 Discuss challenges American adolescents face in making the transition from school to work and ways to help them attain satisfying, well-paid employment. (639-640)

STUDY QUESTIONS

The Importance of Peer Relations

1. What traits are found in maternally reared rhesus monkeys with no peer contact? (598)

_____

2. How do parent and peer associations complement one another? (598)

_____

_____

3. Describe the development of peer-only reared rhesus monkeys. (598)

_____

_____

_____

4. Describe the research findings of Freud and Dann concerning the development of six young German-Jewish orphans who lived together in a concentration camp for several years without close ties to adults. (598)

_____

_____

_____

5. Peers serve as vital sources of _____ in threatening situations and contribute to many aspects of development, but they do so more effectively when preceded by a warm, supportive relationship with a(n) _____. (598)

Development of Peer Sociability

Infant and Toddler Beginnings

1. What types of social acts occur between infants during the first year? (599)

_____

_____

2. Between 1 and 2 years, _____ between peers occurs
more often. (599)

3. Peer sociability in the first two years is fostered by the _____
_____ . (599)

The Preschool Years

1. _____ concluded that social development proceeds in a three-step
sequence. It begins with _____ activity-- unoccupied, onlooker
behavior and solitary play. (599)

2. Describe parallel, associative, and cooperative play. (599)
A. Parallel:_____

_____

B. Associative:_____

_____

C. Cooperative:_____

_____

3. Recent longitudinal research indicates that these play forms (do/do not) form a
developmental sequence in which later-appearing ones replace earlier ones. (599)

4. True or False: Nonsocial activity is still the most frequent form of behavior among 3-
to 4-year-olds. (599)

5. _____ and _____ play remain fairly stable from 3 to 6 years
and together account for as much of the young child's play as highly social, cooperative
interaction. (600)

6. We now understand that it is the _____, rather than the _____, of solitary
and parallel play that changes during early childhood. (600)

7. Define the following cognitive play categories. (600)
A. Functional:_____
B. Constructive:_____
C. Make-believe:_____

361

D. Games with rules:_____

8. True or False: Generally, all kinds of nonsocial activity are cause for concern during the preschool years. (600)

9. _____ play becomes especially common during the preschool years and requires sophisticated cognitive, emotional, and social skills. It also enhances these skills. (600)

Middle Childhood and Adolescence

1. True or False: In middle childhood, children have a greater sensitivity to prosocial expectations than in earlier years. (601)

2. The overall incidence of aggression (increases/decreases) in middle childhood. _____ among boys and _____ among girls persist into adolescence. (601)

3. A form of peer interaction that becomes common in middle childhood is _____ _____ play. It consists of _____ _____. (601)

4. In our evolutionary past, rough-and-tumble play may have been important for the development of _____. (601)

5. True or False: By midadolescence, children spend more time with peers than with any other social partners. (601)

Influences on Peer Sociability

Parent Encouragement

1. List three ways that parents influence their children's peer relations. (602)
A._____
B._____
C._____

Play Materials

1. Quantity of play materials (does/does not) affect young children's peer interaction. (602)

2. _____, _____, _____, and _____ are play materials that tend to be associated with solitary and parallel play. _____ _____ and _____ objects tend to be associated with cooperative play. (602)

3. Preschoolers use _____ toys to act out everyday roles. _____
materials encourage fantastic role play and more complex social interaction. (602)

Age Mix of Children

1. How do the theories of Piaget and Vygotsky differ on the benefits of same- and mixed-age interaction? (603)

_____

_____

2. True or False: Beginning in infancy, contact with older children seems to foster peer interaction. (603)

3. Mixed-age conditions among preschool and school-age children led to a greater _____ and _____ of interaction by younger children, along with special _____ by older children. (603)

4. The oldest school-age children in mixed-age settings (do/do not) prefer same-age companions. (603)

5. In what ways do children profit from interacting with coequals? (603)

_____

6. What competencies do children acquire from interaction with older and younger children? (603)
A. Younger: _____
B. Older: _____

Cultural Values

1. What forms does peer sociability take in collectivist societies? (603)

_____

_____

2. Caregivers who view play as mere entertainment are (more/less) likely to provide props and encourage pretend. (603)

3. During adolescence, peer contact is particularly strong in (industrialized/less developed) nations. (604)

4. What two factors probably account for the greater amount of time spent by American teenagers with peers? (604)
A._____
B._____

1. _____ refers to likability--the extent to which a child is viewed by agemates as a worthy social partner. (604)

2. Researchers usually assess peer acceptance with self-report measures called _____ _____ techniques. (604)

3. The four different categories of social acceptance yielded by sociometric techniques are: _____ children, who get many positive votes; _____ children, who are actively disliked; _____ children, who get a large number of positive and negative votes; and _____ children, who are seldom chosen, either positively or negatively. (604)

4. Peer acceptance is a (weak/moderate/strong) predictor of current as well as future psychological adjustment. (604)

5. _____ children, especially, are unhappy, alienated, poorly achieving children with a low sense of self-esteem. (604)

6. Peer rejection during middle childhood is strongly associated with _____ _____, _____, _____, _____, and _____ in adolescence and _____ _____ in young adulthood. (604)

7. True or False: Researchers are certain that peer relations are a major causal factor for a wide variety of later life problems. (605)

Origins of Acceptance in the Peer Situation

1. Physical attractiveness (is/is not) salient for children; their physical self-judgments correlate with overall self-worth (more/less) than other self-esteem factors. (605)

2. What evidence indicates that partiality for certain facial features may be innate? (605)

_____

_____

3. True or False: During early and middle childhood, children are likely to attribute negative behaviors to agemates who are unattractive. (605)

4. True or False: Teachers, but not parents, show a "beauty-as-best" bias in their attitudes and behavior toward children. (605)

5. Research findings indicate that by age 5, unattractive children were (more/less) aggressive with other children than were attractive children. What may explain these findings? (605)

_____

6. Describe how children with various sociometric ratings interact with their peers. (606)

A. Popular:_____

B. Rejected-aggressive:_____

C. Rejected-withdrawn:_____

D. Controversial:_____

E. Neglected:_____

7. Compared to bullies and well-adjusted adolescents, victims of peer abuse are chronically _____, _____, _____, _____, and _____. (607)

8. In what ways do the majority of peer-victimized children reinforce bullies? (607)

_____

9. Victims of bullies have histories of _____ attachment, _____ child rearing, and (among boys) _____. (607)

10. By elementary school, _____ percent of children are harassed by aggressive agemates. (607)

11. Children (do/do not) feel less discomfort at the thought of causing pain and suffering to victims than nonvictims. (607)

12. True or False: The most extreme victims of peer abuse are also very aggressive. (607)

13. What are two interventions used with victimized children? (607)
A._____
B._____

14. In what ways can adults help reduce bully-victim problems? (607)

_____
_____

Helping Rejected Children

1. Most interventions for improving the peer relations and psychological adjustment of rejected children involve _____, _____, and _____ positive social skills. (608)

2. An additional intervention designed to help rejected-aggressive children is intensive _____. This intervention improves their school achievement and social acceptance. (608)

3. In addition, techniques aimed at reducing rejected-aggressive children's antisocial behavior including _____ against antisocial acts and _____ for engaging in them led to better social acceptance. (608)

4. _____ interventions, such as training in perspective taking and social problem solving, have also produced favorable outcomes. (608)

5. Why is it often necessary to increase rejected children's expectations for social success? (608)

_____

_____

6. True or False: Interventions focusing only on the rejected child are likely to be sufficient. (608)

Peer Groups

---

1. What are the characteristics of a peer group? (608-609)

_____

_____

2. In what ways do children's experiences in peer groups provide a unique context for social learning? (609)

_____

Peer Group Formation

1. In the Robbers Cave study by Sherif and his colleagues, at what point did a strong group structure emerge? (609)

_____

2. In the Robbers Cave study, what happened to the groups' norms and social structures when they engaged in competitive games? (609)

_____

_____

3. To reduce intergroup hostility, the camp staff planned events with _____ _____ goals in which all campers joined forces to solve common problems. (609)

Group Norms

1. Group norms are evident by the end of _____. (609)

2. Late childhood and adolescent peer groups are organized around _____, small groups of about five to seven members who are good friends and usually alike in age, race, ethnicity, SES, personality, attitudes, and values. (609)

3. The cliques within a typical high school can be identified by their _____ and _____. (609)

4. Adolescents also form larger, more loosely organized groups called _____. Membership is based on _____ and _____. (610)

5. _____ are important in determining to which cliques and crowds teenagers belong. (610)

6. Indicate the type of groups to which teenagers whose parents engage in particular child rearing styles are likely to belong. (610)
A. Authoritative:_____
B. Permissive:_____
C. Uninvolved:_____

7. Cultural variations in group norms exist. For instance, the emphasis Asian parents place on _____ and _____ carries over to peer affiliations. (610)

8. Family experiences (do/do not) affect the extent to which adolescents become like their peers over time. (611)

9. Mixed-sex cliques form in (early/late) adolescence. (611)

10. What is the function of mixed-sex cliques? (611)

_____

_____

11. What vital functions does the clique serve during the teenage years? (611)

_____

12. What function does the crowd serve for adolescents? (611)

_____

Group Social Structures

1. In all groups, members differ in _____ or _____, an arrangement that fosters _____ and _____ _____. (611)

2. A(n) _____ is a stable ordering of individuals that predicts who will win when conflict arises between group members. (611)

3. The dominance hierarchy becomes (more/less) stable during middle childhood and adolescence. (612)

4. What adaptive function does a dominance hierarchy serve? (612)

_____

5. True or False: Peer groups seldom differ in their normative concerns, and high status tends to accrue to the same people in almost all situations. (612)

Peer Relations and Socialization

Peer Reinforcement and Modeling

1. Children's responses to one another serve as _____, modifying the extent to which they display certain behaviors. (612)

2. True or False: Research finds that initially nonaggressive children may steadily increase in aggressiveness in the face of peer hostility. (612)

3. Peer imitation occurs (less/more) often between familiar than unfamiliar peers. (612)

4. Carefully planned peer tutoring programs lead to benefits in _____ and _____ for both tutors and tutees. (613)

Peer Conformity

1. Conformity to peer pressure (is/is not) greater during adolescence than in childhood or young adulthood. (613)

2. True or False: Adolescence is a period in which young people blindly do what their peers ask. (613)

3. In what areas is peer pressure greatest in adolescence? (613)

_____

_____

4. Compared to other areas, pressure toward misconduct in adolescence is (high/low). (613)

5. (Early/Older) adolescents are more likely to give in to peer pressure. (613)

6. Parents have more impact on teenagers' _____ and _____ _____. Peers are more influential in matters such as _____, _____, and _____. (613)

7. True or False: In the United States, teenage alcohol and drug use is higher than in any other industrialized nation. (614)

8. Teenage experimenters with drugs and alcohol (are/are not) headed for a life of decadence and addiction. (614)

9. List two reasons why adolescent drug experimentation should not be taken lightly. (615)
A._____
B._____

10. Describe the typical drug abuser. (615)
_____
_____

11. To treat drug abuse, _____ is often a necessary and even lifesaving first step. (615)

12. Comprehensive drug abuse treatment programs have relapse rates of from _____ to _____ percent. (615)

13. _____ parenting is related to resistance to unfavorable peer pressure, whereas adolescents who experience extremes of parental behavior tend to be (less/highly) peer oriented. (614)

Television

1. _____ percent of American homes have at least one television set, over _____ percent have two or more, and a TV set is switched on in a typical household for _____ hours per day. (617)

2. In the study of a Canadian town, school-age children showed a decline in _____ _____ and _____, a rise in _____ beliefs, and an increase in _____ and _____ aggression 2 years after TV reception became available. (617)

How Much Television Do Children View?

1. The average American school-age child watches _____ hours of TV per week. (617)

2. Which children tend to watch the most TV? (617)

_____

Development of Television Literacy

1. Learning to understand television's specialized code of conveying information is known as _____. (617)

2. Describe the two parts of television literacy. (617)
A._____
B._____

3. True or False: Young children understand much of televised information. (618)

4. At age _____, children fully grasp the unreality of TV fiction. (618)

5. _____ and _____ lead to gains in television literacy. (618)

Television and Social Learning

1. The National Television Violence Study concluded that _____ pervades American TV. (618)

2. A wide variety of studies has concluded that television violence teaches children _____. (618)

3. True or False: Highly aggressive children have an average appetite for violent TV. (619)

4. Watching television violence (does/does not) make children more willing to tolerate it in others. (619)

5. Heavy TV viewers believe that there is much more _____ and _____ in society. (619)

6. How are African-Americans and other ethnic minorities depicted on TV? (619)

_____

7. Contrast the portrayal of women and men on TV. (619-620)

_____

_____

370

8. Explain what is meant by a bidirectional relationship between TV viewing and gender stereotyping. (620)

_____

_____

9. Although children can distinguish a TV program from a commercial as early as _____ years of age, below age _____ they seldom grasp the selling purpose of the ad. (620)

10. True or False: Older children no longer find TV commercials alluring. (620)

11. Although TV can increase children's prosocial behavior, prosocial TV has positive effects only when it is free of _____. (620)

Television, Academic Learning, and Imagination

1. _____ was created with the goal of strengthening school performance, especially among low-SES children. (621)

2. True or False: Children's "Sesame Street" viewing is related to their higher scores on tests of vocabulary and basic academic knowledge. (621)

3. The rise in syndicated shows that feature toys as main characters (increases/decreases) children's imagination; children tend to _____ what they see on TV rather than experiment with ideas. (621)

4. Some experts argue that television encourages reduced _____ and _____. (621)

Improving Children's Television

1. True or False: Today there are more restrictions than there once were on program content and advertising for children on TV. (621)

2. The average American child finishing elementary school has seen more than _____ violent acts on television. (622)

3. What restricts the federal government's regulation of TV? (622)

_____

4. Instead of regulatory control, what two actions does the federal government require of broadcasters, and what one action must TV manufacturers comply with? (622)
A. _____
B. _____
C. _____

5. List three strategies for regulating children's TV viewing. (623)

A._____

B._____

C._____

6. How did the Canadian television industry respond following a teenager's violent crime? (623)

_____

7. Public education about the impact of television is vital, since _____ _____ is a powerful instrument of change. (623)

Computers

1. By 1997, almost all American public schools had integrated _____ into their _____. (621)

Computers in Classrooms

1. True or False: Children are far more likely to collaborate when working with the computer than with pencil and paper. (623)

2. Describe the features of CAI programs. (623-624)

_____

_____

3. Why should the use of drill-and-practice activities on the computer not be overemphasized? (624)

_____

4. Why should word processing be used to enhance, not replace, other classroom writing experiences? (624)

_____

5. Computer programming leads to improvements in _____, _____, and _____. (624)

6. What gains for children are derived from the process of detecting errors in computer programs? (624)

_____

7. What are some advantages for children in opened-ended programming contexts? (624)

_____

_____

372

8. True or False: Electronic communications technology appears to enhance children's understanding of other cultures. (624)

Home Computers

1. About _____ percent of American families own a personal computer. Yet computers appear most often in the homes of economically well-off children, and as a consequence are believed to widen _____ performance gaps between _____ SES children and between boys and girls. (624-625)

2. Speed-and-action videogames foster _____ and _____ skills. (625)

3. Studies indicate that playing _____ videogames duplicates the effects of violent _____ --it promotes _____ and desensitizes children to violence. Furthermore, videogames are full of _____ and _____ stereotypes. (625)

4. True or False: Research suggests that home computing is associated with an increase in leisure time spent with family members. (625)

5. What do research findings suggest about the quality of social relationships on the Internet and the impact of heavy Internet use on psychological adjustment? (625)

_____
_____
_____
_____

Schooling

Class and Student Body Size

1. In a field experiment, (regular-class/small-class) pupils scored higher in reading and math achievement. Even after all pupils were returned to regular-size classes, children who experienced the (small/large) classes remained ahead in _____. (626)

2. Why is small class size beneficial? (626)

_____
_____

3. What are the benefits of a small student body size in secondary school? (627)

_____
_____

4. A special advantage of small schools is that potential dropouts are far more likely to

_____, _____,
and _____. (627)

5. Small school size (is/is not) associated with better achievement. (627)

Educational Philosophies

1. In a(n) _____ classroom, children are relatively passive in the learning process. The _____ is the sole authority for knowledge, rules, and decision making. Pupils' progress is evaluated by how well they keep pace with a _____ _____. (627)

2. In a(n) _____ classroom, children are viewed as active agents in their own development. The teacher assumes a(n) _____ authority role, sharing decision making with pupils, who learn _____. Children are evaluated by considering their progress in relation to _____. (627)

3. The prevalent style in classrooms today is the _____. (627)

4. Older school-age pupils in _____ classrooms have a slight edge in academic achievement. However, pupils in _____ classrooms are more critical thinkers, and they value and respect individual differences in their classmates more. (627)

5. True or False: Traditional-classroom kindergartners achieve less well in grade school than their open-classroom counterparts. (627-628)

6. List three themes of Vygotsky-inspired educational innovations.(628)
   A._____
   B._____
   C._____

7. Describe the Kamehameha Elementary Education Program (KEEP). (628)

_____
_____
_____

8. A(n) _____ collaborates with community agencies to provide children and adolescents at risk for poor achievement with health and social services they need to benefit fully from education. (629)

School Transitions

1. List three ways to prepare preschoolers for the challenges of kindergarten. (629)
A. _____
B. _____
C. _____

2. True or False: Research reveals that with each school change, adolescents' course grades decline. (630)

3. What are some observations of junior high students concerning their teachers? (630)
_____

4. A comprehensive study by Simmons and Blyth indicated that participation in extracurricular activities declined more in (6-3-3/8-4) arrangements, especially for (boys/girls). (630)

5. In the Simmons and Blyth study, self-esteem of (boys/girls) in (6-3-3/8-4) schools declined with each school change, whereas their (6-3-3/8-4) counterparts gained throughout the secondary school years. (630)

6. Why do girls in 6-3-3 schools fare poorest? (631)
_____

7. _____ and _____ young people show an especially sharp drop in school performance after the transition to junior high school. (631)

8. Describe some ways to ease the strain of moving from elementary to secondary school. (631)
_____
_____
_____
_____

Teacher-Pupil Interaction

1. Class time devoted to _____ and _____ is consistently related to achievement test scores. (632)

2. American elementary school teachers emphasize _____ more than _____. (632)

3. Studies indicate that students are (more/less) attentive when teachers emphasize higher-level thinking than basic memory exercises. (632)

4. What types of pupils experience positive interactions with their teachers? (632)

_____

5. Teachers especially dislike children who _____
_____ . (632)

6. What is an educational self-fulfilling prophecy? (632)

_____

7. How do self-fulfilling prophecies interact with teacher and student characteristics? (632-633)

_____
_____
_____
_____

8. When teachers hold (accurate/inaccurate) views, students achieving poorly are more affected. (633)

9. When teachers are _____, many children respond with improved performance. However, biased teacher judgments are usually slanted in a (positive/negative) direction, resulting in more (favorable/unfavorable) classroom experiences and achievement. (633)

10. _____ and _____ children tend to receive less favorable feedback from teachers than do white children. This undermines their _____
_____ . (633)

Grouping Practices

1. How can homogeneous grouping widen the gap between high and low achievers? (633)

_____
_____

2. True or False: Self-esteem and attitudes toward school are more negative in multigrade arrangements. (633-634)

3. (Homogeneous/Heterogeneous) groups yield poorer-quality interaction than do (homogeneous/heterogeneous) groups composed of above-average pupils. (634)

4. True or False: By high school, homogeneous grouping tends to perpetrate educational inequalities of earlier years. (634)

5. True or False: SES differences in quality of education and academic achievement sort American students less drastically than is the case in other countries. (634)

Teaching Pupils with Special Needs

1. The _____ (Public Law 101-475) mandates that schools place children who require special supports for learning in the "least restrictive" environments that meet their educational needs. (634)

2. _____ refers to the placement of pupils with learning difficulties in regular classrooms for part of the school day, whereas _____ refers to placement for these children in regular classrooms full time. (634-635)

3. Some mainstreamed pupils with _____ show problems in adaptive behavior, or _____; however, the largest number of mainstreamed pupils have _____; they have difficulties with one or more aspects of learning believed to be due to faulty brain functioning. (635)

4. Achievement differences between mainstreamed pupils and those taught in self-contained classrooms (are/are not) great. (635)

5. Why are mainstreamed children often rejected by peers? (635)

_____

_____

6. True or False: Special-needs children should not be educated in regular classrooms. (635)

7. Describe three ways in which teachers can promote peer acceptance of mainstreamed children. (635)
A. _____
B. _____
C. _____

Parent-School Partnerships

1. How can schools increase parent involvement? (636)
A. _____
B. _____
C. _____
D. _____
E. _____

Cross-Cultural Research on Academic Achievement

1. In international studies of mathematics and science achievement, Americans score no better than at the _____. (637)

2. In the most recent assessment, by twelfth grade U.S. math and science general knowledge scores were near the (top/bottom) in relation to 21 countries. (637)

3. True or False: In a comparison of elementary school children in Japan, Taiwan, and the United States, large differences in math achievement in kindergarten became greater with increasing grade. (637)

4. True or False: Asian pupils are higher achievers because they are more intelligent than American students. (637)

5. The achievement of U.S. elementary and secondary school students (has/has not) improved over the past decade in math and science. (637)

6. Why might limited natural resources in Japan and Taiwan result in higher academic skills in their students? (638)

_____

7. Japanese and Taiwanese parents and teachers believe that (few/all) children have the potential to master challenging tasks, whereas American parents and teachers regard (effort/ability) as the key to academic success. (638)

8. Compared to Asian parents, American parents are far (more/less) satisfied with the quality of their children's education, hold (higher/lower) standards for their children's academic performance, and are (more/less) concerned about how well their youngsters are doing in school. (638)

9. Describe the method of teaching in Japanese and Taiwanese classrooms. (638)

_____
_____
_____

10. How is time used more effectively in Japanese and Taiwanese classrooms? (638)

_____
_____

11. How do Japanese and Taiwanese teachers communicate with parents? (638)

_____
_____

12. True or False: The highest performing Asian students are poorly adjusted. (638)

Making the Transition from School to Work

1. Approximately _____ percent of American adolescents graduate from high school without plans to go to college. (639)

2. Why is a heavy commitment to jobs held by adolescents harmful? (639)

_____

_____

3. Work-study programs are related to _____, _____
_____, and _____.
(639)

4. True or False: Compared to European nations, the United States invests more in training systems designed to prepare its youths for skilled business and industrial occupations and manual trades. (639)

5. List three major challenges of implementing an apprenticeship system. (639-640)
   A._____
   B._____
   C._____

ASK YOURSELF...

15.1 Three-year-old Bart lives in the country, where there are no other preschoolers nearby. His parents wonder whether it is worth driving Bart into town once a week to play with his 3-year-old cousin. What advice would you give Bart's parents, and why? (p. 604)

15.2 In kindergarten, Miranda prefers to draw pictures, work puzzles, and look at books by herself. She rarely plays with other children. Jezebel is also a solitary child, but she spends most of the day wandering around the room, anxiously hovering near peers without joining their play. Which child is likely to have a neglected social status? How about a rejected-withdrawn status? Explain.
(p. 608)

15.3 Phyllis likes her 14-year-old daughter Farrah's friends, but she wonders what Farrah gets out of hanging out with them at Jake's Pizza Parlor on Friday and Saturday evenings. Explain to Phyllis what Farrah is learning. (p. 615)

15.4 "I can't control him, he's impossible," Robbie's mother complained, referring to his impulsive, aggressive behavior. At home, Robbie often turns on the TV and watches prime-time shows with high doses of violence. Why might Robbie be attracted to violent television? Suggest some strategies his parents can use to shield him from harmful TV messages. (p. 626)

15.5 Ray is convinced that his 5-year-old son, Tripper, would do better in school if only Tripper's kindergarten teacher would provide more teacher-directed lessons and worksheets and reduce the time devoted to learning-center activities. Is Ray correct? (p. 636)

15.6 Tanisha is finishing sixth grade. She could either continue in her current school through eighth grade or switch to a much larger junior high school. What would you suggest she do, and why? (p. 636)

15.7 Sandy, a parent of a third grader, wonders whether she should support her school board's decision to teach first, second, and third graders together, in multigrade classrooms. How would you advise Sandy, and why? (p. 636)

15.8 Explain how education in Japan and Taiwan illustrates findings presented earlier in this chapter on aspects of schooling that promote high achievement.
(p. 639)

CONNECTIONS

15.1 What aspects of adult-child interaction probably contribute to the relationship between attachment security and young children's peer sociability? (See Chapter 10, page 431.)

15.2 Explain how peer interaction contributes to young children's concepts of distributive justice and to their capacity to distinguish moral from social-conventional and personal matters. (See Chapter 12, pages 501 and 503.)

15.3 How can parents help shy, inhibited children overcome their social wariness, thereby reducing their risk for peer rejection and later maladjustment? (See Chapter 10, pages 417 and 420.)

15.4 Consider what children learn from participating in large peer networks versus interacting with one or two close friends. How might boys' preference for large groups and girls' preference for small clusters contribute to sex-related differences in friendship quality and personality traits? (See Chapter 11, page 471, and Chapter 13, pages 548-552.)

15.5 How can excessive TV viewing negatively affect children's health? (See Chapter 5, page 197.)

15.6 How are teachers' optimistic and pessimistic views of pupils' academic competence, which create self-fulfilling prophecies, likely to affect children's attributions for success and failure in achievement situations? (See Chapter 11, pages 453-455.)

15.7 Do Chinese child-rearing beliefs and practices complement the experiences Taiwanese children typically encounter in school? Explain. (See Chapter 14, page 569.)

PUZZLE 15

Across

4 ___ uses computers to practice academic skills
7 Child plays near others with similar materials but does not interact
8 Loosely organized peer group
11 Play activity is directed toward a common goal
12 Placement of pupils with learning difficulties in regular classrooms for all or part of the day
13 ___ groups have unique norms and structures of leaders and followers
15 Children become frequent targets of attack in peer ___
16 ___ activity is unoccupied, onlooker behavior and solitary play
17 Play in which children engage in separate activities but interact by exchanging toys
19 Full ___ is placement of pupils with learning difficulties in regular classrooms full time
20 Learning ___ are specific learning difficulties that result in poor school achievement
22 ___-and-tumble play involves friendly fighting
23 Children who get many positive votes on sociometric measures
25 Television ___ is understanding of TV's code of conveying information
26 ___-service schools provide services to students at risk for poor achievement
27 Classroom based on the educational philosophy that children are active agents

Down

1 Children with ___ mental retardation have IQs between 55 and 70
2 Children seldom chosen, either positively or negatively, on sociometric measures
3 ___ techniques ask peers to evaluate one another's likability
5 Rejected-___ children engage in high rates of conflict and are hyperactive and impulsive
6 ___ hierarchy limits aggression within the group
8 Children who get many positive and negative votes on sociometric measures
9 Classrooms where children are passive learners
10 Group of 5 to 7 good friends
14 Children who are actively disliked
18 Rejected-___ children are passive and socially awkward
21 ___-fulfilling prophecy, in which a pupil adopts a teacher's attitudes toward him or her
24 Peer-___ rearing, or nonhuman primates reared together from birth without adults

384

PRACTICE TEST

1. The form of play in which children engage in separate activities, but interact by exchanging toys and commenting on one another's behavior is _____ play. (599)
    A. cooperative
    B. associative
    C. parallel
    D. integrated

2. From research on play, we now know that: (600)
    A. later-appearing play forms replace earlier ones.
    B. nonsocial activity is cause for concern among preschoolers.
    C. extensive functional play among preschoolers may be cause for concern.
    D. solitary and parallel play decline rapidly from 3 to 6 years.

3. What contributes to the view that rough-and-tumble play may have an adaptive function? (601)
    A. The overall incidence of aggression remains stable from earlier years.
    B. This type of play may assist children in establishing dominance relations.
    C. Rough-and-tumble play permits children to hurt each other.
    D. Rough-and-tumble play increases during adolescence when individual differences in strength become clear.

4. Peer interaction of young children: (602)
    A. tends to be more socially complex when playing with nonspecific materials.
    B. seldom involves parental encouragement or assistance.
    C. is not influenced by child-rearing styles of parents.
    D. tends to take the form of cooperative play when puzzles are provided.

5. Which of the following is NOT true of the age mix of children? (603)
    A. Piaget emphasized that children profit from interacting with older, more capable peers.
    B. Babies with older siblings are more socially responsive to same-age playmates.
    C. Mixed-age conditions on problem-solving tasks lead to greater complexity of interaction by younger children.
    D. The oldest children in mixed-age settings prefer same-age companions.

6. Research on peer acceptance indicates that: (604)
    A. all children fit into one of four different categories of social acceptance.
    B. controversial children, especially, are unhappy and alienated.
    C. peer rejection during middle childhood is associated with delinquency in adolescence.
    D. peer relations are clearly a major causal factor in later-life problems.

7. Physical attractiveness: (605)
   A. has little bearing on peer acceptance.
   B. of children does not affect the attitudes of parents and teachers.
   C. of an unfamiliar adult influences the play of 12-month-old infants.
   D. is not associated with popularity among children who know each other well.

8. Research on social behavior indicates that: (606)
   A. neglected children are usually well adjusted.
   B. rejected-aggressive children display a blend of positive and negative social behaviors.
   C. controversial children are at risk for abuse at the hands of bullies.
   D. rejected-withdrawn children are relatively happy and comfortable with their peer relationships.

9. The Robbers Cave experiment demonstrated that: (609)
   A. a strong group structure did not emerge until it was necessary to compete with outsiders.
   B. new leaders and normative behaviors appear when a group competes with others.
   C. joint recreational activities in the final phase were sufficient to create friendly interaction.
   D. competition for desired resources is not sufficient to create hostility between groups.

10. Research on group norms indicates that: (610)
    A. adolescents with authoritative parents are likely to be members of the brain, jock, and popular groups.
    B. cliques are large, loosely organized groups.
    C. crowds are small groups based on friendship.
    D. cliques increase in importance in late adolescence.

11. Research on group social structures indicates that: (612)
    A. the dominance hierarchy limits aggression among group members.
    B. the dominance hierarchy is extremely unstable during middle childhood.
    C. hostility within a dominance hierarchy is common.
    D. social power and leadership in dominance hierarchies is always concentrated in the strongest, most aggressive children.

12. Research on peer reinforcement and modeling indicates that: (614)
    A. initially nonaggressive children seldom increase in aggressive behavior, even in the face of peer hostility.
    B. peer imitation occurs more often between unfamiliar peers.
    C. peer tutoring only benefits tutees.
    D. authoritative parenting is consistently related to resistance to unfavorable peer pressure.

13. Research on adolescent substance use and abuse indicates that: (615)
    A. alcohol and drug use has increased during the last decade.
    B. experimenters are headed for a life of addiction.
    C. drug abusers are seriously troubled and inclined to engage in antisocial acts.
    D. comprehensive drug abuse treatment programs are highly effective for almost all participants.

14. Television viewing: (617)
    A. actually results in an increase in creative thinking, as shown by the Canadian study.
    B. is greater among children with higher IQs.
    C. is associated with extensive comprehension of programming, even among young children.
    D. consumes more of American children's time than any other waking activity.

15. Research on television and social learning indicates that: (619)
    A. although not recommended, exposure to violence on TV has no lasting effects on children.
    B. highly aggressive children have a greater appetite for violent TV.
    C. boys who watch many violent programs at 8 are no more likely to have committed serious criminal acts by 30.
    D. violent television does not affect children's attitudes toward social reality.

16. Research on television and social learning indicates that: (620)
    A. a bidirectional relationship between TV viewing and gender stereotyping may exist.
    B. even 5-year-olds understand the selling purpose of commercials.
    C. programs that mix prosocial and violent content have positive effects on children.
    D. authoritarian parents have children who watch more prosocial programs.

17. Which of the following is NOT supported by research on children's television viewing? (621)
    A. The more children watch "Sesame Street," the higher they score on tests of vocabulary.
    B. Programs with violent content are detrimental to children's imaginative play.
    C. When children play with the toys featured on television programs they tend to experiment with ideas in their play.
    D. Television viewing replaces activities children would otherwise engage in, such as reading, playing, and interacting with adults and peers.

18. Which of the following is not required of broadcasters or TV manufacturers by the federal government? (622)
    A. regulatory control
    B. 3 hours per week of educational programming for children
    C. a rating of television content
    D. TV sets containing V-chips

19. Computers: (623)
    A. have been integrated into the instructional programs of a small minority of American public schools.
    B. are less interesting to children than TV.
    C. divert children from other worthwhile classroom activities.
    D. promote collaboration among children.

20. The use of computers for: (624)
    A. computer-assisted instruction mainly emphasizes active, meaningful experimentation.
    B. word processing helps children learn to spell more accurately than when they write by hand.
    C. word processing should replace other classroom writing experiences.
    D. programming leads to gains in metacognitive knowledge and self-regulation.

21. Which of the following is NOT a concern about computers? (624-625)
    A. Computers tend to be found in the homes and schools of economically well-off children.
    B. Preschool and elementary school pupils prefer using computers socially.
    C. Videogames are full of ethnic and gender stereotypes.
    D. Videogames account for most out-of-school recreational use of computers.

22. Research on the effects of class and student body size of schools indicates that: (626)
    A. as classes drop to 13 to 17 pupils, academic achievement improves.
    B. small schools are associated with gains in achievement.
    C. adolescents in large schools report a greater sense of personal responsibility.
    D. a greater percentage of students in large than small high schools are actively involved in the extracurricular experiences.

23. Which of the following is NOT true of traditional classrooms? (627-628)
    A. In traditional classrooms, children are relatively passive in the learning process.
    B. Traditional classrooms are prevalent today.
    C. Traditional-classroom kindergartners achieve less well than their open-classroom counterparts.
    D. Traditional classrooms are inspired by Piaget's vision of the child.

24. Research regarding teacher-pupil interaction does NOT reveal that: (632-633)
    A. African-American and Mexican-American children often receive less favorable feedback than do white children.
    B. elementary school teachers emphasize higher-level thinking more than rote.
    C. unruly pupils are often criticized and rarely called on.
    D. well-behaved, high-achieving pupils typically experience positive interactions with teachers.

25. Research on teaching pupils with special needs indicates that: (635)
    A. mainstreaming works best for all pupils.
    B. mainstreamed pupils are generally fully accepted by peers.
    C. mainstreamed pupils achieve at a substantially higher level than those in self-contained classrooms.
    D. often these pupils do best when they are in a resource room part of the day and mainstreamed for the remainder.

PUZZLE 1.1

PUZZLE 1.2

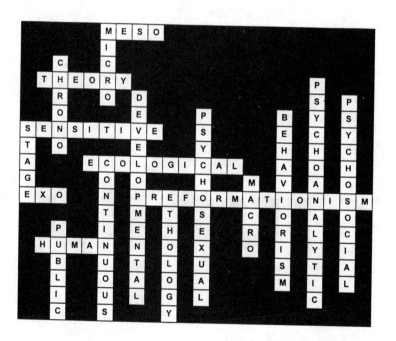

390

PUZZLE 2.1

PUZZLE 2.2

PUZZLE 3.1

PUZZLE 3.2

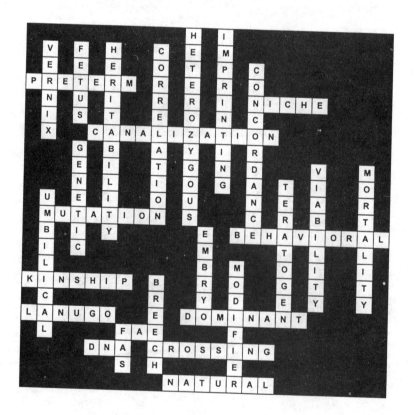

PUZZLE 4.1

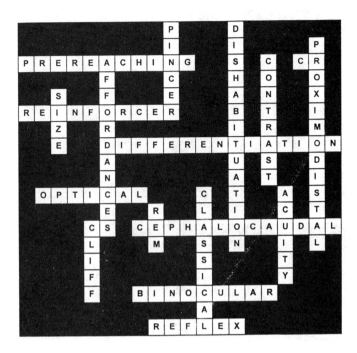

PUZZLE 4.2

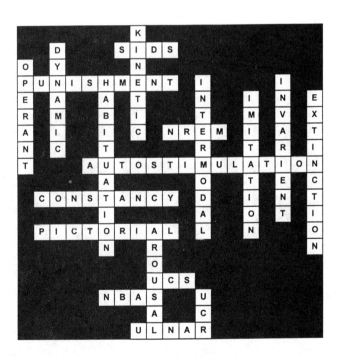

PUZZLE 5.1

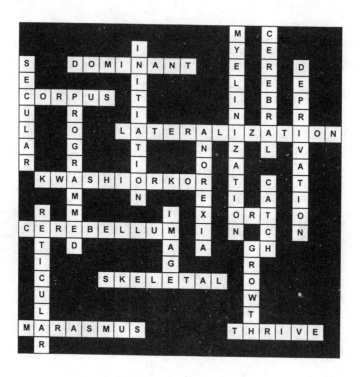

PUZZLE 5.2

PUZZLE 6.1

PUZZLE 6.2

PUZZLE 7.1

PUZZLE 7.2

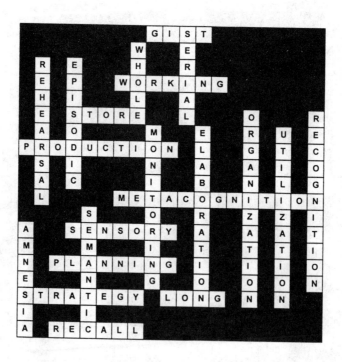

PUZZLE 8

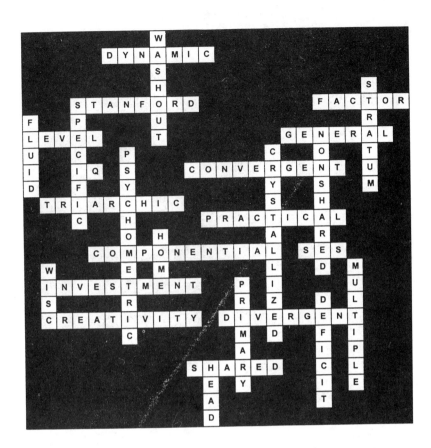

PUZZLE 9.1

PUZZLE 9.2

PUZZLE 10

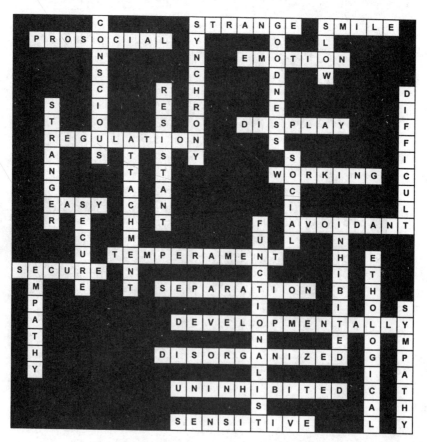

PUZZLE 11

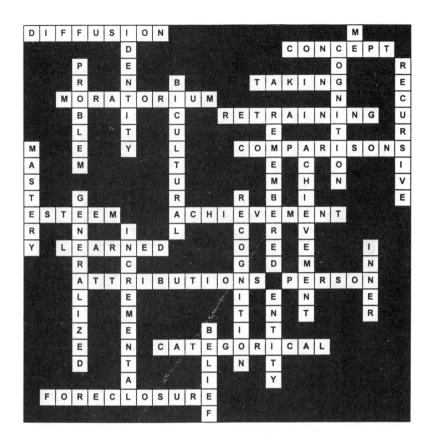

PUZZLE 12

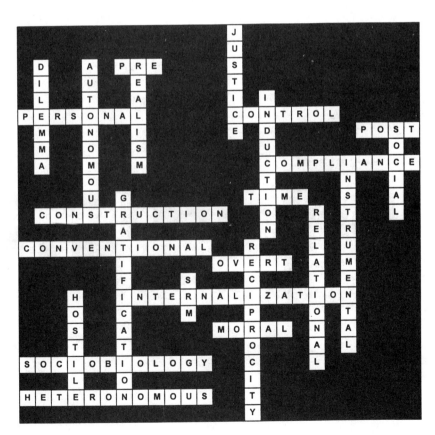

PUZZLE 13

PUZZLE 14

PUZZLE 15

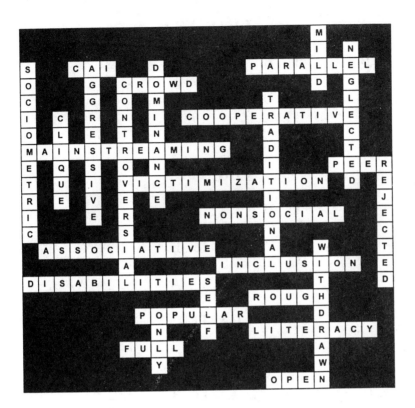

ANSWERS TO PRACTICE TESTS

CHAPTER 1

1. C	6. B	11. B	16. B	21. B
2. D	7. A	12. A	17. D	22. C
3. C	8. C	13. D	18. B	23. A
4. A	9. C	14. A	19. C	24. B
5. C	10. D	15. A	20. C	25. A

CHAPTER 2

1. C	6. B	11. D	16. A	21. A
2. D	7. A	12. C	17. A	22. C
3. D	8. D	13. C	18. D	23. C
4. A	9. A	14. C	19. D	24. C
5. B	10. A	15. C	20. A	25. A

CHAPTER 3

1. C	6. A	11. A	16. C	21. D
2. B	7. B	12. B	17. A	22. C
3. D	8. C	13. C	18. B	23. C
4. C	9. D	14. A	19. B	24. A
5. D	10. C	15. C	20. B	25. B

CHAPTER 4

1. C	6. A	11. D	16. B	21. D
2. B	7. C	12. C	17. D	22. B
3. C	8. A	13. C	18. C	23. A
4. A	9. B	14. A	19. D	24. D
5. B	10. B	15. B	20. C	25. C

CHAPTER 5

1. A	6. C	11. B	16. A	21. D
2. C	7. C	12. D	17. C	22. B
3. C	8. D	13. B	18. A	23. D
4. C	9. B	14. D	19. C	24. C
5. C	10. D	15. A	20. D	25. C

CHAPTER 6

1. C	6. A	11. C	16. C	21. D
2. B	7. A	12. D	17. B	22. B
3. C	8. B	13. B	18. A	23. A
4. A	9. B	14. B	19. A	24. C
5. C	10. B	15. D	20. C	25. B

CHAPTER 7

1. A	6. B	11. D	16. C	21. A
2. D	7. D	12. B	17. A	22. B
3. B	8. A	13. D	18. B	23. D
4. C	9. C	14. B	19. C	24. B
5. D	10. B	15. A	20. C	25. A

CHAPTER 8

1. C	6. A	11. D	16. B	21. B
2. B	7. C	12. C	17. C	22. A
3. A	8. A	13. A	18. B	23. B
4. B	9. D	14. C	19. C	24. D
5. C	10. A	15. C	20. A	25. C

CHAPTER 9

1. C	6. A	11. B	16. A	21. C
2. B	7. C	12. C	17. C	22. C
3. B	8. D	13. A	18. B	23. D
4. D	9. B	14. A	19. C	24. C
5. C	10. C	15. B	20. A	25. A

CHAPTER 10

1. A	6. A	11. C	16. C	21. A
2. D	7. B	12. B	17. C	22. C
3. B	8. A	13. B	18. C	23. D
4. C	9. B	14. A	19. C	24. A
5. D	10. A	15. A	20. A	25. C

CHAPTER 11

1. C	6. C	11. B	16. B	21. D
2. B	7. B	12. D	17. C	22. A
3. A	8. D	13. C	18. B	23. D
4. D	9. D	14. A	19. C	24. D
5. D	10. A	15. C	20. C	25. A

CHAPTER 12

1. A	6. A	11. D	16. D	21. B
2. C	7. B	12. D	17. B	22. B
3. B	8. C	13. B	18. C	23. A
4. C	9. A	14. D	19. A	24. C
5. D	10. B	15. C	20. C	25. C

CHAPTER 13

1. D	6. A	11. B	16. B	21. D
2. D	7. D	12. B	17. C	22. C
3. B	8. D	13. D	18. B	23. D
4. C	9. C	14. A	19. B	24. A
5. C	10. A	15. A	20. A	25. C

CHAPTER 14

1. D	6. A	11. D	16. B	21. B
2. B	7. B	12. A	17. B	22. D
3. C	8. D	13. B	18. C	23. A
4. C	9. A	14. A	19. A	24. C
5. B	10. A	15. A	20. A	25. D

CHAPTER 15

1. B	6. C	11. A	16. A	21. B
2. C	7. C	12. D	17. C	22. A
3. B	8. A	13. C	18. A	23. D
4. A	9. B	14. D	19. D	24. B
5. A	10. A	15. B	20. D	25. D

NOTES

NOTES

NOTES

NOTES

NOTES

NOTES